HISTORY AND REPETITION

WEATHERHEAD BOOKS ON ASIA Weatherhead East Asian Institute, Columbia University

COLUMBIA UNIVERSITY PRESS   *New York*

KOJIN KARATANI

HISTORY AND REPETITION

EDITED BY SEIJI M. LIPPIT

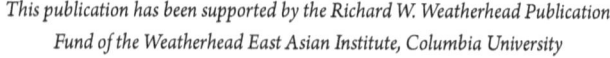

This publication has been supported by the Richard W. Weatherhead Publication
Fund of the Weatherhead East Asian Institute, Columbia University

COLUMBIA UNIVERSITY PRESS
Publishers Since 1893
NEW YORK   CHICHESTER, WEST SUSSEX
cup.columbia.edu

Copyright *Rekishi to hanpuku* by Kojin Karatani © 2004 Kojin Karatani.
Originally published in Japanese by Iwanami shoten, Publishers, 2004
Introduction and translation copyright © 2012 Columbia University Press
All rights reserved

Library of Congress Cataloging-in-Publication Data
Karatani, Kojin, 1941–
[Rekishi to hanpuku. English]
History and repetition / Kojin Karatani ; Edited by Seiji M. Lippit.
p. cm. — (Weatherhead books on Asia)
Includes bibliographical references and index.
ISBN 978-0-231-15728-5 (cloth) ISBN 978-0-231-15729-2
(pbk.) ISBN 978-0-231-52865-8 (e-book)
1. Historiography. 2. Japan—History—1868—Historiography.
I. Lippit, Seiji M. II. Title.

D13.K2913   2011
952.0072—dc22   2011012631

CONTENTS

Author's Preface to the English Edition vii
Editor's Introduction: On Repetition, Singularity, and Historicity xv

1. Introduction:
On *The Eighteenth Brumaire of Louis Bonaparte*
1

2. History and Repetition in Japan
29

3. The Discursive Space of Modern Japan
47

4. The Allegory of Ōe Kenzaburō:
Football in the Year Man'en 1
87

5. The Landscape of Murakami Haruki:
Pinball in the Year 1973
Translated by Hisayo Suzuki
117

6. The End of the Modern Novel
Translated by Michael K. Bourdaghs
151

7. Buddhism and Fascism
173

Glossary 211
Works Cited 223
Index 235

AUTHOR'S PREFACE TO THE ENGLISH EDITION

From ancient times, it has been said that history repeats itself. In truth, people study history precisely because it is not a onetime phenomenon but rather maintains the possibility of recurrence. For example, historians often say that those who are ignorant of history are doomed to repeat it. Does that mean, then, that those who have knowledge of history will be able to avoid its recurrence? Does the repetition of history actually exist? Such questions have never been properly considered. For even if they intuitively acknowledge the repetition of history, scholars, aspiring to be scientific, refrain from taking on the issue for fear of rendering their work unscientific. I believe in the existence of historical repetition, as well as in the possibility of engaging such repetition scientifically. Of course, what is repeated is not the event itself but rather the structure. In a process of structural repetition, an event may at times also appear to be repeated. One should not be swayed by the similarity of historical events, however, for it is only the structure that recurs.

I wrote most of the essays contained in this volume in the environment that existed around 1989. It was a time when an age was coming to an end, as symbolized by the collapse of the Soviet Union and the death of the Shōwa emperor in Japan. Around this time, I became aware of a correspondence between the events of the Shōwa period [1926–1989] and the events of the Meiji period [1868–1912] in Japan. That realization formed the genesis of these essays. This type of correspondence does not represent a random coincidence, I thought. For clearly it conceals within it a geopolitical structure distinctive to East Asia as well as to the structure of the modern world system. Yet it is actually difficult to directly engage this type of repetitive structure. Historians and sociologists tend to avoid it. On the other hand, the major novelists of contemporary Japan all thematized the repetitive quality of modern Japan. For this reason, I first wrote these essays in the form of literary criticism.

These essays were written entirely within the Japanese context, for a Japanese readership. At the same time, I realized that these issues were not limited to Japan. Consequently, in order to take up the problem in a more universal context, I appended the essay on Marx's *The Eighteenth Brumaire of Louis Bonaparte* to the beginning of the volume. In general, Marx's view of history is based on stages of development, and thus it appears unrelated to the question of repetition. In fact, however, Marx actually thought deeply about the structure of repetition. The repetitive structure that he discerned in *Capital* was the business cycle, and especially the economic crisis, distinctive to the capitalist economy. On the other hand, in *The Eighteenth Brumaire*, Marx deals mainly with the repetitive structure unique to the state. In a certain sense, the latter is more important than the former.

After entering the 1990s, however, I stopped writing about these issues. For one thing, increasing numbers of people pointed out the return of the prewar period and the repetition of the 1930s. Yet conversely, I began gradually to think that this type of perspective was incorrect. For example, the "economy of grand space" [*Grossraumwirtschaft*] proclaimed in 1930s Germany or the Greater East Asia Co-Prosperity Sphere proclaimed in Japan were, in a certain sense, repeated in the 1990s. The obvious example is the European Union, but in East Asia as well the plan of an economic and political community has been raised from a variety of perspectives. To that extent, one can indeed discern a type of repetitiveness. At the same time, however, it cannot be denied that such phenomena are far different from those of the prewar period. For these reasons, I was dissatisfied with the contents of this book, which was essentially based on a 1980s consciousness. But I soon realized that there was no need to make any fundamental corrections; instead, what was required was to see the repetitiveness of history in a span not of 60 years but of 120 years.

In truth, the situation following 1990 resembled less the situation of 60 years ago than that of 120 years ago. The politics and economics of post-1990 have been referred to as "neoliberalism," but they are, in fact, quite similar to those of post-1870 imperialism. For example, many today are surprised by the emergence of China, India, and Russia as great powers, but when the situation is compared with the world of 120 years ago, there is no great reason for surprise. People are conscious of and try to avoid the repetition of 60 years ago, but when it comes to 120 years ago, they are not even aware of the repetition.

In East Asia, for example, there is no doubt that the problems of the prewar period still cast shadows on relations between China, Taiwan, South Korea, North Korea, and Japan. Focusing only on this, however, we may overlook just how different the present is from the prewar period. China, which then lay in a fragmented state, exposed to imperialist invasion, has by now become a political and economic giant. The same can be said of Taiwan, South Korea, and North Korea. If anything, it is better to go back to the 1880s in order to understand the present circumstances. At the time, the Qing dynasty was a world empire of massive scale. In the peripheral country of Japan, the old system was overthrown, opening the country to the outside. In response, the Yi dynasty in Korea suppressed pro-Japanese anti-isolationists, attempting to maintain its closed-country policy with the Qing dynasty as suzerain state. Ultimately, this led to confrontation between Japan and the Qing dynasty—that is, to the Sino-Japanese War of 1894/1895. The institutions of the modern nation-state and industrial capitalism were established in Japan, which was in the process of a conversion to imperialism. At the same time, by this point the Qing dynasty not only was massive but possessed modern military arms. As a result, at the time of the Sino-Japanese War the Japanese were quite fearful of the Qing dynasty. Seen in this light, the current state of affairs much more closely resembles that of the 1880s than the 1930s. The current political tensions in East Asia—including those surrounding Taiwan, which Japan colonized as a result of the Sino-Japanese War—have their origins in the events of this period. A repetitive structure exists in this way in East Asia.

It goes without saying that this type of problem is not confined to East Asia. For example, it applies as well to Russia and to the Middle East. Or rather, one should say that this type of repetitive structure exists on a global scale. In the Japanese Iwanami edition of this book, I included a diagram of the "Stages of Global Capitalism," which presents a linear development of the stages of world capitalism, including mercantilism, liberalism, and imperialism. In other words, this represents a view of development according to stages, based on the evolution of productive forces. Seen from this perspective, the 1990s would be characterized by a transition from durable consumer goods to information industries. Yet this linear view obscures the repetitive structure.

On this point, I learned from Immanuel Wallerstein (1980) to think of "liberalism" and "imperialism" as cyclical processes rather than as historical stages. According to his thinking, the age of "liberalism" describes the world system in which there are nation-states that have achieved an overwhelming hegemony. In contrast, in the age of "imperialism," hegemonic nation-states are in the process of decline, but new nations have not yet gained enough power to usurp them, and thus a period of struggle continues.

According to Wallerstein, only three nations have achieved hegemony in the world economy: the Netherlands, Great Britain, and the United States. When the Netherlands as hegemonic nation was liberalist, the backward Britain was mercantilist (protectionist). In addition, politically the Netherlands was not an absolute monarchy but rather a republic. The nation's capital, Amsterdam, was an exceptional city where Descartes and Locke went into voluntary exile and where Spinoza was able to live in peace. When the Netherlands lost its hegemony, there was a period of political and economic strife between Britain and France, which aimed to be its successor; this is referred to as the age of mercantilism. On the other hand, although the Netherlands was overtaken by Britain in the latter half of the eighteenth century in terms of manufacturing, it continued to maintain hegemony in the areas of commerce and finance. It was in the nineteenth century that Britain achieved an overall superiority, establishing what is known as the stage of liberalism (1810–1870).

After 1870, Britain began to decline as a result of the rise of Germany, the United States, Russia, Japan, and others, and a fierce political and economic competition ensued between those countries. This is referred to as the stage of imperialism. Yet if we see the stage of imperialism not as being defined by various historical characteristics, as Lenin prescribed, but rather as a stage in which the hegemonic nation is in a state of decline, but before a successor nation has been established—thus leading to a state of conflict—then one can say that this stage came to an end in the late 1930s when the United States established its hegemony.

I include here the same chart with the additional row of "Hegemonic nation" (table 1). This category illustrates why the repetitive structure becomes visible within a 120-year rather than a 60-year span. It is generally believed that in the 1990s, the United States achieved overwhelming hegemony on the order of the British Empire in the nineteenth century. Yet it was prior to 1990 that the United States was a hegemonic nation; from the

TABLE 1 Stages of Global Capitalism

	–1810	1810–1870	1870–1930	1930–1990	1990–
Global capitalism type	Mercantilism	Liberalism	Imperialism	Late capitalism	Neoliberalism
Hegemonic nation	(Imperialist)	Great Britain (Liberalist)	(Imperialist)	United States (Liberalist)	(Imperialist)
Capital	Merchant capital	Industrial capital	Finance capital	State monopoly capital	Multinational capital
Global commodity type	Woolen textiles	Fiber textiles	Heavy industry	Durable consumer goods	Information
State	Absolutism	Nation-state	Imperialism	Welfare state	Regionalism

1970s, as illustrated by the removal of the dollar from the gold standard, it had entered into a period of economic decline corresponding to the rise of Germany and Japan. After 1990, the United States remained dominant in the realms of finance and commerce, but this is a common experience for a hegemonic nation in decline, as illustrated in the cases of the Netherlands and Britain.

For this reason, one should locate the American stage of "liberalism" not in neoliberalism but rather in what is referred to as the Cold War period (1930–1990). During that time, the various advanced capitalist nations cooperated in opposing the Soviet bloc as a common enemy while, on the domestic front, advancing policies of social welfare and the protection of labor. Despite their hostile and revolutionary outward appearances, the Soviet bloc and the domestic socialist parties, far from presenting a threat to world capitalism, worked to supplement and stabilize it.

What came to the fore in the advanced capitalist nations beginning in the 1980s were the policies of Reaganism and Thatcherism, which reduced the taxation and regulation of capital. This is referred to as neoliberalism. Such policies, however, do not contradict imperialism. Hannah Arendt (1973) claimed that one of the distinguishing characteristics of imperialism that became clear in the 1880s was that the state was freed from the boundaries of the nation. That is to say, imperialism describes a condition in which the state and capital rush headlong into global competition, even at the cost of sacrificing the nation. For example, "the export of capital" is one of the distinguishing characteristics cited for late-nineteenth-century imperialism. Yet this signifies the search for cheap overseas labor at the expense of domestic labor. In that case, the situation is the same in the globalization and neoliberalism of the 1990s. The decline of the welfare state allows capital and nation to escape from financial burdens and enter into global competition. It cannot be helped that this leads domestically to class disparity. This type of thinking is nothing more than a reprise of the ideology of social Darwinism—the survival of the fittest—that held sway after 1870. In this sense, the state of affairs following

1990 should be seen not from the perspective of liberalism but rather from that of imperialism.

Michael Hardt and Antonio Negri (2000) have claimed that since the 1990/1991 Gulf War, the United States has no longer been an imperialist power. They assert that its power differs from modern imperialism, which represents the extension of the nation-state, and resembles instead the kind of "empire" of the ancient Roman Empire. In truth, the way that the United States acted in the Gulf War, with the support of the United Nations, appeared different from its previous actions. Furthermore, there is also a certain basis for the claim that what the United States defended was global capitalism and the world market rather than the interests of one nation. However, the United States' trying at the time to obtain the backing of the United Nations was not in order to act as a new "empire" but rather simply because it had lost the financial resources to act as a hegemonic nation. The fact that the United States was not a world empire was demonstrated in the 2003 Iraq War, in which it ignored the United Nations and acted alone. At that time, what became more and more clear was that Europe had emerged as a megastate to oppose the United States and furthermore that China, India, as well as the new Russia had also emerged as powers to oppose it. No doubt there will unfold a competition between these states over which will emerge as the next hegemonic power. In this sense, one must say that post-1990 represents the stage of imperialism.

This is the perspective that I hold at the moment. Of course, this is not something that predicts future events. However, at the least there can be no doubt that the repetitive structure inherent in state and capital will continue. If we do not pay attention to this, we will indeed be fated to repeat history.

EDITOR'S INTRODUCTION

ON REPETITION, SINGULARITY, AND HISTORICITY

SEIJI M. LIPPIT

History and Repetition is a translation of volume 5 of *Teihon Karatani Kōjin shū* (*Selected Writings of Karatani Kōjin: Standard Edition*), published by Iwanami shoten in 2004. Many of the essays included in this book were first published in journals in 1989 and were subsequently collected in the book *Shūen o megutte* (*On Endings*), published by Fukutake shoten in 1990. These include "Kindai Nihon no gensetsu kūkan" (The Discursive Space of Modern Japan), which first appeared in the January 1989 issue of *Kaien*; "Ōe Kenzaburō no aregorī" (The Allegory of Ōe Kenzaburō) (*Kaien*, October 1989); "Murakami Haruki no fūkei" (The Landscape of Murakami Haruki) (*Kaien*, November–December 1989); and "Kindai bungaku no owari" (The End of Modern Literature, translated here as "The End of the Modern Novel"), a combination of "Dōitsusei no enkan" (The Cycle of Identity) (*Kaien*, March 1988) and "Shōsetsu to iu tōsō" (The Struggle That Is the Novel) (*Gunzō*, June 1989).

These essays were substantially revised and in some cases expanded for their inclusion in the 2004 Iwanami edition. Furthermore, two additional chapters were included in the Iwanami volume: "Josetsu: *Rui Bonaparuto no Buryumēru jūhachinichi*" (Introduction: On *The Eighteenth Brumaire of Louis Bonaparte*)—earlier versions of which had appeared in the journal *Hihyō kūkan*, no. 7 (1995), and as part of a new Japanese translation of the first edition of Marx's text published by Ōta Shuppan in 1996—and the newly written "Nihon ni okeru rekishi to hanpuku" (History and Repetition in Japan). These chapters provide a theoretical framework for the book's analysis of historical repetition and its application to Japanese history. The volume concludes with "Bukkyō to fashizumu" (Buddhism and

Fascism), a shorter version of which initially appeared in *Hihyō kūkan*, no. 18 (1998).

As Karatani notes in his preface to this edition, the essays thus first appeared in a period of dramatic historical transformation, both on a global scale and in Japan. On the world stage, the collapse in 1989 of the Berlin Wall and subsequently of the Soviet Union marked the end of the Cold War order (which had provided the political framework of postwar intellectual and cultural discourse in Japan as elsewhere) and generated the confident proclamation (simultaneously belated and premature) of the "end of history."[1] In Japan, the death in January 1989 of the Shōwa emperor, who had been on the throne since 1926 and who embodied in his person an ineluctable link between the wartime and postwar periods, underscored the widespread sense of a watershed historical break. Within a year or so, the collapse of the high-flying bubble economy (marked by the crash of the stock market and the implosion of real-estate values) led to a sustained period of economic stagnation that called into question widely held assumptions about the nature of Japanese capitalism and the nation's place in the global economy, and that was (in hindsight) a prefiguration of the worldwide financial collapse of 2008. In this sense, this book can be considered a critical intervention, by one of Japan's premier intellectuals, into a moment of radical historical transition that continues to unfold.

The conjunction of these two moments of "ending," existing simultaneously in Japan and on a global scale, can be seen to underwrite the analysis contained in this book, which originated, in effect, with a consideration of the parallax (to use one of Karatani's key concepts) existing between different discursive systems. In particular, the theme of repetition emerged from Karatani's examination of the gap between the Western (Christian) calendar and the Japanese practice of periodizing history according to imperial era names. Thus in "The Discursive Space of Modern Japan," Karatani points out the pattern of

---

[1] On the belatedness of the proclamation of the end of history, see Derrida (1994:15–16).

repetition that exists between the Meiji (1868–1912) and Shōwa (1926–1989) periods—both in the specificity of, for example, the ritual suicides of General Nogi Maresuke and the novelist Mishima Yukio, which occurred in Meiji 45 and Shōwa 45, respectively, and in broader political movements (or processes) such as the Meiji Restoration and its "re-presentation" as the Shōwa Restoration. But the key analytical move, for Karatani, occurred when he situated this repetition internal to Japanese history in the broader context of historical shifts in the stages of global capitalism. In effect, it is in the gap between these two practices of periodization that the theme of historical repetition comes into focus.

Parallax, which literally refers to the apparent displacement of an object's position when viewed along two different lines of sight, is a concept that Karatani has developed in a philosophical context most extensively in his *Transcritique* (2001; English translation 2003), a tour de force cross-reading of Kant and Marx that Slavoj Žižek has called "one of the most original attempts to recast the philosophical and political bases of opposition to the empire of capital of the current period" (2004:121). There, it indicates for Karatani an antinomy between different positions (or discursive systems) that never resolves into any unified or static positionality. Žižek writes,

> Karatani starts with the question: what is the appropriate response when we are confronted with an antinomy in the precise Kantian sense of the term? His answer is that we should renounce all attempts to reduce one aspect of it to the other (or, even more, to enact a kind of "dialectical synthesis" of the opposites). One should, on the contrary, assert antinomy as irreducible, and conceive the point of radical critique not as a determinate position as opposed to another position, but as the irreducible gap between the positions—the purely structural interstice between them. (121)[2]

---

2 Žižek subsequently further developed this conception of the "parallax gap" into an organizing concept for his book *The Parallax View* (2006).

In a sense, the conceptualization of parallax as the "purely structural interstice" between different discursive systems and positions, as well as the exploration of intellectual figures who have wrestled with such parallax in the domains of modern philosophy, literature, and history, has been an underlying theme of Karatani's work throughout. This includes the first two books of his translated into English, *Origins of Modern Japanese Literature* (*Nihon kindai bungaku no kigen*, 1980; English translation 1993)—in which the novelist Natsume Sōseki is seen to maintain an intermediary position between the literary institutions of East and West, allowing him to construct a singular theoretical critique of literature—and *Architecture as Metaphor* (*In'yū to shite no kenchiku*, 1981; English translation 1995),[3] which explores the gap between the construction and the deconstruction of form in various fields of knowledge.

In *History and Repetition*, one can say that the difference represented by parallax is framed by the essentially temporal relation formed through the inexorable process of historical repetition. Repetition, in Karatani's analysis, is not defined by the recurrence of events, nor is it a question of the eternal recurrence of the same. Instead, he notes that "repetition is possible only in terms of *form* (structure) and not *event* (content)." Rather than the repetition of history, in fact, it may be useful to speak of repetition *as* history, as defining, in particular, two different conceptions of historicity that are woven throughout Karatani's analysis. Thus, on the one hand, repetition is defined as the recurrent moment of violent crisis that attends major transitions in the historical development of capital. Karatani writes that "the accumulation and expansion of capital takes place only according to the violent selection brought about by recession and depression," while noting that the transitions in the stages of capitalism have resulted in "total reorganizations and transformations of society, while also leading inevitably to the alternation of hegemonic nations within global capitalism." In this sense, repetition is the necessary function of a historical process defined by the

---

[3] The English translation of *Architecture as Metaphor* incorporates elements from a number of other works by Karatani. See Kohso (1995:xvii).

structural renewal of capital. Yet, on the other hand, one can say that the recurrent crises also expose another kind of historicity, one that exists outside this kind of "structural causality" and that Karatani refers to as "singularity."

In volume 2 of his work *Investigations* (*Tankyū*), a philosophical treatise that he completed just before a number of the essays in this book first appeared, Karatani develops a conception of singularity (*tandokusei*) that stands in contradistinction to particularity (*tokushusei*) (1989b:9–32).[4] Karatani notes that in philosophical discourse, the concept of the particular is in fact defined by the possibility of its belonging to the category of the general. He fixes instead on a conception of the singular that exists radically exterior to any such dialectical circuit, resisting assimilation into categories of universality. Singularity is, for Karatani, essentially tied to the function of the proper name, while also indicating a historicity that "differs from history as structure, history as narrative, or history as law" (15). Ultimately, what underlies Karatani's conception of singularity, what is signified by the "irreplaceability" of the proper name, is an essential relation to alterity. As Hosea Hirata has written, in Karatani's analysis the proper name—always bestowed by others—marks the site of a primary encounter between self and other. Hirata writes, "As an exemplary signifier, it floats outside me, yet at the same time I feel that it is inside me, as a most integral part of me. This contradictory gap between the inside and the outside of my 'self' revealed through my proper name is the space of the Other" (2005:75). In fact, in *Investigations* Karatani situates the concept of singularity in an analysis that is often spatial in orientation; he develops, for example, the conception of a "communicative space" located in between communities, a place of radical exteriority and intercourse (*kōtsū*) where a genuine encounter with others (those who do not share common rules) is possible.[5]

---

4 The essays in *Investigations* were originally serialized in the journal *Gunzō* from 1986 to 1988 and published as a book in 1989. For discussions of Karatani's conception of singularity, see Kohso (1995:xxii–xxvi) and Hirata (2005:71–76).
5 On this point, see also Karatani (1993a).

In turn, it is the *temporal* dimension of such an interstice that can be seen to form one of the underlying subjects of *History and Repetition*, which focuses on the moment of historical transition (crisis) opened up by the compulsive process of repetition existing at the heart of economic, political, and discursive systems. Thus the book explicates the brutally violent mechanism of repetition at work in various systems of representation. Karatani conceptualizes this process through a powerful rereading of Marx's *The Eighteenth Brumaire of Louis Bonaparte* as a theory of the state to parallel the theory of political economy found in *Capital*. While the two works appear fundamentally different (a systematic, theoretical analysis of capitalism, on the one hand, and a journalistic account of contemporary politics, on the other), Karatani argues that an analogous analytical framework underlies both works: where Marx, in his analysis of industrial capitalism, returns to the earlier form of merchant capital, in *The Eighteenth Brumaire* he places the bourgeois state in relation to the archaic form of absolute monarchy, which the modern nation-state has supposedly overcome. Yet it is precisely in its moment of crisis, Karatani argues, that the bourgeois state evokes (re-presents) the absolutist monarch of the past.

This conception of a political and economic return of the repressed in turn underwrites the examination of emperor-system fascism in Japan; as Karatani emphasizes, fascism in Japan emerged following the establishment of Taishō democracy, which introduced universal male suffrage (just as Louis Bonaparte, and later the Nazi Party, came into power through the representative system). Karatani rejects the kind of exceptionalism that would seek to exclude the Japanese historical example from the category of fascism, arguing instead that in both European and Japanese cases, fascism should be understood as a dynamic process (a counterrevolution deployed against the threat of socialist revolution) enmeshed in a historical repetition compulsion. For Karatani, fascism originates in the field of representative democracy, which, in its moment of political and economic crisis, calls forth once more the repressed figure of the absolutist monarch. In the Japanese case, the

"Shōwa Restoration" (a slogan claimed by fascists) represented an imperial restoration as the repetition of the Meiji Restoration. But in Karatani's analysis, it is not the figure of the emperor himself who fulfills the role of Louis Bonaparte in this representation but rather Konoe Fumimaro, who twice served as the nation's prime minister and whose conception of a "new order" established the basis for economic and political reforms whose impact would carry over into the postwar period.

At the same time, however, there is also a certain slippage that takes place in this ineluctable process of historical repetition: Karatani argues that at the heart of this mechanism lies a "hole," a lacuna that can never be filled but that nevertheless fundamentally structures systems of representation (discursive, economic, and political). For Karatani, the historical repetition compulsion marks the return of this repressed fissure, which is precisely what any system of representation both tries to obscure but cannot do without: Karatani thus writes that this "unrepresentable" void is what "makes such systems of representation possible. This hole is not in any way invisible but in fact exists everywhere. Yet for that very reason, its nature as a hole is hidden." In effect, it exists both inside and outside the system of representation, constituting the site of its functioning while also always maintaining the possibility of systemic crisis.[6] In Karatani's examination of this invisible yet central hole at the core of the process of historical repetition, the domain of literature comes to have a key role.

The middle chapters of this book consist of a series of important analyses of a number of the central figures of contemporary Japanese literature, including Ōe, Murakami, Mishima, and Nakagami Kenji. In one sense, literature—and in particular the modern novel—is a privileged site for this analysis because it brings into focus the connection between the proper name and historicity. Or, more precisely, it is in the process of modern literature's demise that this connection comes into the open. As Karatani notes in his brilliant analysis of *Football in the Year*

---

6 For a discussion of Karatani's argument in relation to Lacanian psychoanalysis, see Endo (2002:2–3).

Man'en 1 (*Man'en gannen no futtobōru*, 1967; translated as *The Silent Cry*), Ōe's novel is characterized by a use of proper names that lies outside the conventional practices of modern realism, including the use of allegorical "type names" for his main characters (Mitsusaburō and Takashi) as well as the notable elision of important place-names, such as that of the remote village (and nearby "provincial city") on the island of Shikoku where much of the narrative takes place. Karatani argues that Ōe's work is deliberately presented as a negation of the realist novel, which in effect came into being through the substitution of "ordinary" names for allegorical ones. Focusing on the particular, "realistic" details of everyday experience, the modern novel was seen as providing access to the universal: this dialectic between the particular and the universal was precisely the basis for the Romantic differentiation between symbol and allegory.[7] In turn, according to Karatani, Ōe's rejection of realism is not in fact a negation of history but rather the opposite: through his deployment of allegory, Karatani argues, Ōe resists the dissolution of particularity into generality, thereby attempting to gain access to a certain singular, historical "truth."[8]

Ultimately, in Karatani's analysis, this historicity is related to what Takeuchi Yoshimi has referred to as the "aporias of modern Japanese history," and what Karatani, for his part, refers to as its parallax. In Ōe's novel, it is located in the interstitial space framed by the conjunction of the local era name "Man'en" and the universal, global designation "1960" (the year of the anti–U.S.-Japan Security Treaty uprising), an opposition that comes into view by way of the reenactment of the Man'en

---

7 In his discussion of symbol and allegory, Karatani cites Walter Benjamin's *Origins of German Tragic Drama*, but we can also perhaps discern here shades of Paul de Man's analysis in his well-known essay "The Rhetoric of Temporality" (1983).

8 One of the running motifs of Ōe's novel is the possibility of unveiling an abject and horrific "truth," what is described as an "absolute truth which, if a man tells it, leaves him no alternative but to be killed by others, or kill himself, or go mad and turn into a monster. The kind of truth that once uttered leaves you clutching a bomb with the fuse irretrievably lit" (1974:157).

rebellion as the game of football organized by Takashi more than a century later. In "The Discursive Space of Modern Japan," Karatani argues that the intellectual terrain of modern Japan is framed by competing identifications with Asia and with the West, an opposition exemplified by the contrasting discourses of Fukuzawa Yukichi's "de-Asianization" on the one hand and, on the other, of Okakura Kakuzō's assertion of Japan as the museum of Asian civilization and his proclamation that "Asia is one" (1970:1). For Karatani, this oppositional structure is further complicated by continually shifting orientations toward national rights and popular rights.

In effect, Karatani's presentation of the coordinate space of modern discourse, as well as the continual shifting between quadrants, helps to explicate the mechanism underlying the recurrent phenomenon of ideological conversion (*tenkō*), which was shaped by the double inscription of modern Japan as both belonging to and existing outside the West.[9] This contradiction, most dramatically and violently realized in Japan's status as non-Western imperial power, could not be transcended through any simple declaration of the overcoming of modernity. In Karatani's reading, Ōe's novel is an attempt to grasp this parallax that structures Japanese modernity, and the impossibility of resolving it into any unified positionality (a recognition that, in effect, amounts to the rejection of the concept and practice of *tenkō*) is figured through the depiction of a recurrent historical violence associated, throughout the novel, with the topos of Asia.

---

9 The practice of ideological conversion is typically associated with the apostasy of Marxist intellectuals and activists in the 1930s under pressure by the state. A number of critics, including Yoshimoto Takaaki (2008:99–119) and Fujita Shōzō (1997:45–52), have shown, however, that the practice of *tenkō* in that context was not based simply on a renunciation of Marxism but rather involved a shift in the terms of political struggle from one based on class to one based on ethnicity. In effect, it was a shift in positionality, from an opposition between classes to one between nations, that allowed for the conversion of Marxism into nationalism. For an insightful discussion of *tenkō*, see Bourdaghs (2003:39–44).

In turn, Karatani reads Murakami's *Pinball in the Year 1973* (*1973-nen no pinbōru*, 1980; translated as *Pinball, 1973*) as a parody of *Football in the Year Man'en 1* and, more specifically, as an attempt to overcome the type of historical violence and struggle captured in Ōe's allegorical narrative. In Murakami's early fiction, Karatani points out, proper names are almost entirely excluded. In their place are differential signs (indicating difference internal to the system of representation rather than any necessary connection to the object of representation), reflected in the prevalence of numbers. For example, Ōe's novel is structured around the conflict between the two brothers, Mitsusaburō and Takashi, who represent an opposition between reflection (interiority) and violence (action) that is seen to exist at the core of modern history and that is reflected in the allegorical meanings embedded in their proper names (Mitsu = nectar; Taka = hawk). In place of this sibling rivalry, in *Pinball* we find the nameless female twins, who are referred to by the narrator as 208 and 209, numbers that represent a completely arbitrary designation. "Names here are nothing more than differential signs for distinguishing things that are completely indistinguishable," Karatani writes. "In other words, proper names are dissolved into language in general."

In turn, Murakami's works are replete with specific historical markers: references to the student movement of the 1960s and early 1970s, to Mishima's suicide in 1970, and so on. Yet for Karatani this pervasive citation of history in fact marks an evacuation or emptying out of history, through the operation of a certain type of Romantic irony. For example, Murakami's sentence "That was in 1960, the year Bobby Vee sang 'Red Rubber Ball'" (1985:17) expresses an irony analogous to that undergirding Kunikida Doppo's "Those Unforgettable People" (*Wasureenu hitobito*, 1898), which for Karatani serves as one of the foundational texts of the institution of modern literature. In Doppo's story, those who are ultimately deemed "unforgettable" are not important figures who should remain fixed in memory (those who are given proper names, in other words) but rather those who are eminently anonymous and nameless. In

Origins of Modern Japanese Literature, Karatani names this process the "discovery of landscape," a necessary component of the establishment of interiority and, in turn, of a consciousness of national community. In the same way, while being keenly aware of the political meaning of 1960, Murakami ironically associates it with a "meaningless" artifact of a global popular culture. In this sense, Murakami repeats the discovery of landscape, but this time on a transnational, rather than a national, scale.

And just as Karatani argues that in Doppo's case the establishment of interiority signified the transcendence of political struggle, Murakami's fiction too is positioned as emerging through the overcoming of the conflicts of modern Japan, and most immediately those of the 1960s. This is, in effect, the meaning of Murakami's substitution of "pinball" for "football." Karatani notes that Ōe's football is the kind of game that Claude Lévi-Strauss analyzes in *The Savage Mind*: one that structures society according to a set of asymmetrical relationships, of which the most fundamental is the difference between winner and loser. Yet pinball is a game that is engaged not with others but with a machine:

> On the one hand, pinball appears to create the outcome of asymmetrical relationships of winner and loser, in the same way as football. However, the idea of a machine as victor is odd. It is also odd for the player to be the loser. Victory and defeat do not become events (it is another matter if one is competing against another player). In one sense, the player always loses. Yet this does not constitute an event, for players need only to replay. They act only within the rules of this machine, and what is tested is nothing more than the extent to which they have (physically) mastered those rules.

When the narrator finally comes face-to-face with the long-sought-after pinball machine, his conversation with it, Karatani points out, is a monologue: "'She' is not an other like 'Naoko.' That is, she does not place limits on 'I.' The love that 'I' has for the machine is nothing but self-love." In this way, for Murakami, the game of pinball indicates entry into a virtuality ("It is hardly necessary to point out," Karatani writes, "that today's computer games are the descendants of pinball") devoid of genuine encounter or struggle with others.

If, in this comparison between *Origins of Modern Japanese Literature* and *History and Repetition*, Murakami can be seen to occupy the position of Doppo, the role of Sōseki is taken up by two figures: Takeda Taijun and Sakaguchi Ango, around whom the last chapter of the book revolves. If the establishment of interiority signified the overcoming of political struggle, a similar gesture of transcendence was repeated in the discourse of overcoming modernity in the midst of the Pacific War, exemplified by the 1942 symposium "Overcoming Modernity" (Kindai no chōkoku), which brought together some of the central intellectual figures of the time. As Takeuchi Yoshimi's analysis shows, what this attempt ultimately signified was the overcoming of the core conflicts and contradictions of modernity (what Takeuchi articulates as the "aporias" of modern Japanese history); in this sense, it can be considered as precisely structurally equivalent to the establishment of interiority (as transcendence of political struggle), which was for Karatani the founding gesture of modern literature. In contrast, Takeda and Ango, writing at around the same time as such calls to transcend the modern, provide a counterdiscourse that instead engages the contradictions of modernity. Karatani sees in these two figures a reflection of the "radical core of Buddhist thought," mediated by their own complicated relations with institutional Buddhism and with Marxism, that formed the intellectual basis for their resistance to fascism.

For Takeda, the alternative to the discourse of overcoming modernity (and to the violence of empire) was expressed in his study of the venerable Chinese historian Sima Qian in *Sima Qian: The World of the "Historical Records"* (*Shiba Sen: Shiki no sekai*, 1943), which begins with the line "Sima Qian was a man who lived on in shame" (1972c:25). Karatani notes that this shame refracts Takeda's own experience of falling away from both Marxism and the Buddhist clergy, as well as his participation in the invasion of China—the object of his lifelong study—as a soldier in the imperial army. But more fundamentally, Karatani argues, shame (as opposed to guilt) is a sentiment that is necessarily situated in relation to others: for this reason, while there can be "salvation" from guilt, no such possibility is available to overcome shame. In *The World of the "Historical Records,"* Takeda unfolds a spatial delineation of a world existing without center (or, more precisely, possessing multiple centers); furthermore, it is a world that had passed through multiple experiences of "ruin" (*metsubō*). As Karatani notes, this analysis no doubt contained within it a prediction of the collapse of the Japanese empire. Indeed, in the aftermath of the war, Takeda, who was living in Shanghai at the time of the defeat, depicted the collapse of empire as an experience of "absolute ruin" unprecedented in Japanese history (1972a:94).

For his part, Ango analyzes the postwar collapse through the concept of "fallenness" (*daraku*).[10] In 1942, the same year as the "Overcoming Modernity" conference, Ango published "A Personal View of Japanese Culture" (Nihon bunka shikan), in which he counters the German architect Bruno Taut's laudatory account of traditional Japanese architecture (including, most famously, such landmarks as the ancient temple Hōryūji and the seventeenth-century Katsura Detached Palace) with the beauty embodied in such artifacts of modern society as a factory, a destroyer, and a prison. It is surely no accident that Ango here points to emblems of industrial, military, and disciplinary power—his rejection of traditional aesthetics (he wrote that he would not have any problem with Hōryūji being turned into a parking lot) is connected, in this way, to the irreducibly modern sites of subjectification that also served as

---

10 *Daraku* is typically translated as "decadence," but I follow Joseph Murphy's lead in avoiding this translation and rendering it instead as "fallenness." Murphy points out that Karatani's discussion of Ango's conception of *daraku* counters the typical placement of that author's work in the context of postwar nihilism. See Karatani (2001:542n.7).

the core apparatus of the wartime regime. He thus implicitly underscores the fundamental contradiction underlying the proclamation of overcoming modernity during wartime. In turn, in his postwar essay "On Fallenness" (Darakuron),[11] Ango situates the debasement of falling away from transcendent ideals as the basis for the recovery of an authentic humanity.

Karatani in this way demonstrates that Takeda and Ango, as symbolized by their conceptions of "ruin" and "fallenness," articulated a sensibility that was diametrically opposed to the trajectory of transcendence that marked the wartime calls to overcome modernity. And, in the moment of absolute collapse that the end of the war represented, the two writers conceptualized both the terror and the potentiality of an existence placed outside nation and culture. As Karatani notes, however, for Ango the sense of being thrust outside the familiar structures of home had always been, in a sense, the core meaning of literature. In his essay "The Home of Literature" (Bungaku no furusato, 1941), Ango writes of finding the essence of literature in a certain exceptional experience of reading, an experience of "being suddenly thrust out, feeling confusion as though our preconceived understandings have been betrayed." Karatani writes, "Just as he does with the word 'fallenness' [*daraku*], Ango overturns the accepted meaning of the word 'home' [*furusato*]. For Ango, home is not something intimate or familiar but instead signifies a state of being thrust into alterity." For Karatani, then, Ango's "fallenness," like the concept of shame in Takeda, signifies an exposure to others—piercing the enclosure of interiority, it thrusts one into an inevitable encounter with alterity. In this sense, we might say that for Takeda and Ango, the concepts of *metsubō* and *daraku* denote precisely the space of exteriority and historicity that Karatani designates by the word "singularity."

In recent years, Karatani has spurred a great deal of debate in Japan (and elsewhere) with his proclamation of the "end of modern literature." His pronouncement points to the dissi-

---

11 For complete English translations of "Darakuron," see Sakaguchi (1986, 2010).

pation of the central role that literature (or, more specifically, the novel) played in modernity, especially in the formation of national languages and the imagining of national community. At the same time, it also indicates intellectuals' (including Karatani's) loss of faith in literature as an effective arena for the contestation of philosophical and intellectual thought, such that Jean-Paul Sartre had once written that "literature is, in essence, the subjectivity of a society in permanent revolution" (1988:139, cited in Karatani 2005:38). The middle chapters of this volume, which trace the thematics of repetition in contemporary writers from Mishima, Ōe, and Nakagami to Murakami, essentially establish the analytical groundwork for this later declaration of the demise of modern literature (in fact, chapter 6 of *History and Repetition* was originally titled "The End of Modern Literature"). Yet it is perhaps not surprising that these essays, which essentially lay out the case for literature's absolute decline as a medium for political or historical critique, constitute some of the most important statements on literature that Karatani has made. For he had always maintained a critical perspective and sense of distance in relation to literature. In an environment in which contemporary theoretical discourses had in some sense internalized Sartre's conception of literature as revolution (Julia Kristeva's *Revolution in Poetic Language* being but one prominent example), *Origins of Modern Japanese Literature* stands as a pioneering critique of the institution of literature as one of the sites of modern subjectification. For Karatani, the history of modern literature as an institution is, in effect, a history of continual attempts to overcome the political conflicts that attend Japanese modernity. And it is always on the critical margins of this institution—such as in the case of Sōseki's theoretical critique carried out in *Theory of Literature*—that the essence and import of literary practice come to the surface. In this regard, the figures of Ango and Takeda, who stand against the discourse of overcoming modernity not only of the 1940s but also in its "postmodern" iteration, are no exception. In their explorations of conceptions of *daraku* and *metsubō*, they in effect identify the core meaning of what Karatani has always seen as the possibility of literature, which, for him, emerges precisely in its state of fallenness and ruin.[12]

A Note and Acknowledgments

Japanese names are rendered in this book in the customary Japanese order, surname first. A number of authors are typically referred to by their pen names—such as Sōseki, Ōgai, Ango, and Doppo, among others—and I have also followed Japanese convention in this regard. As much as possible, I have tried to relegate explanatory material to the glossary at the back of the book. The footnotes contained in the original Japanese Iwanami edition are designated as "Author's note"; all other notes are from the translators, as are parenthetical citations in the text.

Translations of the preface and all other chapters in the book are my own, with the exception of chapters 5 and 6; I am grateful to Hisayo Suzuki and Michael Bourdaghs for their careful translations of those two chapters. Earlier versions of several chapters (as indicated in footnotes to those chapters) have previously appeared in English; I benefited greatly from being able to consult the earlier work of translators, including Sandra Buckley, Sabu Kohso, and Joseph Murphy. I am also grateful to Jennifer Cullen, Timothy Goddard, Koichi Haga, Yukio Lippit, and Franz Prichard for their help at various stages of this project. Jennifer Crewe of Columbia University Press provided unflagging support and helpful advice, and I was also aided by the suggestions of two anonymous readers for the press as well as by expert editing by Mike Ashby and Irene Pavitt. Above all, I would like to thank Kojin Karatani for his invaluable guidance and continued support.

---

12 On this point, see Lippit (2004:101–12). There, I cite a statement by Derrida that—although his approach to literature is quite different—sheds light on the repetition of origins at the end of literature: "But given the paradoxical structure of this thing called literature, its beginning *is* its end. It began with a certain relation to its own institutionality, i.e., its fragility, its absence of specificity, its absence of object. The question of its origin was immediately the question of its end. Its history *is constructed* like the ruin of a monument which basically never existed" (1992:42).

HISTORY AND REPETITION

1 INTRODUCTION

ON THE EIGHTEENTH BRUMAIRE OF LOUIS BONAPARTE

1

When the communist system collapsed at the end of the 1980s and—as symbolized by Francis Fukuyama's (1998) assertion of "the end of history"—an optimistic outlook based on the globalization of representative democracy and liberal market economics was proclaimed, it appeared as if works by Marx such as *Capital* or *The Eighteenth Brumaire of Louis Bonaparte* had entirely lost their meaning. Yet if anything, it was at that point that these works began to emit a dull yet powerful luster. Since then, we have witnessed a worldwide structural recession and the dysfunction of representative democracy. This does not portend, however, the collapse of capitalism or of the modern nation-state. Rather, it exposes the fact that history exists within a kind of repetition compulsion.

It is precisely the problem of such a repetition compulsion that *Capital* and *The Eighteenth Brumaire* address. What Marx grasped in *Capital* is the repetition compulsion inherent in capital's movement toward accumulation. Capital is driven to self-reproduction through a ceaseless process of differentiation, and this process is unable to avoid the repetitive business cycle of recession, prosperity, economic crisis, recession. For its part, *The Eighteenth Brumaire* elucidates the repetition compulsion that cannot be resolved by the political form of the modern nation-state, a repetition compulsion that is in fact inevitably set in motion by the very attempt to resolve it. What must be

---

An earlier version of this chapter was translated by Sabu Kohso as "Representation and Repetition: *The 18th Brumaire of Louis Bonaparte* Revisited" (Karatani, n.d.).

recognized in the 1990s is that we still find ourselves in such a repetition compulsion.

For example, there were many who predicted that in reference to the emergence of a global economic crisis and the breakdown of the parliamentary system, the 1990s would resemble the 1930s. This type of thinking may appear to be nothing more than the familiar catastrophism on the part of the Left. But in the present context, at a time when the old-line Left has fallen from grace, I think this problem is worth serious scrutiny. This type of repetition points to the approximately sixty-year business cycle in global capitalism known as the Kondratieff wave.[1] Seen from an economic perspective, there was a transition to "late capitalism" in the 1930s; sixty years earlier, in the 1870s, there was a transition from liberalism to imperialism. In this sense, the 1990s will no doubt give rise to the transition to a global market economy. My intent, however, is not to examine this phenomenon in detail here. What I am interested in analyzing is the repetition compulsion that transcends the particular differences of each of these historical moments, and which in fact is the basis for the creation of new stages themselves.

Repetition in history does not signify the recurrence of the same events, for repetition is possible only in terms of *form* (structure) and not *event* (content). Events themselves are able to evade repetition, whereas a given structure—such as the business cycle—is unable to do so. This is precisely the type of repetition compulsion that I take up here. As Freud wrote, the compulsion to repeat marks the return of the repressed that can never be remembered; instead of being remembered, it is repeated in the present. What we are able to remember is nothing more than events. For this reason, to compare the *events* of the 1870s, 1930s, and 1990s is no doubt to lose sight of the "return of the repressed" that exists there. In order to see this process, we must turn to *Capital* and especially to *The Eighteenth Brumaire*. After all, from the very opening passages of this latter text, Marx problematizes the question of repetition in history.

---

1 That is, the theory of the "long wave" authored by N. D. Kondratieff [1892–1938]. For further details, see Mandel (1980). [Author's note]

What then does "the repressed" signify in this context? The answer is intertwined with the question of representation in the parliamentary system as well as in the capitalist economy, as mentioned at the outset. It is true that these systems are "repressive." Their compulsion to repeat, however, is not based on that type of repression. Instead, the "repressed" that remains absolutely unrepresentable is the "hole" that makes such systems of representation possible. This hole is not in any way invisible but in fact exists everywhere. Yet for that very reason, its nature as a hole is hidden.

In the capitalist economy, for example, one can say that money is just such a hole. In *Capital*, Marx made clear that money is a being—or rather a Heideggerean being-as-nothingness—that is driven to a perpetual movement of self-reproduction exceeding any human will. Classical economics mocked the perversity of the bullionist (the mercantilist), who worships money. Yet in times of financial panic, when the system of trust has collapsed, it is precisely money to which people rush. For classical or neoclassical economists, money is nothing more than a standard to express value, a means of payment—in other words, a visible "being." For just this reason, however, that which makes it possible for money, as a being = nothing (or to put it another way, as a "thing"), to exist in the commodity form (the value form) is concealed. It is in times of economic crisis—whether or not the crisis itself comes into being in dramatic fashion—that people are receptive to it. At such times, however, people kneel down before money. At that moment, money is not merely a thing but rather a sublime fetish. To put it conversely, money exists as something unrepresentable, and it is during the economic crisis as repetition compulsion that people experience this.

In *The Eighteenth Brumaire*, the "hole" that exists in the system of representation is the "king" who was banished by this system. We see that in its place, the "emperor" Bonaparte is restored to life. Kings, emperors, and presidents actually exist, just as money exists. But what is important is the fact that they are the "nothingness of being" that makes possible the system of representation. For this reason, it is not important who the "king" or "emperor" is, or even whether they are actually called king or emperor. What is at stake is that the parliamentary (representative) system created in modern times contains a hole that can never be filled, one that exists quite apart from the actual, visible king, president, or emperor; furthermore, it is precisely this hole that is repeated as the "return of the repressed."

The reason that I take up *The Eighteenth Brumaire* here is that it analyzes as a symptom what was repeated in the 1870s and the 1930s and that is likely being repeated in the 1990s. The events in France that it examines contain something that prefigures the later phenomena. It is not the events themselves, however, that lead me to believe this but rather Marx's penetrating analysis of them. Undeniably, *The Eighteenth Brumaire* is a journalistic work analyzing the contemporaneous French political situation; from the standpoint of modern-day historiography, it is bound to be inadequate. That one must consider more complex factors regarding the actual Louis Bonaparte or the Second Empire is self-evident. What I find in *The Eighteenth Brumaire*, however, is a fundamental consideration of the state, rather than actual history. This is similar to the relationship between *Capital* and British economic history. *Capital* does of course consider British economic history as its source material, but one can—and should—read *Capital* quite apart from it.

In *Capital*, Marx attempted to explicate the phantasmatic system organized by money. Nevertheless, this system should not be designated as the economic base. Instead, it belongs to the superstructure, organizing as well as concealing the economic base; in other words, it is the system of representation. For precisely this reason, it continually maintains within it the danger of collapse. For its part, *The Eighteenth Brumaire* takes up the unavoidable danger contained in another kind of system of representation, that of representative democracy. If *Capital* engaged economy as a question of representation, *The Eighteenth Brumaire* engages politics along the same lines. Similarly, if *Capital* is a critique of modern economics, *The Eighteenth Brumaire* is a critique of modern political science. Furthermore, in Bonapartism the two forms of representation come together. Thus the problems taken up by *The Eighteenth Brumaire* not only belong to the past but also emerge once more in the fascism of the 1930s as well as in the state of affairs since the 1990s.

There are several advantages to taking *The Eighteenth Brumaire* as a starting point. In considering 1930s fascism, for example, we should not think of it as a phenomenon specific only to Germany and Italy, for we would then lose sight of problems that emerged in the 1930s on a global scale. Furthermore, such a narrow focus would not provide an opportunity to think about the question of "repetition" in the 1990s. For, as I have already stated, events themselves cannot be repeated. In this sense, fascism would be considered merely a problem of the past. However, as long as the problems that burden the parliamentary system and the capitalist economy do not disappear, the problems of the past will continue to linger in the future.

The Eighteenth Brumaire is, for example, an indispensable text for understanding the fascism of 1930s Japan. Theories of fascism tend to be modeled on the experience of Germany and Italy, and such models do not necessarily apply smoothly to the Japanese case. As a result, nonsensical assertions such as those denying the existence of fascism in Japan are able to gain a fair amount of currency. There is, however, a limit to how much the concept of fascism alone can explain the phenomenon that emerged in advanced capitalist countries in the 1930s. This phenomenon was, in the first place, a counterrevolution in reaction to the Russian Revolution. In other words, it had to contain a certain degree of socialism itself. The movement of counterrevolution was spurred on by the Great Depression of the 1930s. For example, in America a president—Roosevelt—emerged who represented all parties and classes and who propelled wartime policy. This was not fascism, but neither was it liberalism. What is necessary in order to see such a phenomenon from a universal viewpoint? The answer is *The Eighteenth Brumaire* (I address the Japanese case in chapter 2).

The Eighteenth Brumaire is filled with insights that make possible a fundamental analysis not only of the imperialism of the 1870s and the fascism of the 1930s but also of the new state of affairs that has emerged since the 1990s. For example, in *The Eighteenth Brumaire*, Bonaparte's seizing of power is preceded by the collapse of the "Left" in 1848. This fact, despite differences in historical particulars, is also held in common by the 1870s, the 1930s, and the 1990s. To put it simply, I believe that fascism is one form of Bonapartism. But what is important is to see this as a dynamic process of the sort depicted in *The Eighteenth Brumaire*. Otherwise, the result would be nothing more than the production of another sterile definition.

For example, Engels defined Bonapartism as follows. In the conflict between the bourgeoisie and the proletariat, when a balance of power emerges between them and neither is able to seize state power, a temporary state power that maintains a certain autonomy from both is established. For Engels, Bonapartism refers to the character of an autocracy formed in this manner. Marxists have tended to follow this definition of Bonapartism without properly reading *The Eighteenth Brumaire*.

If one is talking only of a balance of class power, however, then one can also say that the absolutist monarchy was established in the equilibrium between feudal forces and the bourgeoisie. For this reason, one cannot understand the distinguishing feature of Bonapartism only by the fact that class conflict had shifted to that between the bourgeoisie and the proletariat. The difference between absolutist monarchy and Bonapartism—which emerges from within the bourgeois state formed through the overthrow of the absolutist monarchy—exists above all in the process of how the class equilibrium is achieved. It is obvious that in the latter case it is realized through the representative system based on popular elections and through the coalition of various political parties.[2] And, without

---

[2] Imprisoned in Italy, Gramsci viewed Bonapartism as a form of Caesarism. According to his thinking, coalition government is a form of Caesarism. However, one can say that his view of Bonapartism as a form of Caesarism was, if anything, meant to oppose Engels's view of Bonapartism, which had taken root among Marxists. Gramsci tried to analyze Bonapartism by going back to Caesar's actions in the Roman senate. But was it not Marx himself who had seen Bonaparte as a "repetition" of Caesar in *The Eighteenth Brumaire*? For this reason, my usage of the term "Bonapartism" also applies to the following matters that Gramsci discusses regarding Caesarism:

this basic understanding, it is impossible to grasp the meaning not only of Bonapartism but also of the subsequent forms of counterrevolution, including fascism.

2. The Question of the Representative System

In *The Eighteenth Brumaire*, Marx considers the question of representation on at least five different levels. The first is that of the parliamentary (representative) system. The February Revolution of 1848 gave birth for the first time to popular elections in a republic that had overthrown the monarchal system. In truth, however, it was this parliament that gave rise to the strange events that occurred thereafter. The events described in *The Eighteenth Brumaire* are unthinkable outside the system of popular suffrage. Marx points out the existence of actual social classes in the background of such a representative system. And subsequently, Engels would view Marx's great achievement as the discovery of the "laws of history," whereby in the background of political, religious, philosophical, and other ideological representations there exist socioeconomic class structures and conflict.

> In the modern world, Caesarist phenomena are quite different, both from those of the progressive Caesar / Napoléon I type, and from those of the Napoléon III type—although they tend towards the latter. In the modern world, the equilibrium with catastrophic prospects occurs not between forces which could in the last analysis fuse and unite—albeit after a wearying and bloody process—but between forces whose opposition is historically incurable and indeed becomes especially acute with the advent of Caesarist forms. However, in the modern world Caesarism also has a certain margin—larger or smaller, depending on the country and its relative weight in the global context. For a social form "always" has marginal possibilities for further development and organizational improvement, and in particular can count on the relative weakness of the rival progressive force as a result of its specific character and way of life. It is necessary for the dominant social form to preserve this weakness: this is why it has been asserted that modern Caesarism is more a police than a military system. (1971:222) [Author's note]

Yet what Marx actually discerned in these historical events was, conversely, a phenomenon that appears to advance independently of, or even counter to, such a socioeconomic class structure, and he tried to explicate its functioning. Clearly this function resides in the representative system. As Hans Kelsen would later state, in contrast to the assemblies of estates, "representation" in the parliament based on popular suffrage was nothing more than a fiction.[3] In other words, there can be no necessary relationship between those who represent and those who are represented. Marx emphasizes the independence of the political parties and their discourse from actual classes. Or rather, the latter constitute what Kenneth Burke refers to as "class unconsciousness," and they are rendered conscious as "classes" only in the place of the former's discourse (1966:70). This is also clear from Marx's comments on smallholder peas-

---

3 In "On the Essence and Value of Democracy" (1929), Kelsen wrote as follows:

One wanted to create the appearance, as if parliamentarism gave undiminished expression to the idea of democratic freedom, and *only* to this idea. The *fiction of representation* serves this purpose—the idea that parliament is only the *representative* of the people, that the people can express its will only in parliament, only through parliament—although the parliamentary principle is connected in all constitutions, without exception, to the provision that the representatives are to take *no binding instructions* from their voters, and that *parliament* is thus in its function legally *independent of the people*. Yes, it was with this declaration of independence by the parliament with regard to the people that the modern parliament first emerged, clearly distinguishing itself from the old assemblies of estates, whose members were bound by the imperative mandate of their groups of voters and were responsible to them. (2000:97)

In works such as *The Reasoning of Marxism* [*Marukusu shugi no riron*, 1974] and *On Engels* [*Engerusu-ron*, 1968], Hiromatsu Wataru emphasized that it was Engels who played "first violin" in the formation of historical materialism. I agree with this opinion—not in order to stress the importance of Engels but rather to point out that Marx's essence lies elsewhere. Engels's *The Peasant War in Germany*, written several years before *The Eighteenth Brumaire*, demonstrates what he called "the laws of history." Yet it is not only because of its lack of Marx's literary genius that this work cannot be compared to *The Eighteenth Brumaire* but also because it lacks any consciousness of systems of representation. [Author's note]

ants. First, he explains the arbitrariness of the relationship between the representatives and the represented as follows:

> Only one must not form the narrow-minded notion that the petty bourgeoisie, on principle, wishes to enforce an egoistic class interest. Rather, it believes that the *special* conditions of its emancipation are the *general* conditions within the frame of which alone modern society can be saved and the class struggle avoided. Just as little must one imagine that the democratic representatives are indeed all shopkeepers or enthusiastic champions of shopkeepers. According to their education and their individual position they may be as far apart as heaven from earth. What makes them representatives of the petty bourgeoisie is the fact that in their minds they do not get beyond the limits which the latter do not get beyond in life, that they are consequently driven, theoretically, to the same problems and solutions to which material interest and social position drive the latter practically. This is, in general, the relationship between the *political* and *literary representatives* of a class and the class they represent....
>
> The parliamentary party was not only dissolved into its two great factions, each of these factions was not only split up within itself, but the party of Order in parliament had fallen out with the party of Order *outside* parliament. The spokesmen and scribes of the bourgeoisie, its platform and its press, in short, the ideologists of the bourgeoisie and the bourgeoisie itself, the representatives and the represented, faced one another in estrangement and no longer understood one another. (Marx 1963:50–51, 102–3)

The fact that the relationship between the "representatives" and the "represented" is in this way fundamentally arbitrary made it possible for the industrial bourgeoisie as well as other classes to abandon their original "representatives" in favor of Bonaparte. On February 4, 1848, the various parties appeared as differences between "representatives"—that is, in the place of discourse. Three years later, however, Bonaparte seized power as someone representing everyone. Marx rejects reducing this to Bonaparte's own ideas, strategies, or character. None of these perspectives can explain the secret of how Louis Bonaparte—who, on February 4, 1848, had nothing to recommend him other than the fact that he was Napoléon's nephew—was able to attain the seat of power.

In *Capital*, Marx says that it is easy to see that money is a commodity, but that the real problem is to explain how and why a commodity is able to become money. He makes a similar statement with regard to Bonaparte. In response to Victor Hugo, who heaped "bitter and witty invective" upon Bonaparte, Marx writes that he will "demonstrate how the *class struggle* in France created circumstances and relationships that made it possible for a grotesque mediocrity to play a hero's part" (1963:8). Indeed, no matter how many times one repeats the type of criticism that Hugo unfurls, it amounts to the same thing as pointing out that money is no more than a piece of paper: nothing is revealed by such a critique. At the same time, the mystery raised by Marx cannot be unlocked simply by the phrase "class struggle." Rather, the mystery that made an emperor of Louis Bonaparte is hidden in the fact that the mechanism of the representative or discursive system exists autonomously, that "class struggle" can be made conscious only by way of such a mechanism, and furthermore, that this system maintains within it a hole that can never be filled.

In thinking of fascism, or of the current political trajectory, it is of decisive importance that all of this emerges only by way of representation in a general election. Marx points out that among the "representatives" and the "represented" there exists a class with neither its own representatives nor a discourse that would protect and generalize its own class interests, and that therefore must be represented by someone else. These are the smallholder peasants:

> In so far as millions of families live under economic conditions of existence that separate their mode of life,

their interests and their culture from those of the other classes, and put them in hostile opposition to the latter, they form a class. In so far as there is merely a local interconnection among these small-holding peasants, and the identity of their interests begets no community, no national bond and no political organization among them, they do not form a class. They are consequently incapable of enforcing their class interest in their own name, whether through a parliament or through a convention. They cannot represent themselves, they must be represented. Their representative must at the same time appear as their master, as an authority over them, as an unlimited governmental power that protects them against the other classes and sends them rain and sunshine from above. The political influence of the small-holding peasants, therefore, finds its final expression in the executive power subordinating society to itself. (Marx 1963:124)

In concrete terms, these peasants, who emerged for the first time onto the political stage via popular suffrage, cast their ballots for Louis Bonaparte. Yet they supported Bonaparte less as their own representative than as "emperor." Ultimately, the force that propelled Bonaparte beyond the presidency onto the imperial throne was contained there.

We have seen that it was precisely this type of class that served as fascism's main base in the twentieth century. In that context, however, what is of perhaps greater importance is the representative system based on popular suffrage that allowed peasants to stand on the political stage. For example, Hitler emerged from within the model representative system of Weimar Germany, and furthermore—although this fact is often ignored—the rise of Japan's emperor-system fascism also came after the universal male suffrage law of 1925. In 1930s Germany, Marxists viewed Hitler as nothing more than an agent of rescue for the crisis in the bourgeois economy and believed that they merely had to expose this fact. Just like the Nazis, they also viewed the Weimar parliament as deceitful. Contrary to their expectations, however, one cannot explain Nazism's "representation" of the masses only through concepts of violence or tactics. In the first place, the Communist Party is itself another "representative" and maintains no necessary link to the "represented."

Hitler became chancellor by way of parliamentary elections in the republic that was established after the banishment of the German emperor in the wake of World War I, and he became führer by way of a general election. The Frankfurt school Marxists determined that they could not explain these confusing developments by way of Marxism (dialectical materialism) and therefore brought in psychoanalysis. One can see a similar phenomenon in Japan, where Marxists who were stumped by the question of emperor-system fascism introduced social psychology or cultural anthropology. They thought that they were thereby compensating for Marx's theoretical failings.

If we analyze these phenomena by way of *The Eighteenth Brumaire*, however, there is no special need to bring in psychoanalysis. For in this text, in which he analyzes the dreamlike events that occurred in a brief period of time, Marx in effect prefigures Freud's *Interpretation of Dreams*. What Marx emphasizes is not the "dream-thoughts"—in other words, the actual relationships of class interest—but rather the "dream-work," in other words, the ways in which class unconsciousness is condensed and displaced. Freud writes as follows:

> The dream is seen to be an abbreviated selection from the associations, a selection made, it is true, according to rules that we have not yet understood: the elements of the dream are like representatives chosen by election from a mass of people. There can be no doubt that by our technique we have got hold of something for which the dream is a substitute and in which lies the dream's psychical value, but which no longer exhibits its puzzling peculiarities, its strangeness and its confusion. (1965:14)

Freud likens the "dream-work" to a parliament elected by popular suffrage. This being the case, instead of applying psychoanalysis to Marx's argument, we should instead read psychoanalysis from the perspective of *The Eighteenth Brumaire*. Althusser opposed the established theory of economic determinism and tried to explain the relative autonomy of the superstructure by the concept of "overdetermination," derived from the application of Lacanian theory. Yet this amounts to nothing more than the general reinterpretation of dialectical materialism.

What Marx demonstrates in *The Eighteenth Brumaire* is more specific and elaborate. He does not fail to overlook the symbolic form that is the representative system. Furthermore, he points out that the representative system itself has a twofold structure. The first resides in the parliament, that is, in legislative power, while the other resides with the president, that is, in executive power. The latter is elected by a direct national vote. In truth, in response to the republicans' attempt to restrict the number of electors, Bonaparte announced the general election and gained popularity as "the representative of the people"; furthermore, just as Hitler would do years later, he appealed a number of times to the national vote.

3. Legislative Power and Executive Power

The difference between parliament and the presidency is not merely one in electoral format. As Carl Schmitt has noted, the parliament, insofar as it is a form of rule that operates via debate, is liberalist, while the presidency, insofar as it represents the general will (Rousseau), is democratic. According to Schmitt, dictatorship runs counter to liberalism but not to democracy. He writes that Bolshevism and fascism "are, like all dictatorships, certainly antiliberal but not necessarily antidemocratic. . . . The will of the people can be expressed just as well and perhaps better through acclamation, through something taken for granted, an obvious and unchallenged presence, than through the statistical apparatus that has been constructed with such meticulousness in the last fifty years" (Schmitt 1988:16).

This problem had already been clearly put forward by Rousseau. Rousseau ridiculed the British parliament (representative system) as follows: "Sovereignty cannot be represented for the same reason that it cannot be alienated; it consists essentially in the general will, and the will cannot be represented" (2002:221). He also writes that "as soon as a nation appoints representatives, it is no longer free; it no longer exists" (223). Rousseau took the direct democracy of ancient Greece as his model and rejected the representative system. The logical end point for this kind of thinking, however, is no doubt Hegel's discernment of the "general will" in the executive power (bureaucracy) as opposed to the parliament, or else in the negation of the representative, parliamentary system in favor of the "directness" of a national vote. Of course the "directness" of a national vote is merely one variation on the representative system.

This problem is not limited to the question of the political representative system. The difference between parliament and the presidency as forms of representation corresponds to the question of representation in epistemology. On the one hand, Cartesian thought posits that truth can be deduced from a priori evidence, while on the other, the Anglo-Saxon tradition posits that truth is nothing more than a provisional hypothesis based on an agreement with others. In political terms, the former can be seen to correspond to the view that the "general will" is represented by a being that transcends the various opposing classes and people, while the latter corresponds to the view that this will is represented by agreement based on debate. Of course both, as Heidegger says, are modern ways of thinking that discern truth in representation.

Heidegger carried out a fundamental critique of such ways of thinking. In a political sense, he rejected both parliament and president. According to Heidegger, truth was something that would be directly unveiled by Being through a poetic thinker or leader (führer). For example, Heidegger asserts that the national election carried out by Hitler was not and should not be part of the representative system.[4] It should be obvious,

---

[4] On the occasion of the national vote of 1933, Heidegger asserted that it is not and should not be the selection of representatives. What he emphasized is that rather than a "representative" to be chosen by national vote, the führer must be a "master," an emperor before whom one bows down:

however, that this was nothing more than another form of representation—in other words, an imaginary unification of fragmented, contradictory classes. Heidegger argued that the führer was not a "representative" to be selected by a national vote but should rather be an "emperor" that one kneels before. But is that not precisely the re-presentation (revival) of the absolutist monarch?

In a bourgeois democratic state, the people are supposed to be sovereign, and the government they select is supposed to represent their will. Seen from that perspective, the absolutist monarch / sovereign is already a concept to be ridiculed. However, Carl Schmitt (1985), who wrote during the Weimar Republic, noted that if one thinks only within the framework of the nation-state, the sovereign remains invisible, but in exceptional situations (such as war), the sovereign as decision maker comes out into the open. By way of this theory, Schmitt would subsequently legitimize Hitler as a decision-making sovereign, but his thinking contains within it questions that cannot simply be rejected.

What Marx discerns in *The Eighteenth Brumaire* is the process whereby Louis Bonaparte emerged as "a decision-making sovereign" following the 1848 Revolution, which overthrew a monarchy that retained traces of absolutist sovereignty. What Marx makes clear is that the state itself emerges within the crisis of the representative parliament or the capitalist economy. The emperor and führer are its personifications and are nothing other than the return of the repressed (absolutist sovereignty).

In this way, we see in the process of Bonaparte's becoming emperor the first popular election in world history, the crisis of the representative system, as well as its imaginary sublation. In this sense, *The Eighteenth Brumaire* anticipates the essential

German teachers and comrades! *German Volksgenossen and Volksgenossinnen!* The German people has been summoned by the Führer to vote; the Führer, however, is asking nothing from the people. Rather, he is giving the people the possibility of making, directly, the highest free decision of all: whether the entire people wants its own existence [*Dasein*] or whether it does *not* want it. Tomorrow the people will choose nothing less than its future. (1993:49) [Author's note]

elements of the political crises that would subsequently emerge in the modern nation-state. It can be seen that these crises begin with the system of representative democracy. Representative democracy emerges via the elimination of the absolutist monarch, yet it contains within it a hole that can never be filled. The "repetition compulsion" within the system of modern democracy is faced with the task of filling that hole in times of crisis.

4. The Lumpen Proletariat and the State Apparatus

The smallholder peasants are not the only class that has a representative to whom it can relate only by way of obeisance. The military and bureaucracy are much the same. Marx writes as follows: "This executive power with its enormous bureaucratic and military organization, with its ingenious state apparatus, embracing wide strata, with a host of officials numbering half a million, besides an army of another half million, this appalling parasitic body, which enmeshes the body of French society like a net and chokes all its pores, sprang up in the days of the absolute monarchy, with the decay of the feudal system, which it helped to hasten" (1963:121). Indeed, the military and bureaucracy exalted Bonaparte in the context of the general election. As I explain later, the cyclical worldwide panic of 1851 had an important role here. This crisis marked the emergence of the bureaucratic and military organization—or, in other words, the "state" itself—which had appeared hidden under the parliamentary system of the general election. "Only under the second Bonaparte does the state seem to have made itself completely independent. As against civil society, the state machine has consolidated its position" (122). In other words, at the moment when the bourgeois economy has reached a dead end, the state apparatus, under the direction of an "emperor"-like leader, actively intervenes.

Furthermore, in *The Eighteenth Brumaire*, Marx repeatedly refers to a class "that does not form a class." This is symbolized by the Society of December 10 accompanying Bonaparte. In contrast to the smallholder peasants, its members have fallen out of any substantive class and appear to exist only according to a contentless "discourse." Marx refers to them derisively as the *Lumpenproletariat*. Yet in no way were they powerless. It was precisely by way of the lumpen that the Bonaparte camp was able to use the power of the press effectively.

Bonaparte needed to represent all people. As seen in his nickname, "Saint-Simon on horseback," he championed a kind of national socialism. Therefore, he needed to represent the working class, while also needing to represent the capitalist class beaten down by economic crisis. Furthermore, he needed to represent the peasants as well. Yet how is it possible to represent everyone? "Bonaparte would like to appear as the patriarchal benefactor of all classes. But he cannot give to one class without taking from another," Marx writes (1963:133). He adds, "Driven by the contradictory demands of his situation and being at the same time, like a conjurer, under the necessity of keeping the public gaze fixed on himself, as Napoléon's substitute, by springing constant surprises, that is to say, under the necessity of executing a *coup d'état en miniature* every day, Bonaparte throws the entire bourgeois economy into confusion, violates everything that seemed inviolable to the Revolution of 1848" (135). In effect, what was possible for him was to create the *image* of doing something rather than actually doing it.

One can say that Bonaparte was the first politician who consciously put into practice the maxim that the media-created image shapes reality. In the first place, his very existence was based on nothing other than the image of his being Napoléon's nephew. The thoroughgoing use of the image also applies to the world expositions that he twice held after becoming emperor. For him, these were less ceremonial rituals than the daily "*coup d'état en miniature*." In fact, Bonaparte's own actual coup d'état was carried out as a similar type of performance rather than as a military overthrow of the state.

In *The Prince*, Machiavelli wrote that the sovereign has no need to be a good man yet must appear to be a good man. He had already discerned that modern politics is based on the image.

To put it into other terms, it was an insight that the meaning of a sign is separate from its referent. That Machiavelli has continued to be criticized by those in power—who are in fact much more unscrupulous "Machiavellians" themselves—is analogous to criticism of the sign's autonomy from its referent among realist authors, who in truth have been putting this autonomy to their own uses. Of Bonaparte, Baudelaire said that anyone who used the press in this way could become president. Yet the Symbolist movement in poetry that began with Baudelaire in fact runs parallel to Bonapartism in terms of the historical shift in the use of the image.

In some sense, *The Eighteenth Brumaire* exposes tendencies that would be seen more clearly in the Nazism of the 1930s or in the postmodernism of the 1980s than in the nineteenth century. One can say that these tendencies are the early signs of "mass society." Those who participated in the Revolution of 1848 were less the proletariat of whom Marx wrote than the urban masses of whom Benjamin would write. They, too, are a class that does not form a class. Or rather, one should say that at the time of the 1848 Revolution in France there already did not exist, among those who were "represented," any classical form of class segmentation.

Certainly, Marx's analysis did not extend to such matters. He criticizes, or rather scorns, the sign without referent, political discourse that does not connect to substantive classes. But one should note that his book is not written in the style of nineteenth-century realism. Edmund Wilson has compared Marx's satire to that of Jonathan Swift (2003:286), but if anything, one can say that in this work Marx displays, with a Rabelaisian touch, a certain scatological affection toward the "scum, offal, refuse of all classes" (Marx 1963:75). Only such a style could, no doubt, contend with the perverted matters surrounding Bonaparte. In truth, exiled revolutionaries such as Marx who gathered in Paris were, like Bonaparte and others, a type of *bohème*. Contemporary historians who quibble over historical facts overlooked by *The Eighteenth Brumaire* have themselves failed to notice that the work is a literary text of the first order, one that depicts a farce.

5. The Repetition of History

The next question of representation to be raised is that of re-presentation, the question of repetition. Of course, this relates to the famous opening lines of *The Eighteenth Brumaire*: "Hegel remarks somewhere that all facts and personages of great importance in world history occur, as it were, twice. He forgot to add: the first time as tragedy, the second as farce. Caussidière for Danton, Louis Blanc for Robespierre, the *Montagne* of 1848 to 1851 for the *Montagne* of 1793 to 1795, the Nephew for the Uncle" (Marx 1963:15).

The repetition of history cited here by Marx is in relation to the first French Revolution, of 1789, and the second French Revolution, of 1848. In both cases, a revolution that overthrew the monarchy and aimed to establish a republic resulted ultimately in imperial rule. But there is more. In the words following these opening lines, Marx points out that the "Revolution of 1789 to 1814 draped itself alternately as the Roman republic and the Roman empire" (1963:15). In other words, the events following the first Revolution, of 1789, were already constituted as a repetition of the past.

According to Marx's thinking, the three-year span following 1848 was a repetition of the period from 1789 to Napoléon's coup d'état. The first Revolution, while itself taking the form of a repetition of antiquity, in fact enacted a bourgeois revolution. With the 1848 Revolution, on the other hand, there was nothing new to be realized. For this reason, Marx refers to it as farce. Yet there was, in fact, something that Bonapartism aimed to achieve. This was the dissolution, by executive power, of the class conflicts engendered by capitalism, to make unnecessary all revolutions in the future—such was the content of *Des idées napoléoniennes* that Louis Bonaparte authored. In contrast to the military exploits of his uncle, he emphasized peace and industrial development. Of course, this did not prevent Louis Bonaparte from dispatching troops to block Italian independence. Externally, his rule was imperialistic.

Marx adds to the passage quoted above as follows: "Men make their own history, but they do not make it just as they please; they do not make it under circumstances chosen by themselves, but under circumstances directly encountered, given and transmitted from the past. The tradition of all the dead generations weighs like a nightmare on the brain of the living" (1963:15). The repetition that Marx focuses on here, however, is not this sort of general truth but rather the fact that in a certain sense the 1789 Revolution—in other words, the emergence of Emperor Napoléon from within a republic that had been formed through the killing of the king—was a repetition of nothing other than the history of Caesar.

This is clear from Marx's citation of Hegel. When Marx writes that "Hegel remarks somewhere," that *somewhere* no doubt refers to Hegel's remarks on Caesar in *The Philosophy of History*. Yet Hegel's words have a different meaning from what Marx has in mind. Hegel writes that "in all periods of the world a political revolution is sanctioned in men's opinions, when it repeats itself. Thus Napoléon was twice defeated, and the Bourbons twice expelled. By repetition that which at first appeared merely a matter of chance and contingency, becomes a real and ratified existence" (1991:313).

According to Hegel's thinking, Caesar is a world historical figure, and the events that he mentions are also world historical events. The reason for this is that they transformed the principle of the nation based on the folk or the city-state into the broader principle of the empire that transcends the various folks. Caesar attempted to become emperor at a stage when Rome had expanded and could no longer continue as city-state or republic, and he was assassinated by Brutus and others who tried to protect the republican form of government. Yet after they killed Caesar, who they thought was trying to destroy the republic, they realized that the republic could no longer be maintained. In other words, they realized that the expanded Rome could not be governed according to the principles of the republic. At that point, although Caesar died, the emperor subsequently came into being. In truth, Caesar himself can be said to have become emperor, in the sense that his name was transformed into a common noun signifying emperor (i.e., kaiser, czar).

In effect, those involved in the French Revolution repeated, in temporally compressed form, this Roman history. By way of the Revolution, they were able to form a republic, which, however, culminated after a period of chaos in the imperial reign of Napoléon. Nevertheless, while appearing superficially to be a repetition of Roman history, it was quite different, for the political and economic mechanisms of each context were different. What the French Revolution achieved was the establishment of a bourgeois economic system and the nation-state. And the European federation that Napoléon proclaimed was nothing other than a kind of "imperialism" that aimed to defend the French national economy against British industrial capital. This was an extension of the nation-state and was never comparable to the Roman Empire. On this matter, Hannah Arendt pointed out the following:

> Conquest as well as empire building had fallen into disrepute for very good reasons. They had been carried out successfully only by governments which, like the Roman Republic, were based primarily on law, so that conquest could be followed by integration of the most heterogeneous peoples by imposing upon them a common law. The nation-state, however, based upon a homogeneous populations' active consent to its government ("le plébiscite de tous les jours"), lacked such a unifying principle. (1973:125)

Arendt furthermore noted that this had already occurred with Napoléon: "The inner contradiction between the nation's body politic and conquest as a political device has been obvious since the failure of the Napoleonic dream" (128). Napoléon's policy of conquest gave birth to nationalism and independence movements in the various countries. In other words, Napoléon ultimately transmitted the French Revolution to each of the regions. This is indeed the "cunning of reason," to use Hegel's words. Imperialism as an extension of the nation-state was subsequently never able to resolve this contradiction. This analysis also applies to the politics of Napoléon III. His policy of invasion, contrary to its intended effect, gave rise to German and even Italian unification. And the various European imperialisms that subsequently emerged ultimately gave birth to nation-states around the globe.

Yet in Europe, attempts to reconstruct the Roman Empire have continued unabated. This is related to an internal problem existing within the modern nation-state. The modern nation-state emerged at the point when absolutist monarchies established their sovereignty independent of Roman law and the Catholic Church and entered into military and industrial competition with one another. In this context, the will to transcend the condition of the modern sovereign nation more or less recalls the Roman Empire. In truth, what this will actually accomplished was imperialist control of one nation over another. Nevertheless, the nation-state is unable to discard the drive to negate itself and move toward "empire." This is the repetition compulsion of the nation-state itself. It is apparent that today's European Union represents another repetition of this drive.

6. The Business Cycle as Repetition

The other question of representation addressed by Marx in *The Eighteenth Brumaire* belongs to the capitalist economy. The monetary economy exists as a system of representation, and its crisis is manifested as economic crisis. Marx writes that the economic crisis of 1851 moved the bourgeoisie at one stroke to support Louis Bonaparte. What the bourgeoisie desired at that moment was not a kind of liberalist or legislative state but rather a strong administrative state; in other words, they desired Bonaparte as emperor. In a certain sense, he responded to this desire. To add to Marx's analysis, the policies of Bonaparte as emperor were themselves filled with contradictions. The bourgeoisie of the time, in terms of economic policy, was split in two. The first opinion, as Saint-Simonist Michel Chevalier stated, was that the marketplace must be opened and that France must enter the worldwide economy; at the same time, however, the state should intervene in the economy to spur industrial development. The other view, as stated by conservative Adolphe Thiers, aimed to preserve a balanced system centered on agriculture. Within this opposition, Louis Bonaparte presented himself as a conservative at heart who in practice was a Saint-Simonist. In other words, he emerged as a figure that promised to erase or mediate this serious opposition.[5]

Marx understood Bonaparte as a figure who erased the oppositions between the various classes, but these oppositions were closely related to the particular problems of France, which was under pressure from the British economy during this time. At the same time, this question can be generalized into the opposition between global capitalism and the national economy. For example, the choice between liberalization of the market, which sacrifices the national economy, versus the protection of the national economy is one of the greatest points of political contention today. Those politicians who act as if they can fulfill all these desires can be called "Bonapartists." Of course, they are not limited to fascists only. The fascism that emerged in Germany and Japan in the 1930s can most appropriately be viewed as different modes of Bonapartism. One of the benefits of understanding the phenomena of the 1930s as Bonapartism is that it can also explain what occurred in the United States during that time. President Roosevelt, who was able to gain the support from both the Right and the Left, and from all parties, classes, and ethnicities, can be seen as a Bonapartist. In practice, he broke through the traditional framework of the two-party system.

The 1851 economic crisis mentioned in *The Eighteenth Brumaire* was part of an approximately ten-year-long business cycle. What Marx grasped in *Capital* was this type of short-term business cycle. This differs from the roughly sixty-year, long-term cycle of global capitalism—Kondratieff's "long wave." The principle that generates such cycles, however, is the same. It is, in

---

5 The above analysis owes a debt to Sakagami (1977). [Author's note]

other words, related to the decrease in the general rate of profit and the use of more fundamental technological innovation. Such cycles have not only generated worldwide crises but also led to transitions in the core commodities (world commodities) of capitalist production, transitions from textiles to heavy industry, to durable consumer goods, and to the information industry. Such transitions could not help but engender total reorganizations of society. It is because of such structural causality that the long-term business cycle cannot be explained by way of the economic register alone.

Yet, to repeat: in terms of principle, such long-term waves do not differ from short-term business cycles. In other words, they should be seen as one part of the process whereby the "organic composition of capital" is dramatically increased. According to this process, the capitalist economy enters a new stage. However, such a new stage does not go beyond the understanding expressed in *Capital*—that is, beyond the limits of the capitalist economy itself. Without such violent reorganizations engendered by economic depression, the accumulation / expansion of capital cannot be achieved. And capital exists as such only when it is increasing; it is unable to cease its movement of accumulation. One cannot analyze this phenomenon only within the framework of a single nation.

While Marx appears to take the single country of England as a model for his analysis in *Capital*, he was in fact addressing global capitalism. On the one hand, for example, he seems to treat foreign trade as something secondary. At the same time, however, he states that capitalism cannot exist without foreign trade. Thus, in the third volume of *Capital*, Marx writes of the "decreasing tendency of the rate of profit" and notes that this tendency can be checked by foreign trade:

> Capital invested in foreign trade can yield a higher rate of profit, because, in the first place, there is competition with commodities produced in other countries with inferior production facilities, so that the more advanced country sells its goods above their value even though cheaper than the competing countries. In so

far as the labour of the more advanced country is here realized as labour of a higher specific weight, the rate of profit rises, because labour which has not been paid as being of a higher quality is sold as such. The same may obtain in relation to the country, to which commodities are exported and to that from which commodities are imported; namely, the latter may offer more materialized labour *in kind* than it receives, and yet thereby receive commodities cheaper than it could produce them. Just as a manufacturer who employs a new invention before it becomes generally used, undersells his competitors and yet sells his commodity above its individual value, that is, realizes the specifically higher productiveness of the labour he employs as surplus-labour. He thus secures a surplus-profit. (2001:314–15)

British laborers were able to counter the "impoverishment rule" that Marx mentions and were able to attain wealth because capital was able to extract surplus value from foreign trade. The impoverishment was generated not domestically but rather among people abroad. Therefore, it is incorrect to consider surplus value within the enclosed confines of a one-nation model. The general tendency for decreasing rates of profit, as well as the movement to counter it, continue to generate the increase in capital's organic composition as well as the globalization of capitalism.

The principle of foreign trade as an escape route from the "decrease in the rate of profit" continued to function essentially unchanged in subsequent eras. In Marx's late years, for example, the "general decline in the rate of profit" was manifested as chronic recession, and the "export of capital" began. This is the stage of imperialism of which Hobson and Lenin wrote and that ultimately led to World War I. Furthermore, the 1930s witnessed the creation of economic blocs, which led to World War II. The postwar period was characterized by the U.S.–Soviet Cold War structure. In this case, the collapse of the Soviet-bloc economy garners the most attention, but on the capitalist side as well, the Fordism of "mass production / mass consumption," which had continued since the 1930s, had also reached its limit. It had succumbed precisely to the "tendency for the decline in the general rate of profit." One cannot resolve this problem by way of policies based on single nations. As Marx says, foreign trade is essential.

What emerged at that point were the policies of "globalization." This was a form of free trade that would completely envelop developing countries and that works to weaken the framework of the nation-state. At the same time, it produces a counterreaction. Furthermore, the form of "empire" that predated the nation-state is revived in a different form. In this way, the repetition compulsion immanent to the capitalist economy is layered on the repetition compulsion immanent to the nation-state. I believe that in *Capital* and *The Eighteenth Brumaire*, Marx fundamentally grasped the principle of these repetition compulsions.

2

HISTORY AND REPETITION IN JAPAN

1

There are two meanings to repetition in history. The first is when people evoke events or people of the past when doing something new. It is this form of repetition that Marx notes in the opening passages of *The Eighteenth Brumaire of Louis Bonaparte*. There is a certain inevitability to the fact that, when faced with circumstances completely unknown to them, people try to understand them through their knowledge of what is familiar but in fact end up doing something entirely different. The second type of repetition is when the past, despite being rejected and forgotten, is nevertheless repeated. This compulsion to repeat is what Freud referred to as the "return of the repressed." And this type of repetition can be seen as the essential characteristic of state and capital, which structure the modern world. It too is inevitable.

What I would like to attempt here is to think about modern Japanese history from the perspective of such repetition. In the 1930s, for example, Marxists in Japan engaged in a major polemic that is referred to as the debate over Japanese capitalism (or sometimes as the feudalism debate). In the background of this discussion, which unfolded between two groups of scholars known as the Lectures school [Kōzaha] and the Labor-Farmer school [Rōnōha], was the opposition between the Communist Party (the Lectures school) and the Labor-Farmer Party (the Labor-Farmer school) and their respective political programs. As a lawful debate that was carried out in public, however, it drew the interest of intellectuals at large. Its influence extended into many areas, developing into a fundamental rethinking of the Meiji Restoration—and Japanese history in general—as well as of philosophy, literature, and art. Most likely the secondary impact of the debate was more important than the debate itself. Taken as a whole, this exchange is worth noting as a rare case in which Japanese intellectuals grappled on their own with Japanese history and reality.

In rough terms, one can say that this debate was based on the opposition between the following viewpoints. According to the Lectures school, the Meiji Restoration fell short of achieving a bourgeois revolution and was no more than a stage in the reorganization of feudal land ownership. As a result, in rural areas feudal or semifeudal land ownership and serfdom persisted, above which existed the absolutist emperor system. These factors continued to constrain the development of capitalism in Japan. In contrast, according to the Labor-Farmer school's perspective, the Meiji Restoration was indeed a bourgeois revolution, and therefore Japanese society had subsequently come to be governed by the principles of the capitalist market economy. The relationship between landowner and tenant farmer, appearing at first glance to be a feudal one, was in fact a contractual relationship that differed from the relationship between lord and farmer. Even the extremely high tenancy fee was not based on any "feudal" (i.e., extraeconomic) coercion by the landowner but rather on the fact that the excess population of tenant farmers seeking land to lease caused a spike in tenancy fees. As a result of the division of the peasant class into opposite extremes, the peasants were in the process of being transformed into wage laborers. Therefore, according to the Labor-Farmer school's assertions, the remnants of feudal relations that currently persisted would undoubtedly soon disappear.[1]

---

[1] The capitalism debate (feudalism debate) maintains a universal significance. For example, while the Lectures school perceived the remnants of feudalism in Japan's unusually high farm rent paid in kind, Kushida Tamizō of the Labor-Farmer school showed that it was based on a capitalist, contractual relationship. He argued that it was nothing more than that the surplus population of tenant farmers' seeking land to lease led to a sharp increase in rent and that rice, which was used to pay the rent, was in fact functioning as currency (Kushida 1979). This debate would be repeated forty years later in the exchange between Ernesto Laclau, who saw a precapitalist "feudalism" in Latin Ameri-

The Lectures school perspective—that is, viewing the Japanese state as an absolutist state whose economic base is "semifeudal land ownership"—was mistaken, and to this extent the Labor-Farmer school critique of the Lectures school was justified. At the same time, however, the Labor-Farmer school perspective could not account for the emergence of the phenomenon referred to as "emperor-system fascism." The Labor-Farmer school, while focusing on the autonomy of the capitalist economy, ignored the fact that the state existed on its own level. For its part, the Lectures school, while focusing on the level of the state, ignored the autonomy of the capitalist economy. As a result, it reduced the state to the level of "semifeudal land ownership." In this way, both the Lectures school and the Labor-Farmer school were unable to grasp the level of the state.

Each of these two groups based its thinking on Marx's *Capital*. Yet they read *Capital* as a book of history. For example, in *Capital* society is said to be divided into the three classes of capitalist, landowner, and laborer. In response to this there is, on the one hand, the view that such class divisions develop in all nations, while, on the other, there is the view that since this analysis was based on the English model, it is not directly applicable to backward nations, for which multiple forms of development should be considered instead. However, what Marx explicated in *Capital* was class as an economic category, not historically or actually existing classes. One need only take a look at *The Eighteenth Brumaire* to see the extent to which Marx was sensitive to the multiplicity of actual classes. The analysis in *The Eighteenth Brumaire* does not apply only to a backward capitalist nation like France. From this perspective, England also had multiple

ca, and Immanuel Wallerstein, who criticized this view, arguing that what appears as feudal is actually formed in the periphery or semiperiphery of world capitalism (Laclau 1979). One finds, for example, forms of serfdom and slavery in world capitalism. These are not precapitalist remnants, however, but rather institutions formed under capitalism. That is to say, in places where a surplus of labor exists, laborers have no choice but to enter into contracts for work, no matter how severe the labor or how low the wages. In other words, even if the mode of production appears to be feudalism or slavery, it is based on economic rather than extraeconomic coercion. [Author's note]

classes with complicated political histories—in this case, too, to a greater or lesser extent, "the tradition of all the dead generations weighs like a nightmare on the brain of the living" (Marx 1963:15).

In *Capital*, Marx tries to analyze the capitalist economy through its forms or categories, which structure all of society. For this reason, he went back to the *logical* starting point of the value form. This is different from its historical origin. In this type of work, it is only natural that the state would be placed in brackets. Here, Marx attempts to grasp the unique, autonomous dimension maintained by the monetary economy and, because he was deeply immersed in this work, does not really think about the state. Thus the Marxist theory of the state has been based on assembling and reorganizing his fragmentary thoughts on the subject since his early years. In this regard, however, I believe that the greatest importance should be attached to *The Eighteenth Brumaire*.

In order to analyze the capitalist economy in *Capital*, Marx moves backward from the national economy (classical economics) to mercantile capitalism; in other words, he tries to rethink capital from the perspective of merchant capital. In the same manner, in thinking about the state we should work backward from the bourgeois state to the absolutist state. The bourgeois state, which appears after the overthrow of the absolutist state, presents itself as being entirely unrelated to its predecessor, but in actuality in times of crisis it recalls the "king" (absolutist monarch) that it had previously killed off. This is precisely what Marx demonstrates in *The Eighteenth Brumaire*. Because it was not written systematically, this book has not been read as a theory of the state. Yet among Marx's writings on the state, only here can one see a method that parallels what is found in *Capital*. It is thus only natural that Marxists who have not properly understood *The Eighteenth Brumaire* can express nothing more than arbitrary thoughts about the relationship between capital and the state.

The Lectures school saw 1930s Japan as an absolutist state and tried to prove this from an economic perspective. They noted, for example, that the emperor was a massive landholder as proof of their argument. However, to refer to a capitalist state characterized by highly developed heavy industry—a state that came to possess a parliament elected by popular suffrage after passing through Taishō democracy—as an absolutist state, and to analyze it through the category of semifeudal land ownership, is a foolish matter. Moreover, to then put forth a political program calling first for the overthrow of the emperor system is sheer folly. It was not external pressure alone that led to the collapse of such a movement. All the same, it is true that the revival of something resembling an "absolutist monarchy" was aimed for in the 1930s—this is what is referred to as "emperor-system fascism." It appeared not at any "semifeudal" stage but in fact at the stage of highly developed industrial capitalism. But in order to explain such a strange phenomenon, do we need any new knowledge that Marx did not possess? As I mentioned earlier, Marxists would have been better off paying even the slightest heed to *The Eighteenth Brumaire*.[2]

In the postwar period, a type of broadly defined Marxism gained prominence in Japan, one that did not reduce

---

2 In the debate over Japanese capitalism, the Labor-Farmer school ignored the state, while the Lectures school, which attached great importance to the state, ended up reducing it to economic process. Among the Labor-Farmer group, Inomata Tsunao was aware of the inseparability of state and capital. But he grasped it only as a distinguishing feature of imperialism. In contrast, Uno Kōzō conceived of the problem of Japanese capitalism and feudal remnants as arising from a backward country importing heavy industry and guiding the development of financial capitalism. This is not only because of the belatedness of capitalist development. If anything, it is capitalist development itself that created "feudal remnants." And when faced with the total crisis of the capitalist economy, it is also the state that aims to solve this crisis. In this sense, though his connections were to the Labor-Farmer school, Uno was much more conscious of the autonomy and agency of the state than not only the Labor-Farmer school but the Lectures school as well. On the other hand, Kamiyama Shigeo (2003), whose connections placed him in the lineage of the Lectures school, criticized the Lectures school for reducing the state to economic process and tried to grasp the autonomous, active topology of the state. For this reason, it is in Uno's theory of capitalism and Kamiyama's theory of the state that the debate on Japanese capitalism can be said to have generated its most productive insight. [Author's note]

emperor-system fascism to the economic base but rather analyzed it through the relatively autonomous level of the superstructure. Consequently, such Marxist thinkers introduced all the scholarly disciplines that had been rejected by classical Marxists, including sociology, social psychology, anthropology, and mythology. The exemplary figure of this group was Maruyama Masao. As I mentioned previously, this is similar to the fact that the Frankfurt school introduced psychoanalysis in its analysis of Nazism. Again, what this analysis lacked was the perspective found in *The Eighteenth Brumaire,* as well as the perspective of *Capital.* Marxists were aware of a static concept of Bonapartism, and even overused it, but they never tried to see the dynamic process whereby Bonapartism emerged from the representative system (the parliament). Instead, they appended various scholarly disciplines such as sociology and anthropology to their analysis. What remained lacking, however, was any consideration of how the state exists and what kind of repetition compulsion it has. For this reason, they failed to grasp the essential point and were unable to offer any insight into subsequent phenomena.

2

Clearly, the form of government in 1930s Japan differed from the type of fascism seen in Italy or Germany. There can be no fascism that worships a king. The Japanese case is therefore referred to specially as "emperor-system fascism," but still there are those who believe the use of the term "fascism" to be inappropriate. Such differences of opinion, however, result from looking at fascism in the context of its academic theory or in its realized forms. What is necessary instead is to see fascism within the totality of its "process."

In general usage, despotic political systems are referred to as fascist. Of course, such usage of the term is not only mistaken but even harmful, for it cannot account for the fact that fascism maintained a certain appeal to people. In a word, fascism was a counterrevolution against the spread of the Russian Revolution (socialism). Counterrevolution is not the same as antirevolution. Fascism itself was revolutionary, and it is for this reason that it drew people in. Fascism was not only anticapitalist but antistatist as well. In Italy, for example, Mussolini was a leader of the Socialist Party until being expelled during World War I for his support for the war, and, furthermore, many anarchists joined with the fascists. In other words, fascism began as a struggle against state and capital. State and capital were ultimately receptive to fascism because they faced a profound crisis that could no longer be resolved through democracy or any simple antirevolutionary suppression. When state and capital assimilated fascism, however, fascism itself was forced to change. Therefore, fascism cannot be defined only by its ideologies and movements or in its fully developed form. Rather, it must be seen within the totality of its "process."

In its early stages, Nazism was an anticapitalist and antistatist movement, and, moreover, the form of the movement was insurrectionist, but it later shifted into parliamentarism, and by the time of its ascendancy to power it was in collusion with the state and capitalist apparatus. In this process, Nazism was greatly transformed. Thus it is not only difficult but in fact meaningless to define Nazism according to one particular stage. If we see it within the totality of its "process," however, then we immediately become aware of the following structure: it was within the representative system of the Weimar Republic, which exiled the "king" after World War I and which was established after the miscarriage of the leftist revolution, that Hitler became chancellor, and he became führer by way of a national vote. What is clear is that this is a homologous process to the one whereby Louis Bonaparte became emperor.

In my view, this type of "process," which Marx presented in *The Eighteenth Brumaire*, is applicable to subsequent developments not only in Germany but in Japan as well. Marx saw the "process" from the 1848 Revolution to Louis Bonaparte's becoming emperor as a repetition of the first French Revolution. This means that the first French Revolution is not confined only to 1789 or a few subsequent years but instead comprises the entire process until Napoléon's ascension to the throne. In the same way, I believe that 1930s "emperor-system fascism" should be seen as a process beginning with the agrarianism [*nōhonshugi*] of Kita Ikki and others and extending through the establishment of Konoe Fumimaro's "new order."

Maruyama (1963) wrote that Japanese fascism lacks the single, charismatic subject who possesses a unified will. Instead, like the portable shrine carried at a festival, it is carried forward by someone until a certain stage, then passed on to someone else at the next stage. However, if we understand fascism within its "process," we can view this process of multiple, differing subjects substituting for one another to achieve a single goal as being equivalent to the process of a single subject continually changing over time. For the purpose of achieving the counter-revolution, it does not matter who the subject is.

Furthermore, throughout this entire process—that is, in the movement from Kita to Konoe's Shōwa Research Association—there was a certain slogan that tied everyone to a single purpose: namely, the "Shōwa Restoration." In other words, the movement was conceived as a successor to—or repetition of—the Meiji Restoration. What, then, does the Meiji Restoration signify in this context? Of course, it too must be seen as a "process." That is to say, the Meiji Restoration is nothing other than the process stretching from the dissolution of the Tokugawa shogunate in 1867 to the promulgation of the constitution (1889) and the establishment of the Diet (1890).

At the time, the Meiji Restoration was thought of as a revival of the emperor's direct rule from antiquity. The contribution of such ancient "costumes" cannot be denied. In truth, the movement affiliated with National Learning [Kokugaku] was an important factor in the Meiji Restoration; as a result, at the time of the Restoration there was a revival of ancient institutions and even an anti-Buddhist movement. Of course, such tendencies were not long lasting.[3] For those who seized state

---

3 Shimazaki Tōson's novel *Before the Dawn* [*Yoake mae*, 1929–1935] includes the description of a revolutionary aligned with National Learning who, disappointed with the outcome of the Meiji Restoration, descends into madness. [Author's note]

power aimed for the establishment of a modern state and a capitalist economic system. The fact that ancient costumes were deployed in the course of the Meiji Restoration is not unique to Japan. The French Revolution is an obvious example, but in the English Revolution of 1648 as well, "Cromwell and the English people had borrowed speech, passions and illusions from the Old Testament for their bourgeois revolution" (Marx 1963:17). What was important in the Meiji Restoration was to strip the many feudal lords of their status and to dismantle the various institutions of feudal society. The revolutionaries of the Restoration thus appropriated, for their own purposes, the ideology of "revere the emperor" that had been used by Tokugawa authorities to support their own power, and they passed the emperor off as a type of absolutist sovereign.[4]

The Meiji Restoration, however, did not end at that point. Subsequently, it developed further in the form of the Seinan War [1877] and the Freedom and People's Rights Movement. It is clear that participants in these events saw them as extending and deepening the Restoration. As a result, somehow or other,

---

4 It is interesting to note that both Napoléon I and Napoléon III (Louis Bonaparte) exerted a great influence on the Meiji Restoration. It comes as no surprise that Napoléon was seen as a hero by both Meiji Restoration royalists and Freedom and People's Rights activists. In *The Unofficial History of the Chinese Revolution* [*Shina kakumei gaishi*], Kita compares the Meiji emperor to Napoléon. From this was born his analysis that, just as Napoléon tried to spread the French Revolution throughout Europe, Japan's advance onto the Asian continent would spread the Meiji Restoration throughout all of Asia. Louis Bonaparte is of further interest. He supported the Tokugawa shogunate, sending a personal letter proposing that the shogun assume the role of absolute monarch by defeating all other feudal lords. The commissioner of finance Oguri Tadamasa tried to move along these lines. In response, however, the revolutionaries of the Satsuma and Chōshū domains pushed the emperor to the fore and, by making him absolute monarch, were able to wrest away the feudal privileges of the lords, including the shogun. Furthermore, the leaders of the Meiji government witnessed Louis Napoléon's cruel defeat in the Franco-Prussian War (1871) as well as the Paris Commune during their trip to Europe, which determined their policy to build the nation on the victorious Prussian model. [Author's note]

the constitution was promulgated and the parliament established. No matter how one looks at it, Japan was not an absolutist monarchy at this point. For the institutions of the modern state and industrial capitalism had already been constructed, and before long, with the Sino-Japanese War [1894–1895], Japan began moving into the stage of "imperialism."

The Meiji emperor essentially became a constitutional monarch, but on the Prussian, rather than British, model. Furthermore, even as the elder statesmen established this constitutional monarchy and parliamentary system, they simultaneously created various devices designed to restrain these institutions. In the constitution, one such device was making the emperor commander in chief of the army and navy. As a result, the military transcended the authority of the Diet and the cabinet. In addition, an example of an extraconstitutional device was the Imperial Rescript on Education. In the 1930s, after the elder statesmen had passed from the scene, such devices would run rampant. Yet to the extent that the military's arbitrary actions themselves had a constitutional basis, they were unable to put an end to the constitution or parliamentary system.

From the beginning, there were conflicting opinions concerning the nature of the emperor system based on constitutional or extraconstitutional controls. Within constitutional theory, a division existed between those who saw the emperor as absolute sovereign and those who saw him as constitutional monarch. In the Taishō period [1912–1926], it was the latter—in other words, Minobe Tatsukichi's "emperor as organ theory"—that was generally accepted. It was in this context that Taishō democracy was established and a universal male suffrage bill approved by the Diet in 1925. The emperor was not a prominent presence in the Taishō period, due in part to his sickly nature. Seen from the perspective of the Meiji period [1868–1912], it was as if the "emperor" had been done away with. In this sense, the "Shōwa Restoration" [*Shōwa ishin*] meant the recalling of the Meiji "emperor"—or, in other words, the enacting of a "reformation" [*ishin*] or social reconstruction in the name of the emperor. Driving this movement was the background of chronic recession following World War I and the spread of socialist movements in the wake of the Russian Revolution.

The first stage in the process of Japanese fascism was the failed coup d'état of February 26, 1936, carried out by young officers in the army's Imperial Way faction. In the background of this action was the state socialist Kita Ikki, who was executed as a result of this incident. Kita's theory can be found in his *General Principles of a Plan for National Reform* [*Kokka kaizōan genri taikō*], 1919, republished in 1923 as *Outline of Proposed Legislation for the Reform of Japan* [*Nihon kaizō hōan taikō*].[5] What national reform meant was, in the first instance, nationalization without compensation of the private wealth of large capitalists above a certain amount, and the nationalization with compensation of the landholdings of large landowners above a certain level. Second, laborers would receive, in addition to wages necessary for the reproduction of the powers of production, half of a company's net profit, and they would actively participate in corporate management. At the same time, in terms of foreign affairs, Kita emphasized the need for Japan to acquire territories from Asia to Australia.[6]

As a means to such a revolution, Kita advocated setting in motion the emperor's supreme power by way of a coup d'état. Kita himself fundamentally supported the "emperor as organ theory," and from the opening passages of *General Principles of a Plan for National Reform* he had considered the emperor to be someone who "represents the nation as the general

---

5 For a complete English translation of the latter text, see Kita (2006).
6 Alongside Kita, another influential thinker of agrarianism was Gondō Seikyō. Using the notion of *shashoku* [a self-governing, mutually assisting agricultural community] as a foundation, he tried to reject the state and capitalism. If anything, Gondō's thinking is closer to anarchism than to Kita's state socialism. Where he differs from anarchists is that he brought forth the emperor as a symbol of this type of agricultural community. Of course, his conception of the emperor was not that of the post-Meiji emperor system, or even of the ancient Yamato court, but rather of a time when Japan had yet to be formed as a nation; in other words, he was nothing more than the priest of a clan community. In reality, however, Gondō's conception of an emperor who transcends the state did not in any way lead to a nullification of the state but rather to the deification of the emperor and the strengthening of the state. [Author's note]

representative of a contemporary democratic state" (1959a:223). Furthermore, he advocated the implementation of universal male suffrage. In other words, for Kita, asserting the supreme power of the emperor did not mean the emperor's deification but rather was no more than a means of realizing a true "representative system." As a result of this attempted coup, however, it was the power of the army's Control faction that was increased instead, and it was precisely the deification of the emperor that was advanced. Thereafter, the military used the supreme power of the emperor (as commander in chief) in order to pursue actions independent of the Diet and the cabinet. In this way, in late 1930s Japan, the parliament (legislative power), the cabinet (executive power), and state apparatus (army and navy, bureaucracy) were all divided, creating an out-of-control situation.

It was Konoe Fumimaro who was able to overcome this division and establish a system of "total mobilization."[7] How and why was Konoe able to achieve this? To answer that question, one should refer to the case of Louis Bonaparte before anything. Louis Bonaparte was the nephew of Napoléon. Without question, it was the halo of this connection to Napoléon that made a difference. But that was not all. Louis Bonaparte was also a man of letters who upheld industrialism and socialism in the manner of Saint-Simon. Marx ridicules him in *The Eighteenth Brumaire*; nonetheless, one must acknowledge that Louis Bonaparte was in his own fashion a capable person who was able to assemble talented people around him. In truth, it

---

7 Just after the May 15 Incident of 1932, when Prime Minister Inukai Tsuyoshi was assassinated and the end of party government as well as the rising tide of military dictatorship became clear, Konoe is said to have stated,

> In order to take back governance from the military as soon as possible, politicians must first acknowledge this way of destiny [that is, the formation of blocs in the world economy, the establishment of a broad economic zone involving Japan, Manchuria, and China] and seize the initiative from the military to enact the various reforms necessary to implement this destiny. If we let this way of destiny slip away from us and think only about restraining the tyranny of the military, governance will never return to the hands of politicians. (quoted in Yabe 1958:54) [Author's note]

was he who remade France into a modern nation. In this sense, the person to whom the label of Bonapartism could most appropriately be applied is Konoe.

Konoe was an aristocrat with ties to the imperial family. There was no one else who could restrain the military, which was parading around under the banner of the emperor's supreme command. Furthermore, Konoe had gathered to himself the support of the Imperial Way faction within the army. Konoe himself was originally a man of letters, as well as a socialist. In truth, his brain trust (the Shōwa Research Association) included Marxists such as Miki Kiyoshi, who gave philosophical signification to the "new order," and Ozaki Hotsumi, who proclaimed the "East Asian Cooperative Community." These Marxists, by infiltrating the inner sanctum of power, believed they were engaging in a pragmatic resistance. In addition, Konoe was supported by reformist bureaucrats, who introduced a Soviet-style five-year plan, and he was also connected to new financial combines [zaibatsu], which contended with the older combines. His ties to the peasant movement were also strong. In other words, he gained support from the entire range of social forces and state institutions.

The political parties all supported Konoe. Under the Meiji constitution, the Diet—or, to put it another way, the prime minister—wielded little power. In this context, Nakano Seigō advocated giving the prime minister special powers, following the example of the American presidency. Diet members believed that the Konoe cabinet would allow them to recover the Diet's power, for, in the end, no one other than Konoe could have restrained the military. For that reason, the parliamentary parties, acting on their own, pushed forward the idea of the unified parliament, under which the parties would be dissolved and unified. It failed because of the opposition of the old Right, which feared turning Konoe into a figure who could threaten the emperor (like the Tokugawa shogunate). Ironically, then, it was the emperor system that hindered Japanese fascism. Seen from the perspective of counterrevolution, however, the Konoe "new order" could be said to have brought the "Shōwa Restoration" to completion.

Konoe served as prime minister three times and, in the first and second instances, made crucial decisions affecting the political course of Japan. In the first instance, during the Marco Polo Bridge Incident, which sparked the Second Sino-Japanese War of 1937, he expanded the war front instead of seeking peaceful conciliation. Second, in 1940 he forged an alliance with Germany and Italy. Both decisions were ones he made on his own. Yet what Konoe tried to accomplish through the system of "total mobilization" should not be tied to the war alone. To begin with, "total mobilization" was something that Ernst Jünger had conceptualized in reflecting on German defeat in World War I. It meant that in contemporary warfare, no distinction exists between the military and the nonmilitary—everything has a military significance—and it is therefore no longer possible to attain victory in war only by strengthening the military. To put it conversely, "total mobilization" was an industrial, rather than a military, concern.[8]

Konoe's new order was regarded as neither socialism nor capitalism, neither liberalism nor totalitarianism. Miki called it "cooperatism" and gave it a philosophical foundation. It is no different from what other Kyoto school philosophers and critics called the "overcoming of modernity." Konoe's new order included within it Kita's "reform proposals." In other words, it was something to advance land reform and dissolution of financial combines while strengthening the rights and participation of laborers. These represented a "reform" of the capitalist state to counter socialism and in that sense corresponded to the transition from the stage of "imperialism" to "late capitalism."

---

8 Noguchi Yukio (1995) pointed out critically that many of the distinguishing features of the postwar Japanese economic system traced their origins to the wartime system of 1940. This point is fundamentally correct. It is not accurate, however, to say that the "wartime system" survived into the postwar period. These reforms were enacted as the counterrevolution of fascism. And, as seen in the example of Spain, fascism does not necessarily mean foreign wars or imperialism. Because of their sublation of the "capitalist," many of the reforms enacted in 1940 were preserved, in spite of the thoroughgoing demilitarization carried out by the American Occupation and the pacifism of postwar Japan. [Author's note]

Ironically, their plans, including land reform and dissolution of the financial combines, would only be truly carried out by American occupation forces after the war. However, postwar Japan's capitalist development was established on the basis of such reform, and in this sense the prewar Konoe new order / overcoming of modernity prepared the way for Japan's "postmodernism," which reached its apex in the 1980s. Just at the moment of its apparent triumph, however, its defeat had also begun: because Japan was so well suited to the stage of late capitalism, it was late making the transition to the stage of neoliberalism / information industry.[9]

In this way, when the particular Japanese context is removed, it becomes clear that the "repetition" in modern

---

9 From the 1970s through 1980s, a new "debate on Japanese capitalism" appeared. It differed from prewar and postwar debates carried out among leftists: instead, it consisted of Japanese businessmen, bureaucrats, and scholars responding to criticism from American businessmen, politicians, and scholars who were confounded by Japan's industrial development, aggressive exports, and nontariff trade barriers. What is of interest is that conservative scholars such as Murakami Yasusuke tried to search for the origins of "Japanese management" in the feudal system—in other words, in the feudal domain / family. In contrast to the prewar Lectures school, this was an unabashed valorization of "feudal remnants." However, just as the high tenancy fee paid in kind, which appears to be a feudal remnant, is in fact formed by the capitalist economy, what is called "Japanese management"—including the seniority system and the participation of labor unions in management—was actually formed under capitalism in its time of crisis. In other words, it began with such institutions as the Konoe system's Industrial Patriotic Association [Sangyō Hōkokukai]. This represented nothing other than a management strategy adopted in order to resolve conflict between labor and management and to increase employee retention rates. Furthermore, American ideologues in the 1980s criticized as exclusionary Japan's "corporate capitalism," in which companies hold one another's stocks, hence weakening the power of the individual stockholder. Meanwhile, this was simultaneously praised by Japanese ideologues as the highest level of capitalism, in which the "capitalist" is sublated. Yet it, too, was something originally formed under policies of the Konoe system, designed to restrict the financial combines by prohibiting stockholder dividends. This version of the "debate on Japanese capitalism" died a natural death after the 1990s, with the bursting of the bubble and the decline of the Japanese economy. [Author's note]

Japanese society existed as one part of the repetition and stages of world capitalism. The business cycle in the capitalist economy is repetition compulsive. The accumulation and expansion of capital takes place only according to the violent selection brought about by recession and depression. Earlier, I pointed out that the long-term waves of the business cycle lead to transitions in global commodities and key industries in capitalist production. In other words, from the textile industry to the cotton industry, then heavy industry, durable consumer goods, and finally the information industry. These changes brought about total reorganizations and transformations of society, while also leading inevitably to the alternation of hegemonic nations within global capitalism. Long-term business cycles cannot be explained solely on the level of economics because of such structural causality. In the case of long-term business cycles, recessions are also long term. And they bring about not only economic crises but also domestic and international political crises. For example, in the Great Depression of the 1930s, there was a shift from heavy industry to durable consumer goods, such as cars and electronic goods. It was during this time that the age of mass production and mass consumption, sometimes also referred to as Fordism, began. In the 1980s, however, it had reached a state of saturation in the advanced countries. Cars and electronic goods continue to be powerful global commodities, but the center of their production and consumption has shifted to "semideveloped" or developing countries. Meanwhile, since the 1990s, the so-called information industries have become the primary, leading-edge industries.

When seen from this perspective, the various stages of global capitalism since the nineteenth century appear roughly as in table 2. The origin of the modern capitalist state lies in mercantilism / absolutist monarchy. Although the modern nation-state rejects the absolutist state, it was from the absolutist state that it inherited conceptions of national community and territory. For that reason, movements that attempt to transcend the nation-state ultimately aim to transcend the absolutist state and, in a sense, recuperate the principle of the old "world empires." But in fact they only end up achieving an imperialism as extension

TABLE 2 Stages of Global Capitalism

	–1810	1810–1870	1870–1930	1930–1990	1990–
Global capitalism type	Mercantilism	Liberalism	Imperialism	Late capitalism	Neoliberalism
Capital	Merchant capital (manufactures)	Industrial capital	Financial capital	State monopoly capital	Multinational capital
Global commodity type	Woolen textiles	Textiles	Heavy industry	Durable consumer goods	Information
State	Absolutism	Nation-state	Imperialism	Welfare state	Regionalism

of the nation-state, as seen, for example, in Germany's "economy of grand space" [*Grossraumwirtschaft*] or Japan's "Greater East Asia Co-Prosperity Sphere" of the 1930s. In the 1990s as well, with the dissolution of the post–World War II Cold War structure between the United States and the Soviet Union, a similar phenomenon appeared. The global market economy has weakened the framework of the nation-state. The nation-state, however, has not been dissolved into a single world market but instead counters by creating an assemblage of multiple regionalisms. In this case, if regionalism, which rejects the framework of the modern nation-state, recalls the communality of premodern civilization (world empire, world religion), it is not because such remnants of an old system still exist strongly today. Rather, it is simply the form of "imagined community" that is required and called forth by the current stage of global capitalism.

What is evident is that in global terms, the Meiji Restoration, which began in 1868, was set in motion during the late stages of liberalism and represented an abrupt transformation toward the stage of imperialism, as would become clear in the 1880s. In turn, the "Shōwa Restoration" of the 1930s was carried out as a transition from the stage of imperialism to the stage of late capitalism. What kinds of discourses were mobilized in the process of this transition are the subject of the next chapter.

3

THE DISCURSIVE SPACE OF MODERN JAPAN

Nothing really comes to any conclusion in the world. Once something happens, it will continue on forever. Only, it keeps changing shape, so people don't recognize it is all.

—NATSUME SŌSEKI, *Grass on the Wayside*

1. Periodization

In Japan, the word "Shōwa" and discourse concerning the Shōwa period [1926–1989] suddenly began to proliferate in the summer of 1987, when news of the emperor's illness spread. At the beginning of 1989, Shōwa came to an end. It ended after so many recountings of "the end of Shōwa" had been consumed. Once it had ended, it became apparent that a "Shōwa period" had existed, and its historical review could begin. But what is the significance of periodizing history according to era names?

Since the Meiji period [1868–1912], Japanese era names have functioned according to the principle of "one reign, one name," but prior to Meiji they were changed frequently. The reasons for change included favorable omens and natural disasters, while some changes were tied to specific years in the sexagenary cycle, according to divination theory. In other words, the change of era names was magical, or ritualistic, and was aimed at the rebirth, through death, of an era = world [世 = 代]. This function has not changed with "one reign, one name." The periods Meiji, Taishō [1912–1926], and Shōwa themselves organize eras (worlds) that possess a beginning and an end. However, these divisions have currency only inside Japan and often give rise to certain illusions.

For example, we are in the habit of saying Meiji literature or Taishō literature, which thereby evokes a certain coherent image. The same applies to the Edo period [1600–1867]: the

This chapter is based on my translation of an earlier version of Karatani's (1991) essay. A prior version of this essay was also translated by Sandra Buckley as "1970 = Showa 45" (Karatani 1989a).

terms "Genroku" [1688–1704] and "Bunka Bunsei" [1804–1830] produce a similar sense of comprehension, which is lacking when we use the Western calendar for the same period. This type of understanding confines us within a strange illusion. This illusion should become clear when we simply think in terms of the Western calendar, but such is not always the case. I became aware of this problem when teaching Meiji literature at Yale University in 1975. For example, modern literature in Japan comes into existence during the Meiji 20s through 30s, but I had never thought about the fact that this period corresponds to what is called the fin de siècle in the West, nor had I thought about the fact that the Taishō period was contemporaneous with World War I (Taishō 3) and the Russian Revolution (Taishō 6). Although I knew both histories well, I had never thought of them "simultaneously." And I am still fixed on the parallax that I discovered then.

Divisions according to era names such as Meiji, Taishō, or Shōwa construct a single, autonomous discursive space and make one forget about relations to the exterior. Yet simply doing away with periodization by era names and thinking in terms of the Western calendar would not resolve this problem. One cannot account for Meiji literature according to the concepts of the nineteenth and twentieth centuries alone; there is something there that disappears when the proper name "Meiji" is removed. This is not to say, however, that there exists a topology unique to Japan, or any internally confined time and space. In fact, what this proper name maintains is a relation to the exterior that does not allow for internal cohesion. Moreover, the image of what is "Meijiesque" or "Taishōesque" does not strictly correspond to the life of the emperor. The terms "Meijiesque" and "Taishōesque," insofar as they symbolize certain historical structures, do in fact exist, and to dispose of them would be to also discard such structures.

This problem is not unique to Japan. For example, the phrase "Elizabethan drama," as opposed to saying English drama of the late sixteenth to early seventeenth centuries, loosely indicates a certain coherent political and social relational structure. This conventional usage of the term is not the same as thinking of history according to court history. Even within Europe, in the same century, people in each country lived in different "discursive spaces." For example, books about "eighteenth-century European thought" deal only with England, France, and Germany, and they pay not the slightest heed to how people were living or thinking in other areas such as Finland or Poland. Yet it is undeniable that each region had its own discursive space, as well as its own form of historical periodization. Such differences disappear when thinking within the Western calendar.

It should also be noted that the Western calendar, while appearing to represent simply a linear chronology, itself contains narrative divisions that are given significance, from the outset, by the narrative of Christianity. Furthermore, the divisions of a hundred years or a thousand years maintain a specific ritual significance. If the calendar were merely a linear chronology, there would most likely be no such thing as the "fin de siècle." The calendar not only projects a fin-de-siècle significance onto events that occur but also in fact itself gives rise to fin-de-siècle phenomena. Even were this not the case, the fact that we view history according to hundred-year divisions, such as the eighteenth, nineteenth, or twentieth centuries, already creates a certain narrative punctuation. In other words, when we think in terms of the Western calendar, we are confined within a system of thought that views a particular narrative as universal.

Of course, the Western calendar is indispensable; it is, however, something on the order of the metric system, and any Christian significance must be abstracted from it. It is indispensable in order to make explicit the fact that each region's historical periodization is based on nothing more than the discursive space of its "world." On the other hand, the universal world can signify only the total, interrelational structure of these multiple worlds.

Earlier, I mentioned that periodization according to era names produces an illusion; we must be aware, however, that any division has the potential to produce such illusions. The divisions of prewar and postwar, for example, are widely used. Certainly World War II is one point of historical demarcation, and the events of 1989, which revealed the end of the postwar

U.S.–Soviet binary, constitute another. These divisions, however, do not account for everything, nor are they the most important. Japan indeed changed after its defeat in the war, but many areas also remained unchanged. Even among the most obvious transformations, there are those that were set in motion before and during the war. Should we then simply discard such divisions?

Periodization, however, is indispensable for history. To mark off a period—that is, to assign a beginning and an end—is to understand the significance of events. One can say that the discipline of history is, to a large extent, contested over the question of periodization, for periodization itself changes the significance of events. Take, for example, the concept of the Middle Ages. A mediocre German historian first began using this term in the eighteenth century, and historians ever since have been fighting over the question of how far the Middle Ages extend. Some argue that they extend as far as the eighteenth century—that even Newton, for example, was a man of the Middle Ages—while others argue that modernity began in twelfth-century Europe. Yet they do not go so far as to discard the period of the Middle Ages itself.

Today, one talks of historical breaks as episteme (Foucault) or paradigm (Kuhn). There is also a school of history (the Annales school) that attempts to view history as a domain without clear demarcations. Things remain essentially unchanged, however. What is put forth under the name of "paradigm" is the production of discontinuous breaks within a science presented as systematic, textbook knowledge, and what is called "episteme" replaces the historical break based on the transcendental subject or idea with the historical break woven by discursive events. Both avoid a teleological viewpoint. Nonetheless, as in any type of periodization, to the extent that they discern a beginning and an end (telos), these perspectives cannot escape a different type of teleological arrangement.

The Annales school examines the transformations and intermingling of differential areas rather than the obvious political and historical divisions, but this too simply puts forth another demarcation, according to which the traditional division / conferral of meaning is altered. Larger demarcations, however, such as before or after the New Stone Age, are also possible. Based on which perspective is taken—years, decades, centuries, millennia—the nature of periodization itself changes. Furthermore, the object, as well as the significance, of history changes. The question, however, is not which particular division is superior. Lévi-Strauss wrote that "history is a discontinuous set composed of domains of history" (1966:259–60). In other words, "history is a method with no distinct object corresponding to it" (262). However, people continue to struggle over the question of "method."

I have no interest in getting involved in such quarrels. Rather, my interest lies in the *parallax* that emerges in the difference between seeing something according to one historical periodization and seeing it according to another, and in what is produced by such a parallax. In other words, in concrete terms, I see, in the parallax between what can be thought in terms of the Western calendar and what can be thought in terms of Japanese era names, a certain structure of repetition in history.

2. Meiji and Shōwa

As I mentioned earlier, "Meiji" and "Taishō" do not strictly correspond to the lives of the emperors and are unrelated to the emperors personally. The emperor is, indeed, only a symbol. The same can be said for Shōwa. Wittgenstein stated that the meaning of words lies in their usage (1958:20). That is, in order to understand the meaning of the word "Shōwa," we need to look at how it is used. Around the time that Shōwa ended, and after it had ended, people began en masse to look back on "Shōwa history." What everyone forgot during this time, however, was that at least until 1987, "Shōwa history" referred to the period before World War II and did not include the postwar period. Many books and articles were written with "Shōwa" in their titles (e.g., *History of Shōwa, Shōwa Literature*), but these generally refer to the prewar period, while the term "postwar" is applied to the period after Shōwa 20 (1945). Similarly, since

1965, the word "postwar" itself has seldom been used. It was around 1965 that people began speaking of the end of postwar literature; parallel to this, the term "Shōwa" lost its significance as a historical division.

For example, phrases such as "early Shōwa" and the "Shōwa 10s" are popular, but this type of phrasing is possible only until the Shōwa 30s. One seldom hears the phrase "Shōwa 40s," because the expression "the 1960s" overlaps with the Shōwa 30s, and after that it is normal to speak of the 1970s or 1980s. Between the Shōwa 30s [1955–1965] and the 1960s there is not only a gap of five years but a significant difference in nuance as well. In contrast to the latter, which is viewed within an international perspective, the former carries with it the context of Japan since the Meiji period. It was perhaps only in the Shōwa 30s that both were able to coexist.

For example, the New Left movement of around 1970 was constituted according to a consciousness of worldwide simultaneity. Looking back from that perspective, the "Ampo struggle of 1960," which erupted over the revision of the U.S.-Japan Security Treaty, appears only as the genesis of that later movement. However, the "Ampo struggle of Shōwa 35" is something fundamentally different. It was, rather, an intensive reexamination of the various questions that had persisted since Meiji. It was only much later, however, that I was able to understand this; at the time, at eighteen, I did not think of these matters at all. I did not understand the perspective of critic Takeuchi Yoshimi, who tried to grasp the Ampo struggle in terms of an opposition between "democracy and dictatorship," nor did I understand why historian Hashikawa Bunzō dwelled on the question of the Japanese Romantic school. What I was able to extract from them was only the fact that Japan's "premodernity" still lingered after the war or, perhaps, was being revived. In effect, I was thinking of history entirely according to the Western calendar.

This is also connected to the fact that I could not understand Mishima Yukio's political transformation in the late 1960s. As I mention later, the issues that Takeuchi raised in 1960 were questions of the Shōwa 10s, and furthermore they were also questions of the Meiji 10s. That is, the ideological questions of the

TABLE 3 Meiji and Shōwa

Meiji		Shōwa	
10	Seinan War	11	February 26 Incident
22	Promulgation of constitution	21	Promulgation of new constitution
27	Sino-Japanese War	26	Peace conference, U.S.-Japan Security Treaty
37	Russo-Japanese War	35	Ampo struggle / New U.S.-Japan Security Treaty
		39	Tokyo Olympics
43	Annexation of Korea, High Treason Incident	43	Zenkyōtō student movement
44	Revision of treaties	44	Return of Okinawa decided
45	General Nogi's suicide	45	Mishima's suicide

Shōwa 10s were, in a sense, the re-presentation of the questions of the Meiji 10s. For example, the February 26 Incident of Shōwa 11 was represented as a "Shōwa Restoration" that would inherit the spirit of Saigō Takamori of Meiji 10 and realize the Meiji Restoration to its fullest extent. For the moment, let us compare the events of post-Meiji 20 and post-Shōwa 20 (table 3). Parallelism that is invisible under the Western calendar becomes apparent here. What all these striking correspondences indicate is the process of Japan's transformation into a nation-state of Western-power status: the establishment of the institutions of the modern state, the achievement of economic development, and the revision of unequal treaties.[1] In the first place, however, such parallelism between Meiji and Shōwa should be seen not only from a perspective internal to Japan but also from that of the movement of global capitalism from one stage to another. It was only the fact that adding Meiji and Taishō together roughly equals sixty years that gave rise to the repetition of Meiji in Shōwa.

1 Following upon the 1936 Berlin Olympics, used by Hitler as a "Fest der Völker," Tokyo had been selected as the site for the next Olympics in 1940—no doubt it was to have been a proud display of the "Greater East Asia Co-Prosperity Sphere"—but it was canceled because of the war. Therefore, the hosting of the Tokyo Olympics in 1964 held great political meaning for Japan. In addition, the Tōkaidō Shinkansen Line, which began operation in conjunction with the Olympics, was in fact a belated actualization of something planned and prepared during the war for military purposes. [Author's note]

Second, this parallelism signifies that the interrelational structure that situates Japan in the West and Asia has not fundamentally changed. To put it differently, we can view what is Meijiesque or Shōwaesque as the discursive spaces exposed by this relational structure. In turn, the discursive space of the Taishō period resembles that of the 1970s because of the combination of a sense of achievement and a self-complacent interiorization, which has repressed this external relational structure.

3. The Discursive Space of Modern Japan

In the late 1950s, Takeuchi attempted to reevaluate the infamous wartime conference known as "Overcoming Modernity." Takeuchi's efforts represent a different undertaking from, say, a contemporary evaluation of the "deconstruction of modernity" in the work of philosopher Nishida Kitarō or the Kyoto school that disregards their political contexts. Takeuchi saw this debate as a failed attempt to resolve once and for all the contradiction-ridden problematics of modern Japan dating back to Meiji; rather than simply rejecting the attempt out of hand, he in fact argued that it should be undertaken anew:

> In a way, the "Overcoming Modernity" symposium represented a condensed version of the aporias of modern Japanese history. Faced with the urgent task of interpreting the idea of eternal warfare at a time of total war, the symposium marked the explosion of such traditional oppositions as those of reactionism and restoration, reverence for the Emperor and exclusion of foreigners, isolationism and the opening of the country, ultranationalism and "civilization and enlightenment," and East and West. It was thus correct to raise these issues at the time, and all the more because they aroused the concern of the intelligentsia. That the symposium produced such poor results is unrelated to the raising of these issues itself, but rather stems from the symposium's failure to dissolve *the war's double nature*, that is to say, its failure

to objectify the aporias of modern Japanese history *qua* aporias. Hence it was impossible to produce a strong thinking subject who could exploit Yasuda's destructive force toward other ends. These important aporias thus vanished into thin air, and the symposium became nothing more than a published commentary on official wartime thought. Combined with the postwar atrophy, the disappearance of these aporias prepared the intellectual ground for Japan's colonization. (2004:145–46; Karatani's emphasis)

By "the war's double nature," Takeuchi means to say that the war was simultaneously a war of aggression against Asia *and* a war to liberate Asia from the Western powers. To put it another way, it was at the same time the Pacific War and the Greater East Asia War. The very "dissolution" of this duality, however, is dangerous, for the two can never be separated: one cannot affirm the one while negating the other.

Takeuchi's logic is also extremely risky, and this is already apparent in his earlier work on nationalism: "If nationalism is desired at all costs, what is to be done? Since it is impossible to evade the peril of ultra-nationalism and maintain only nationalism, the sole path lies rather in drawing out a genuine nationalism from within ultra-nationalism. That is, to draw out revolution from within counter-revolution" (1981a:19–20). Takeuchi's praise of "Overcoming Modernity"—that is, of the Kyoto school and the Japanese Romantic school—functions according to precisely the same logic, a logic that is nearly religious: it is only by passing through evil that salvation is possible.

Modern Japan, however, was located within a structure that compels this type of risky logic. The Meiji Restoration is generally seen as an event that took place in 1868 comprising the fall of the Tokugawa shogunate and the establishment of the Meiji government, but it should more properly be seen as a process that extends through the promulgation of the Imperial Constitution (Meiji 22 / 1889) and the establishment of the Diet (1890). It was during this process that the contradiction-ridden problematics that Takeuchi refers to as "reactionism and

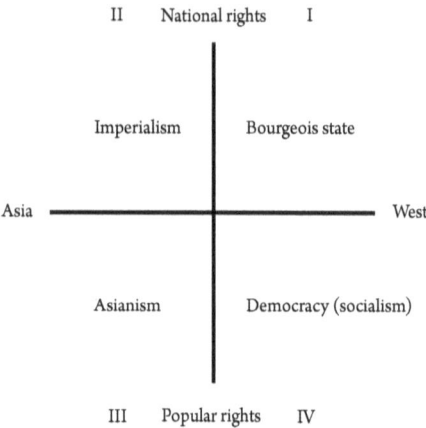

FIGURE 1 The discursive space of modern Japan.

restoration, reverence for the Emperor and exclusion of foreigners, isolationism and the opening of the country, ultranationalism and 'civilization and enlightenment,' and East and West" came into the open. Moreover, these problematics would recur in subsequent years. I would like to present them according to a coordinate space formed by two axes (figure 1). The first presents the choice between national rights and popular rights, two orientations that are entangled with each other in the Meiji Restoration. To the extent that the Meiji Restoration was a revolution, it belonged to popular rights, and to the extent that it aimed to establish a sovereign nation against the Western powers, it belonged to national rights. The early Meiji regime was nothing more than a situation in which revolutionary leaders from the Satsuma and Chōshū domains gained power by raising up the emperor. The regime managed to eliminate the feudal base and establish the economic system of private property and capitalism, but those in power were themselves grounded in a feudal base, and, in addition, there remained old warrior families opposed to the new order. For this reason, this period can be referred to as a system of "absolutist monarchy."

Members of the old warrior class, excluded from the state power monopolized by Satsuma and Chōshū, formed the oppositional Freedom and People's Rights Movement, which called for the establishment of a parliament. In the Meiji 10s, the movement spread to the people at large. In Meiji 14, the government suppressed the movement while simultaneously promising the promulgation of a constitution and the establishment of a parliamentary system. As a result, many people drafted and proposed their own constitutions based on the constitutional politics of England or the ideals of the French Revolution. But in actuality, the government, with Itō Hirobumi taking a central role, drafted the Greater Japanese Imperial Constitution, which was based on the Prussian constitution and was unilaterally promulgated in Meiji 22 (1889). With this action, the structure of the modern nation-state was established, but "freedom and people's rights" were not achieved. Many activists in the Freedom and People's Rights Movement, however, shifted course and cooperated with those in favor of national rights. On the other hand, some of them, as represented by Nakae Chōmin, attempted to expand freedom and people's rights and arrived at socialism.

The above phenomena can be understood in the context of the Western calendar. Yet matters are complicated by the existence of another axis, consisting of the West and the East. That is, this axis represents the choice of moving toward the West or moving in the direction of Asia. The Meiji Restoration was originally an attempt to resist Western colonialism and was essentially anti-Western. There were more than a few types who espoused Westernization but thought of it as no more than a means to fight the West. The motive force of the Meiji Restoration may appear to be a kind of chauvinistic nationalism, of the type represented by the National Learning dating back to the Edo-period nativist scholar Motoori Norinaga. A stronger factor, however, was in fact the revolutionary ideals based on Chinese literature and neo-Confucianism (the Wang Yangming school), as in the case of Saigō Takamori. In terms of both cultural identity and political ideals, such revolutionaries aimed at an Asian solidarity that would oppose the West. Subsequently, this desire would be condensed in the famous statement of Okakura Kakuzō, who participated in the Indian independence movement: "Asia is one" (1970:1).

Following the Restoration, this problem appeared as a deep-seated opposition inside the Meiji government. For example, Saigō, one of the main leaders of the Restoration, proclaimed the need to conquer Korea, an assertion that is considered the opening salvo of Japan's imperialist expansion. However, this is not necessarily the case. Saigō's emphasis was that in order to avoid colonization by the Western powers, there was a need for Korea to open its borders and modernize. This is similar to Trotsky and Che Guevara thinking that the success of their revolutions depended on revolution in Europe and Central America, respectively. The export of revolution is precisely the defense of revolution. In Meiji, the liberation of Asian countries from the imperialist control of the Western powers (i.e., the export of the Meiji revolution) signified the defense of Japan itself. Later there emerged, from among the activists of the Freedom and People's Rights Movement, those who actively engaged in helping to bring about revolution in China based on the same perspective.

On the other hand, Ōkubo Toshimichi and Itō Hirobumi, who, like Saigō, served as central pillars of the Meiji government, rejected Saigō's theory of conquering Korea at the time. They believed that strengthening the Japanese state, rather than the revolution or liberation of Asia, was the first priority. Saigō stepped down from the central government and started a rebellion in Satsuma, in which he died—this was the Seinan War (Meiji 10 / 1877). Soon afterward, however, the Meiji government sent troops to Korea and literally began to put into effect Saigō's argument for conquering Korea. These actions ultimately led to the Sino-Japanese War (Meiji 27 / 1894). At that point, Saigō was recalled as the founder of this type of imperialism.

But Saigō was also remembered as a founding figure from the opposite perspective—that is, as a symbol of popular rights in opposition to national rights, and Asianism in opposition to imperialism. The key point is not to determine which perspective is correct but rather to grasp the very "doubleness" that Saigō maintains. Takeuchi wrote as follows: "Whether to view Saigō as a counterrevolutionary or as the symbol of eternal revolution is not a problem that can be easily resolved. Yet it is difficult to define Asianism outside the context of this problem" (1980a:156).[2] But this type of doubleness cannot be a question confined to Saigō individually. Japan, despite being a country in Asia, aimed for an accelerated Westernization in order to avoid colonization and attain independent status while simultaneously aligning with the Western powers to engage in imperialist expansion in Asia—it was this contradiction-ridden course that pushed not only Saigō but many others as well into a complex topology.

I would like to think about these questions according to the coordinates created by these two axes (see figure 1). The right-hand side of the diagram represents the will to Westernization and de-Asianization.[3] Quadrant I is where the nationalism based on the Prussian model is situated, and in quadrant IV resides the democracy based on the French Revolution. On

---

2 For example, Takeuchi refers to the Seinan War as the "second Restoration." This is to see "eternal revolution," and, further, the founder of Asianism, in the figure of Saigō. Still, although Saigō left office proclaiming "popular rights," there was no element of popular rights in his rebellion. Saigō's troops were formed exclusively of the old warrior class. On this point, the Seinan War was nothing more than the rebellion of the old warrior class dissatisfied with the institutions of the modern nation-state. His army was easily pulverized by the imperial army composed of commoners, which Saigō himself had created. In some sense, one can say that Saigō, by creating a final battleground for the old feudal forces, took care of them in a decisive way, thereby contributing to the consolidation of the new state. Marx says that tragedy exists so that we can part cheerfully from the past. [Author's note]

3 This type of problem is not in any way a phenomenon unique to Japan. Modern nation-states everywhere were established by breaking off and becoming independent from the world empires that preceded them and that were centered on world religions and world languages (Latin, Arabic, Chinese writing, the Cyrillic alphabet). In this process, a nationalism based on an "empathy" proper to the nation, and which rejected the law, religion, and culture of the old empire, was formed. In Japan's case, this was Motoori Norinaga's "National Learning." On the other hand, there is also a movement that seeks the key to transcending the modern nation-state and capitalism in the communality of the previous world empires (civilizations). In Europe, such movements existed from early on and continue to exist today. There is no reason to cease such regionalist movements owing to a fear that they will result, as in the past, in "imperialism." One can no doubt say the same for "Asianism." [Author's note]

the other hand, the left-hand side of the diagram contains that which is related to Asia, with quadrant II representing imperialism and quadrant III, Asianism. Of course, Asianism can be seen as an extension of "popular rights" aiming for the liberation of Asia, and, conversely, imperialism can be seen as an extension of "national rights" aiming at the control of Asia.

However, it is difficult to place individuals within the spaces sketched out by this diagram. For individuals move throughout these domains. It is for this reason that the discursive space of modern Japan becomes so complicated. For example, after the Meiji 20s, many supporters of the Freedom and People's Rights Movement (quadrant IV) shifted to the national rights camp (quadrant I), and furthermore to imperialism (quadrant II). With regard to this phenomenon, Chōmin wrote,

> When I say such things, the average politician in the world will always respond triumphantly that it is nothing more than the stale popular rights doctrine of fifteen years ago, that to trot out such an outdated theory today, when Western nations are all fully engaged in imperialism, is simply behind the times. But even if it is stale in theory, it is fresh in practice. Such a clear theory has been put into practice in Western nations for several centuries, and so in those places it may have become stale. But in our nation, it only sprouted among the people as a theory and was snuffed out by the elder statesmen and self-centered politicians, thus vanishing before ever being put into practice. So as rhetoric indeed it may be exceedingly stale, but as practice it is fresh, and in any case, where does the fault for this lie? (quoted in Maruyama 1961:24–25)

Chōmin wrote these words in 1898—in other words, four years after the beginning of the Sino-Japanese War, which erupted over Japan's imperialist intervention in Korea. At that time, the new "theory" that supplanted popular rights doctrine was the notion of "survival of the fittest" of social Darwinism, which served to support imperialism. At that point, those who had proclaimed "popular rights" fifteen years earlier committed ideological conversion [*tenkō*] en masse and denigrated popular rights doctrine as "an outdated theory behind the times." On the other hand, Asianists who looked up to Saigō—that is, those who aimed for the revolution and liberation of Asia—converted to an imperialism dressed in the guise of Asianism, as typified by the case of Gen'yōsha.

These coordinates are also repeated in Shōwa. In contrast to the Meiji period, industrial capitalism was by then firmly established and class conflict had come out into the open, while, in addition, imperialist expansion was proceeding. It may be seen that in this context Marxism was representative of movements attempting to counter the power of state and capital. In that case, Marxists can be said to belong to quadrant IV. They subscribed to modern rationalism and saw Asia as representative of backward nations in general; there was no element of "Asianism" there. In other words, Marxists were, in the broadest sense, part of the de-Asianization camp. When they faced suppression and underwent conversion, many of them moved toward quadrants I and II, but more than a few moved toward Asianism.

On the other hand, in quadrant II, one can locate agrarianists [*nōhonshugisha*], who opposed capitalism and the centralization of power found in the modern nation-state as well as in Marxism. What they relied on was the ideal of the agricultural community [*shashoku*]. On the one hand, this was related to emperor-system fascism; at the same time, however, since this type of community was something held in common throughout Asia, it was also able to serve as the basis for an ideal of Asian independence. Of course, this was nothing more than an ideal, and in actuality their movement was assimilated into the governing ideology of imperialism. In this way, Asianism and imperialism merged together.[4]

Of equal importance as such conversions are the *reconversions* that took place after the end of World War II. These

---

4 The Marxist Ozaki Hotsumi, part of the brain trust of the Konoe cabinet, proclaimed the "theory of the East Asian Community," but this was replaced by the theory of the "Greater East Asia Co-Prosperity Sphere," which aestheticized Japan's imperialist rule. [Author's note]

re-conversions included movements from quadrant II to I or IV, or from quadrant III to I or IV: in other words, from the left-hand side of the diagram to the right-hand side. Postwar discursive space was formed from the right-hand side of the diagram—that is, from a domain that discarded "Asia." Whether as invasion or liberation, the prohibition against interfering in Asia has dominated postwar discursive space. In actuality, Japan has intervened in Asia even more than in the prewar period and has expanded its economic control there. Yet in terms of discursive space, the left-hand side was situated below the level of consciousness.

It was this postwar discursive space that Takeuchi criticized: "I believe that the aggressive aspect of the Greater East Asia War cannot be denied by any argument. But, by detesting the aggression so much, to reject as well the notion of Asian solidarity that was exposed through the form of aggression is like throwing out the baby with the bathwater. For, in that case, the Japanese would never be able to restore their lost sense of objectives" (1981b:119). Takeuchi did not make such statements in the 1960s to encourage sympathy for Asia. According to his reasoning, the stagnation of Asia (particularly of China) was caused by the resistance to Western civilization. On the other hand, Japan was successful in its modernization because there was no resistance. This was because there had been no "self" to begin with. Takeuchi's Asianism thus reexamines the very question of Japanese identity.

After 1970, however, the type of criticism that Takeuchi wrote was itself canceled out. For example, in the context of the economic development of the 1970s, the fact that a self did not exist was highly valued. It was precisely because of this fact that Japan was able to become a vanguard, hyper-Western consumer and information society. Indeed, there was no self (subject) or identity, but there was a predicative identity with the capacity to assimilate anything, without incurring any shock or giving rise to any confusion. This is what Nishida read as "predicative logic," or "the logic of place," in which he identified the essence of the emperor system. In this sense, after 1970, when Shōwa and Meiji were forgotten and Japan began to exist within a worldwide simultaneity, it is precisely the emperor as zero-degree sign that began to function structurally.

4. Things Taishōesque

Clearly, the fact that "Shōwa" fell out of general usage after 1970, except in official documents, does not signify that the Japanese had distanced themselves from a local perspective tied to the emperor and had adopted an international perspective. Rather, within the discursive space described earlier, it signifies that the Japanese were confined within a dimension eradicating everything outside quadrant I of the diagram. However, this was not the first time such a phenomenon had occurred, for it had earlier come into being during Taishō. If Shōwa repeats Meiji, then the period after Shōwa 45 is a repetition of the period after Meiji 45—in other words, of Taishō.

Just as Shōwa ended, for all practical purposes, in Shōwa 39 (when the Tokyo Olympics displayed Japan's postwar revival both domestically and internationally), Meiji can be said to have come to an end in Meiji 37, with the Russo-Japanese War [1904–1905]. Thus the novelist Natsume Sōseki, who began writing fiction after the Russo-Japanese War, appeared to the contemporary literary world—which was then dominated by naturalism—as a person from the previous age. *Theory of Literature* [*Bungakuron*, 1907], which Sōseki had grappled with desperately in London, appeared only as an antiquated, unfashionable undertaking. In this work, Sōseki took the position that Eastern and Western literature were qualitatively different. It was precisely for this reason that he tried to objectify them both "scientifically," according to the same basis—that is, on the basis of the material, social level of language. Moreover, in this context Sōseki used the phrase "Eastern literature" rather than "Japanese literature." For Taishō intellectuals, however, the type of qualitative differences and tensions between the East, the West, and Japan that troubled such Meiji intellectuals as Sōseki did not exist, except as *quantitative* differences, or as differences in stage. Marxism emerged in Japan as an extension of this situation—the Marxist perspective was based on a consciousness of worldwide simultaneity and homogeneity. In this manner, Marxists analyzed Japanese history prior to the Meiji Restoration within a universal perspective (but one that was actually based on a Eurocentric model).

In the period leading up to the Russo-Japanese War, a consciousness of worldwide simultaneity did not exist, because this was precisely what was being confronted. The war had a simultaneous effect on countries in Asia and around the world that were under colonization by the West. That a non-Western country could defeat a major power such as Russia was an astonishing event. Yet afterward, Japan itself came to participate among the Western powers as a "first-class" nation. And at that point, the sense of external tension and solidarity with Asia that had existed in the Meiji period was lost.

In Japan's Taishō-period war—that is, World War I—such a tension of simultaneity was lacking; it was only a distant event on another shore. Japan profited on the sidelines from this war and did not experience the disastrous effect that it had on Europe. Furthermore, Japan behaved like a Western imperialist power toward Asia. But proportionately, the consciousness of worldwide simultaneity and of a racial perspective strengthened domestically, and, at the same time, "things Japanese," existing independently of foreign culture, began to be emphasized. In the realm of literature, this tendency is represented by the dominance of the I-novel [*watakushi shōsetsu*].

"Things Taishōesque" emerged from a self-complacent consciousness, as tension between Japan and the West began to ease following the Russo-Japanese War and Japan proclaimed its separation from Asia. It should be noted that both Fukuzawa Yukichi's "On Leaving Asia" [Datsu-A ron, 1885] and Okakura's *Ideals of the East* (1903) were written amid the tension that existed prior to the establishment of such a self-complacent consciousness.[5] Both, however, take on a different meaning

---

5 Whereas the Meiji government took Prussian state capitalism as its model and the Freedom and People's Rights group upheld the French Revolution as its ideal, Fukuzawa had in mind English-style politics and economy. As opposed

following the Taishō period. For example, in *The Ideals of the East*, which he composed in English prior to the Russo-Japanese War, Okakura writes,

> The unique blessing of unbroken sovereignty, the proud self-reliance of an unconquered race, and the insular isolation which protected ancestral ideas and instincts at the cost of expansion, made Japan the real repository of the trust of Asiatic thought and culture. . . . Thus Japan is a museum of Asiatic civilisation; and yet more than a museum, because the singular genius of the race leads it to dwell on all phases of the ideals of the past, in that spirit of living Advaitism which welcomes the new without losing the old. . . . The history of Japanese art becomes thus the history of Asiatic ideals—the beach where each successive wave of Eastern thought has left its sand-ripple as it beat against the national consciousness. (1970:5–9)

This passage appears after Okakura's long discourse on India and China. Moreover, Japan's privileged position arises not from the originality of its national essence but rather from its capacity to preserve, as a "repository," the products of Asian intercourse. This type of understanding is unrelated to any

---

to a German-style imperial university, he tried to cultivate the new generation through the private Keiō School, which he established himself. To begin with, ever since his involvement in Dutch learning in the Tokugawa period, Fukuzawa had resented the Confucian ideals that were then dominant. It was his conviction that there would be no new society without a rejection of Confucianism. At first, Fukuzawa anticipated that there would be revolutions in Korea and China, but seeing not the slightest change take place, he grew disillusioned with an Asia governed by Confucianism and wrote an essay whose import was that we must escape from such an Asia. This would subsequently become famous as a theory of "de-Asianization," but it was hardly known at the time. The foundation of Fukuzawa's thought was the establishment of the nation-state. However, the nation-state, when expanded, transforms into imperialism. Fukuzawa never proclaimed imperialism. Nonetheless, he endorsed Japan's transformation into an imperialist power toward Asia following the Sino-Japanese War. [Author's note]

antiforeign nationalism and instead constitutes an attempt to place Japan in an Asian solidarity. Originally, this book was written for the independence of Asia and was, furthermore, written for Asians and Westerners; it was virtually unknown in Japan until its translation years later. Takeuchi writes of Okakura, "In this position, Okakura is more an apostle of transcendental value alienated from the Japanese nation. The Japanese nation would not listen to his appeal, and so he had to take his appeal to the world. And here, Okakura's beauty / spirit / Asia maintains a position similar to the notion of faith in Uchimura Kanzō" (1980b:173).

The Christian Uchimura wrote a text in English explaining the Japanese position in the Sino-Japanese War, but soon after the war ended he realized that it had been nothing more than a manifestation of imperialism, and he engaged in self-criticism. Later, he opposed the Russo-Japanese War, along with socialists such as Kōtoku Shūsui. Uchimura and Okakura were not unpatriotic, but their patriotism was revealed only to Westerners and was not directed internally. Within Japan, Uchimura's God and Okakura's beauty / spirit / Asia existed as an absolute transcendent exteriority that did not allow for the self-sufficiency of the Japanese.

However, in the Taishō period, such exteriority was erased, and people began to seek internally—or, in other words, in Japan's past—for self-identity. At that point, Okakura's statements begin to hold the opposite meaning. Watsuji Tetsurō exemplifies this phenomenon. Watsuji, who had started out as a scholar of Nietzsche and Kierkegaard, wrote *The Revival of Idols* [*Gūzō saikō*] in 1918. Watsuji's "revival of idols" has two meanings: the revival of the "idols" destroyed by Nietzsche and the revival of Buddhist "idols" in Japan. The following year, he wrote *A Pilgrimage to Ancient Temples* [*Koji jun'rei*] and the year after that *The Ancient Culture of Japan* [*Nihon kodai bunka*]. What should be noted, however, is that Watsuji's perspective on Buddhism is entirely aesthetic. In truth, as a student Watsuji attended Okakura's lectures at Tokyo Imperial University on "The History of Far Eastern Art" and was greatly moved by them.

While acknowledging the great impact that Buddhism had on Japanese culture, Watsuji focused on the fact that Buddhism in Japan was still considered to be "foreign thought." He compared this with the reception of Christianity in Europe. For the Germanic peoples, Christianity was a foreign way of thinking, but because it was received in such a way as to repress the non-Christian beliefs that had existed previously, Christianity was not thought of as foreign. Furthermore, in contrast to the length of time it took for the reception of Christianity, Buddhism took root in Japan as soon as it was imported and flowered in the native soil. Watsuji explained this phenomenon as follows:

> Undoubtedly we should discern here not only Buddhism's own lack of combativeness but also the tolerance of the Japanese themselves toward religion. They did not feel that they had to discard their faith in their own gods in order to become devout followers of the Buddha. As can still clearly be seen in contemporary times, it was no contradiction for devout followers to worship both the *kami* and the Buddha. This can perhaps also be seen as a lack of thoroughness in faith. In this way, the Buddhification of the Japanese did not result in a "conversion" signifying the total rejection of non-Buddhist elements. Rather, it was the Japanese who made Buddhism their own. For this reason, despite the long centuries that Buddhism has been the flesh and blood of Japanese culture, it still maintains the possibility of being seen as a "foreign thought." (1962:323)

Elsewhere, I have criticized this type of perspective (Karatani 2004). What I would like to focus on here is that although it appears that Watsuji goes back to the ancient period, in truth he is projecting the post–World War I environment onto the past. Unlike other Asian countries, Japan had accepted Westernization after the Meiji Restoration without resistance; yet after the victory in the Russo-Japanese War, people began to look for a basis of identity in Japanese culture. Such an identity, however, could not be a rejection of Western thought and a substitution of, say, Buddhism or Shinto. The basis of self-identity had to be a certain thinking whereby even Buddhism was seen as "foreign thought," or rather, it had to be a *place* whereby Western thought could be accepted on its own as a "foreign thought." Okakura's image of Japan as "repository" or "museum," in this context, was recast as a "place of nothingness" (Nishida) that could accept anything from the outside without problem.

5. Transformations of Emperor Theory

After Shōwa began in 1926, Japan was suddenly cast into a state of internal and external tension. As a result, in Shōwa discourse the "aporias" that had existed since Meiji were re-presented. In truth, they would be condensed into the image of the Meiji Restoration. In other words, this was the "Shōwa Restoration." It goes without saying that this resulted in war and defeat. Rather than simply comparing the Meiji and Shōwa restorations, however, it is necessary to focus on things "Taishō-esque" that lay between them.

Kita Ikki was executed as an ideologue behind the February 26 Incident of 1936—that is, the attempted coup d'état whereby national reform was to be carried out in the name of the emperor. His thinking, however, was quite distant from the deification of the emperor. He claimed that the pre-Meiji emperor was no different from an "aboriginal chieftain." In truth, as I stated previously, era names prior to Meiji constituted a magical function to control nature. The practice of "one reign, one name" negated this in order to establish the emperor as the sovereign of a modern nation-state. For Kita, the Meiji emperor was a constitutional monarch who existed as an organ of government; in other words, the emperor himself and his ceremonial essence were essentially irrelevant to him. We find a similar conception in Hegel: "It is wrong therefore to demand objective qualities in a monarch; he has only to say 'yes' and dot the 'i,' because the throne should be such that the significant thing in its holder is not his particular make-up" (1967:289).

Prior to the Russo-Japanese War, the emperor was considered a German-style emperor by the Japanese, including Kita. However much he was dressed in the clothes of antiquity, the emperor after Meiji was the sovereign of a modern nation-state. The revolutionaries of the Meiji Restoration concentrated all authority in the emperor in order to eradicate the plural, feudalistic configuration of power. Just as in Europe, this was an unavoidable process in the establishment of the modern nation-state. By making the emperor sovereign, Japan was able to become a modern nation-state. Sovereignty is not, however, only internal to a nation; it maintains an external relation as well. Whether it is sovereignty of the emperor or of the people, we become conscious of the issue of *sovereignty* only in the context of relations to the exterior.

Hegel criticizes the separate treatment of domestic and external sovereignty. According to his thinking, external sovereignty, which emerges with "the relation of one state to another," appears as "something external" and "a happening and an entanglement with chance events coming from without"; but in fact this "negative relation" is "that moment in the state which is most supremely its own" and belongs to the essence of sovereignty (1967:209). In other words, any discourse on the state that is not premised on the existence of other states is merely a discourse on community [*kyōdōtai-ron*].

In the Taishō period, however, the ethnologist Yanagita Kunio saw the prototype of the imperial ritual in village ritual. This was in fact a kind of perspective that sees the emperor as "aboriginal chieftain." Of course, Yanagita was not thereby trying to degrade the emperor system but was, rather, attempting to make it something more familiar to the people. Yet this amounted to separating the emperor from the modern nation-state and thinking of him in terms of the extension of the community (the agricultural community). We should note that around this time, Yanagita began to call his folklore studies "New National Learning" [Shin-kokugaku]. In the beginning, he was interested in the strange existence of the "mountain people" in Japan. In the Taishō period, however, he discarded his hypothesis on the mountain people. In other words, he discarded all sense of exteriority and moved toward the "southern islands." The move was, in effect, a search for identity on the inside. Murai Osamu (1995) has sought the reason for this in the fact that Yanagita was deeply involved in the annexation of Korea as a bureaucrat, for which reason Yanagita had to ignore and repress Korea in his scholarship. In this sense, Yanagita can be seen as a representative of "Taishōesque" discourse.

The ethnological perspective on the emperor emerged only because of the lessening of international tension. It is always when they are aware of international tension that people become conscious of the emperor in Japan, and it is when tension with the outside has weakened that they forget about the emperor. In the closed-country system of the Tokugawa [Edo] period, the emperor existed only for nativist scholars and for the Mito school and did not, in effect, exist for the people at large. When external tension arose at the end of the Tokugawa period, however, the emperor was called forth. He was called forth as sovereign in order to secure the sovereignty of Japan as a nation. In the Shōwa period, too, the emperor was called forth again—hence the "Shōwa Restoration." The fact that the presence of the emperor was weakened in the Taishō period, however, signifies that this period was a temporary release from external pressure. Therefore, to see the emperor from the perspective of ethnology does not signify simply the development of a scientific understanding.

A similar point can be made about the 1970s. It was at this point that cultural anthropology and the historians who imported it began to theorize about the emperor system, but these arguments are ahistorical and lack a political perspective. In essence, they represent the aboriginal chieftain argument. There were, for example, scholars who pointed out the similarity between the emperor system and African kingship (Yamaguchi 2003) or the kingship of Oceania (Ueno Chizuko). Of course, such arguments are presented as attempts to dismantle the emperor system by thinking of it in more fundamental terms, but as I pointed out earlier, even Kita was already aware of this. Furthermore, it is questionable whether such kingship theories can account for even the Nara- [710–784] and Heian-period [794–1192] emperors, much less the modern emperor system.

For example, despite the fact that the Japanese political system prior to the Russo-Japanese War was a constitutional monarchy, it was the elder statesmen (i.e., Restoration leaders from the Satsuma and Chōshū cliques) who ruled, rather than the Diet. The Meiji constitution gave the power of supreme command over the army and navy to the emperor, because the elder statesmen, while accepting the parliamentary system, attempted to secure a power that existed beyond the Diet. In the Taishō period, when the elder statesmen had gone, such theories as the "emperor as organ," which argued that insofar as the emperor followed the decisions of the Diet, the army and navy were also under its control, were able to gain currency precisely because it was a relatively calm period, both internationally and domestically. This is what is referred to as Taishō democracy. In the Shōwa period, however, this constitution became the basis for the autonomy of the army and navy, placing them beyond the control of the Diet. The military sought to justify its arbitrary actions, which had economic recession as its background, by seeking the deification of the emperor. This was entirely different from the notion of "the emperor system that lives among the people," and it arose in the context of international tension. In a similar fashion, until the nineteenth century, a belief existed among the English that their king had healing powers, but this had absolutely no relation to the British Empire.

It is true that in thinking through the question of emperor-system fascism we cannot ignore its mythological structure. In the 1970s, however, all political and economic historicity was ignored. To attempt to discover the origins of the emperor system in the past or among the people appears to be more fundamental, but such attempts actually obscure history. The theories of the emperor that proliferated after 1970 were easily snuffed out by the emperor's illness and by the calls arising from Asian nations to pursue his war responsibility, demonstrating clearly that such theories were based on the erasure of the left-hand side of the discursive space that I outlined earlier.

6. The Death of General Nogi

The weakening of the consciousness of "Shōwa" and of the emperor following Shōwa 40 (i.e., after the Tokyo Olympics) is similar to the sense of achievement and process of interiorization that characterized discursive space following the Russo-Japanese War. As I stated earlier, this interiorization and cosmopolitanism are not contradictory—even as Japan internationalized and maintained a consciousness of worldwide simultaneity, the "outside" was lost. It appears that in order for the transformation of discursive space to become clearly fixed in consciousness, however, some symbolic event must occur. Marx said that we need tragedy in order to part cheerfully with the past, and one can say that Mishima's death in 1970 was such an event.

We are used to speaking of this period as the 1960s, but if we consider the questions of the late 1960s in terms of the Shōwa 40s, a different aspect begins to appear. From the former perspective, this is the high point of the New Left, which in turn is usually situated within a worldwide simultaneity. The New Left movement has been read as a critique of modern Western rationalism; if we look at this period from another perspective, however, that of the discursive space of modern Japan, it can be read as the return, if only temporarily, of the lower half of the coordinate space that had been repressed after the war (see figure 1). For example, Maoism (the Cultural Revolution) was, as Yasuda Yojūrō understood, a kind of pan-Asianism. In addition, the critique of modern, Western rationalism in this period resembles the "Overcoming Modernity" debate of the wartime period. Hence, the closeness that Mishima felt for the New Left was not, in fact, without basis.

We were surprised by Mishima's suicide in 1970. However, if he had committed ritual suicide [*seppuku*] in Shōwa 45, there would not have been much cause for surprise. Mishima himself must have been aware of this. We are used to reading Mishima's action as a re-presentation of the February 26 rebellion, but we should recall instead the *junshi* [following one's lord in death] of General Nogi in Meiji 45. General Nogi's suicide, through its very anachronism, also shocked the people of the time. *Junshi* in relation to an emperor who is the head of a constitutional monarchy is unthinkable. General Nogi adopted a relation of loyalty as to a feudal lord. It is natural that Akutagawa Ryūnosuke and Shiga Naoya, who were raised in the modern nation-state of post-Meiji 20, mocked Nogi's anachronistic action.

However, the event shocked Mori Ōgai and moved him to write "The Last Testament of Okitsu Yagoemon" [Okitsu Yagoemon no isho, 1912]. Thereafter, Ōgai shifted to historical fiction dealing with samurai and people of the feudal world. "Feudal" here signifies the existence of a relation of absolute loyalty to one's direct lord but not to any higher authority. Consequently, a feudal system, as opposed to the modern nation-state, with its centralized authority, is overrun by the revolts of multiple powers. The characters that Ōgai describes in "The Abe Family" [Abe ichizoku, 1913] are willing, because of their loyalty to their lord, to commit treason against the clan.[6] These feudal people maintained an independence that is missing in the individual of the modern nation-state, who is constituted as subject by being entirely subject to one sovereign. In truth, it was not this type of modern individual who supported the Freedom and People's Rights Movement of Meiji 10 but rather the feudal person, with his conceit and sense of independence. However, as the Seinan War of 1877 demonstrates, they were unavoidably led into a civil war aiming to negate national sovereignty.

The instruction in Ōgai's will to be buried as "Iwami native Mori Rintarō" does not signify a nostalgic return to his birthplace but contains within it the negation of the institution of the modern Meiji state, which he himself supported and helped to construct.[7] What captivated Ōgai was not the antiquated quality of the feudal person but rather his sense of indepen-

---

6 English translations of these two works of historical fiction are available in Mori (1977:15–33, 35–69).

7 Rintarō was Ōgai's given name. In his last will and testament, written three days before his death, Ōgai wrote that "I have had connections to both the Department of the Imperial Household and the army, but at the very moment of death I repudiate all outward signs of this connection" (quoted in Bowring 1979:253).

dence and plurality, which had been lost in the modern "interiority" of the Taishō period.

Sōseki was also shocked by this incident and was led to write *Kokoro* (1914). In this novel, Sensei says,

> Then, at the height of the summer, Emperor Meiji passed away. I felt as though the *spirit of the Meiji era had begun with the Emperor and had ended with him*. I was overcome with the feeling that I and the others, who had been brought up in that era, were now left behind to live as *anachronisms*. I told my wife so. She laughed and refused to take me seriously. Then she said a curious thing, albeit in jest: "Well then, *junshi* is the solution to your problem."
>
> I had almost forgotten that there was such a word as "*junshi*." It is not a word that one uses normally, and I suppose it had been banished to some remote corner of my memory. I turned to my wife, who had reminded me of its existence, and said: "I will commit *junshi* if you like; but in my case it will be through loyalty to the spirit of the Meiji era." My remark was meant as a *joke*; but I did feel that the *antiquated word* had come to hold a new meaning for me.
>
> A month passed. On the night of the Imperial Funeral I sat in my study and listened to the booming of the cannon. To me, it sounded like the last lament for the passing of an age. Later, I realized that it might also have been a salute to General Nogi. Holding the extra edition in my hand, I blurted out to my wife: "*Junshi! Junshi!*"
>
> I read in the paper the words General Nogi had written before killing himself. I learned that ever since the Seinan War, when he lost his banner to the enemy, he had been wanting to redeem his honor through death. I found myself automatically counting the years that the general had lived, always with death at the back of his mind. The Seinan War, as you know, took place *in the tenth year of Meiji*. He must therefore have lived for thirty-five years, waiting for the proper time to die.

I asked myself: "When did he suffer greater agony—during those thirty-five years, or the moment when the sword entered his bowels?"

It was two or three days later that I decided at last to commit suicide. Perhaps you will not understand clearly why I am about to die, no more than I can fully understand why General Nogi killed himself. *You and I belong to different eras, and so we think differently.* There is nothing we can do to bridge the gap between us. Of course, it may be more correct to say that we are different simply because we are two separate human beings. (Natsume 1957:245–46; Karatani's emphasis)

The passage contains subtleties that do not lend themselves to summary, so I have included the full quotation. By this time, *junshi* is already an "antiquated word" that can only be a "joke" (and, until Mishima actually died, I considered what he was saying to be a joke). Furthermore, although what Sensei calls "the spirit of Meiji" may not be limited to "the tenth year of Meiji," it undoubtedly represents something prior to Meiji 20.

It is true that Sensei feels guilt at having betrayed his friend K. But he also understands that K did not necessarily die because of failed love or his friend's betrayal. This triangular relationship maintains an entirely different aspect. K was a stoic idealist:

Having grown up under the influence of Buddhist doctrines, he seemed to regard respect for material comfort as some kind of immorality. Also, having read stories of great priests and Christian saints who were long since dead, he was wont to regard the body and the soul as entities which had to be forced asunder. Indeed, he seemed at times to think that mistreatment of the body was necessary for the glorification of the soul. (Natsume 1957:176)

In this light, K appears merely as an eccentric and idealistic youth. Nevertheless, this extreme type seems to be specific to certain periods; take, for example, Kitamura Tōkoku, who turned to Christianity, or Nishida Kitarō, who turned to Zen. In the face of the rapidly forming bourgeois nation-sate, they both took refuge in "interiority" after losing their respective political battles. That is, after the possibilities of the Meiji Restoration were closed off, they tried to position themselves against all worldly things. They were also necessarily defeated by worldly / natural things. Tōkoku committed suicide, and Nishida endured humiliation to enter Tokyo Imperial University as a special-course student (auditor). K can be considered a similar type.

Therein lies the reason that Sensei respects K and follows in his wake. At the same time, however, there is also a malice directed against an unattainable model, which is hidden in the goodwill whereby Sensei says, "In an attempt to make him more human, I tried to encourage him to spend as much time as possible with the two ladies" (Natsume 1957:180). This represents a temptation to make K submit to the worldly / natural things that he has refused. K dies, not because of his friend's betrayal but because of the consciousness of his own impotence and hollowness—of his inability to achieve the independence of his inner self. Consequently, we should say that in the problem of the triangular relationship lies a political question. Both Sensei and K were guilty of betrayal: the betrayal of the multiplicity of possibilities that existed prior to the rapidly consolidating modern nation-state of the Meiji 20s. The same can be said of Sōseki himself.

Sōseki believed English literature to be something on the order of Chinese literature. At first he thought, "If that were so, I believed it was a subject that one could devote one's life to studying without regret," but, "when I graduated I was bothered by a notion that lingered at the back of my mind—that somehow I had been cheated by English literature" (Natsume 2009:43). The "Chinese literature" to which Sōseki was willing to devote his life differed from the Southern school of Chinese painting or the Chinese poetry to which he turned in his later years. It had been something connected to Asia, and to popular rights.

For example, the most widely read works from the Meiji 10s to the 20s were the "political novels" tied to the Freedom and People's Rights Movement. Opposed to this was Tsubouchi Shōyō's "realism" (de-idealism [*botsu-risō*]).[8] It can be seen that the movement to unify speech and writing [*genbun itchi*] rejected the context of Chinese literature such as represented by Kyokutei Bakin and tried to move closer to the type of colloquial *gesaku* fiction represented by Shikitei Sanba. At the time Sōseki rejected this movement, and "Chinese literature" must have signified this rejection for him.

In contrast, English literature was institutionalized as one aspect of Meiji "literary reform" (Shōyō). This fact cannot be separated from the power of the British Empire. What is important is not the ability or sensitivity to enable one to appreciate English literature but rather the position in which "English literature" was placed at the time. One can understand why, within English literature, Sōseki sympathized with Irish-born writers Swift and Sterne. Yet unexpectedly, Sōseki could not help but become the "captain of the Western learning corps" [*yōgakutai no taichō*].

In effect, Sōseki was a remnant of the Meiji 10s. In *Autumn Wind* [*Nowaki*, 1907] and *The 210th Day* [*Nihyaku tōka*, 1906], he depicts protagonists who rage at the workaday world. But seen from the reality of around Meiji 40, when *The Communist Manifesto* had already been translated into Japanese, these characters are old-fashioned. For Sōseki, they are holdovers from the Meiji 10s. What Sōseki referred to as the "spirit of Meiji" was not the spirit of the entire age of Meiji, which he detested. In the "modern literature" that was established in the latter half of the Meiji 20s to the 30s, the kind of "interiority" that Tōkoku and Sōseki possessed was weakened and became nothing more than self-consciousness. In other words, the political origin of "interiority" had been forgotten (Karatani 1993b:11–75). This is what Sensei means by his statement about "belonging to different eras."

8 In 1891 and 1892, Shōyō and Ōgai engaged in a debate over the role of "ideals" (*risō*) in literary criticism, an exchange that is referred to as the debate on "de-idealism" or "antirealism" (*botsu-risō ronsō*). For a discussion of this debate, see Karatani (1993b:136–54).

7. The Death of Mishima Yukio

Sōseki, who was born in the third year of Keiō [1867], may have identified his own life with the reign of Emperor Meiji—hence Sensei's statement about beginning and ending with the emperor. The same may be said of Mishima, who was born in the fourteenth year of Taishō (1925).[9] In a sense, Mishima ended Shōwa by ending his own life.

Although Sōseki wrote *Kokoro*, he was far from committing suicide himself. On his deathbed, he is reported to have said, "I'd like to keep from dying" (Natsume Kyōko 1929:360).[10] This does not mean that Sōseki was afraid of death. Sōseki refused to create a sense of self-closure on his existence and to dramatize his life. He did not leave any testament comparable to Mori Ōgai's "Iwami native Mori Rintarō." He *simply* dropped dead; however, to *simply* die is not to render one's life meaningless.

Sōseki was able to write the tragedy *Kokoro* precisely because he was not the type of person to make his own life into a tragedy. The spirit of Meiji is tragic because it is something that cannot be retrieved. But the spirit of Shōwa is different, for like the Shōwa Restoration, it constantly traces and re-presents or evokes the spirit of Meiji—meaning, of course, the possibilities of pre-Meiji 20.

The critic Yasuda Yojūrō, of the prewar Japanese Romantic school, wrote in 1969, "The fundamental spirit of the Great Asian Revolution was the intention to carry on and complete the Meiji Restoration. Furthermore, it was to carry on the spirit of the great Saigō. This feeling was also alive in the Greater East Asia War" (1988:82). As I mentioned earlier, Yasuda identified, from this perspective, a similar succession in the Red Guards of

---

9 The Shōwa emperor's reign began on December 25, 1926.
10 The account of Sōseki's death is provided by his wife, Kyōko, who stated, "That evening, he was in severe pain, and when I had left his side for just a moment, he bared his chest and said, pour water on me here, and when the nurse sprayed water on him, he said something like, 'I'd like to keep from dying' [*shinu to komaru kara*]. As soon as he spoke, his eyes turned white and he lost all consciousness" (Natsume Kyōko 1929:360).

the Cultural Revolution. Yet the "intention to carry on" signifies that the object to be carried on no longer exists. As Yasuda himself wrote,

> In truth, the period of a void in both literature and thought was appearing in early Shōwa....
>
> Furthermore, early Shōwa was the post–World War I era. And underlying *Cogito*, to the extent that we thought and understood ourselves to be Husserlian, was something like a will to withstand the postwar degeneration, and a movement toward a Japanese reflection. This experience has served as a kind of lesson in terms of the resolve following the Greater East Asian War. Our generation, therefore, is not simply a prewar school, nor obviously, a wartime school. From a world historical viewpoint, we were a post–World War I school. (12, 114)

Yasuda understood this "void" positively, as irony. To put it another way, it is *seriously frivolous*. The spirit of Meiji to which Yasuda succeeds has no content—but to denigrate content, to remain empty, is precisely what defines Romantic irony. Instead of saying "contradiction," Yasuda says "irony." "Contradiction" constructs a problem and then works toward its solution. For Yasuda, it is such solemnity that is contemptible; what constitutes irony is scorn for contradiction and scorn for problems. This irony distinguishes Yasuda not only from the Left but from the conventional Right as well, and it was this absolute irresponsibility and vacuity that attracted people of the generation of Hashikawa and Mishima.

In any case, Yasuda differs from those who attempted to reenact the Meiji Restoration. He was certainly aware, however, that the spirit of Meiji could be re-presented precisely because it was nonexistent. To borrow the words of Marx, the "spirit of Meiji" was tragedy, and the "spirit of Shōwa" that repeated it was farce.

Of course, the Meiji Restoration itself was a re-presentation; it was an "Imperial Restoration." Just as in the case of the French Revolution, ancient designs were mobilized in the Meiji

Restoration. Consequently, as Yasuda said, the spirit of Meiji is linked to the teachings of the medieval poet / emperor Gotoba. There were, however, tasks worthy of realization in the Meiji Restoration, just as there were with Kita and the Shōwa Restoration, but none existed—and could not exist—within the Japanese Romantic school.

In *The Bridges of Japan* [*Nihon no hashi*, 1936], Yasuda claims that he merely wishes to "amplify the ideas" of Okakura (Tansman 2008:264). Yasuda, too, begins with an account of world intercourse in antiquity while praising the "sorrowful and pathetic" (270) bridges of Japan that contrast with the bridges of the West and China. Of course he does not, like a "Japanist" [Nihonshugisha], proclaim a strong Japan or a military Japan. Again, like Okakura, he rejects the Westernization of culture. Furthermore, he rejects "things warrior-like," as well as the view of Japanese history distorted by samurai. Throughout, he recounts "an indulgence in the gentle arts of peace."

After the Russo-Japanese War, Okakura wrote, in *The Book of Tea*, "The average Westerner . . . was wont to regard Japan as barbarous while she indulged in the gentle arts of peace; he calls her civilised since she began to commit wholesale slaughter on Manchurian battlefields. . . . Fain would we remain barbarians, if our claim to civilisation were to be based on the gruesome glory of war. Fain would we await the time when due respect shall be paid to our art and ideals" (1964:2–3). There is a type of Romantic irony contained here; it is, however, of a different order than the play of German Romantic irony, and it maintains a certain historical practicality.

The reason that Yasuda appeared to say the same thing as Okakura, but in reality did not, lies in the fact that Japan actually did "commit wholesale slaughter on Manchurian battlefields." Yasuda identified a "new worldview" in Manchukuo. It is unthinkable that Yasuda, who had been a Marxist, was unable to make the determination that Manchukuo represented nothing other than Japan's imperial domination, yet he necessarily and consciously negates it. For Socrates, irony is "the pretence of ignorance," and Yasuda was precisely feigning ignorance. In this sense, Japanese Romantic school irony is based on the negation of reality and a faith in an unreal beauty. In the terms of Kawabata Yasunari's novel *Snow Country* [*Yukiguni*, 1935–1947], which Yasuda lauded, it is the perception of the beauty of a "sorrowful and pathetic" Japan (represented by the character Komako) beyond the tunnel.[11]

For Yasuda, it was not only that the Shōwa Restoration contained nothing to be realized but also that it constituted a struggle against the very concept of realization, a struggle to discard all thinking since the Meiji Enlightenment. When Mishima, who had been a young member of the Japanese Romantic school, attempted to reenact the Shōwa Restoration in Shōwa 45, it was literally a farce, a fact that Mishima did not attempt to conceal. In the same way, the last character to be reincarnated (repeated) in *The Sea of Fertility* [*Hōjō no umi*, 1965–1971] is a fake. *The Sea of Fertility* ends in a "sea of emptiness."[12]

In this manner, Mishima, by reevoking the spirit of Shōwa, put an end to it. Borrowing the words of Marx, this farce but not tragedy existed so that we could part cheerfully from Shōwa. There is probably no spectacle more ridiculous than conservatives and rightists attempting to appropriate Mishima's death. His action was entirely ironic: what he attempted to realize was the destruction of the very thought that aims at realizing something, and the Japanese culture he aimed to defend not only had nothing of substance to it but also existed as this nothingness itself.

Near the end of *The Decay of the Angel* [*Tennin gosui*, 1970–1971], the last volume in the *Sea of Fertility* tetralogy, the woman questions the protagonist Tōru: "Kiyoaki Matsugae was caught by unpredictable love, Isao Iinuma by destiny, Yin Chan by the flesh. And you? By a baseless consciousness of being different, perhaps?" (Mishima 1974:206; translation modified). Having

---

11 *Snow Country* begins with the famous line "The train came out of the long tunnel into the snow country" (Kawabata 1981:3).
12 Mishima's tetralogy closes with the following lines: "There was no other sound. The garden was empty. He had come, thought Honda, to a place that had no memories, nothing. The noontide sun of summer flowed over the still garden" (1974:236).

been made to realize that he is a counterfeit, lacking in necessity, Tōru plans to commit suicide in order to prove his authenticity, yet fails. However, this suicide attempt was not a search for some "basis" but was carried out in order to achieve the full realization of a "baseless consciousness."

According to Mishima's way of thinking, the emperor should have died in Shōwa 20, even as his supporters predicted at the time. He would have thereby become a god. But with his renunciation of divinity, the emperor lived on as a symbol of postwar national unity. The reincarnated emperor after the war was nothing more than a counterfeit, but it was no different from Mishima's self-contempt at having survived what should have been the "Final War." For Mishima, in order for an object to attain a genuine, absolute beauty (divinity), it must be destroyed, like the Temple of the Golden Pavilion. Mishima's suicide signifies, as well, the killing of the postwar emperor.

8. The Recurrence of Shōwa

The reason that 1970 constitutes a watershed year is not simply Mishima's spectacular death. In the early 1970s, the New Left movement collapsed, as symbolized by the Allied Red Army incidents, and the structure of the postwar world order began to crumble, as indicated by the foreign currency market and the successive oil shocks. Relying on the postwar U.S.–Soviet binary structure that it used unilaterally as it developed, Japan emerged in the 1980s as an economic giant. In terms of consciousness, however, it remained entirely confined to interiority. Every kind of information from the outside was transmitted and consumed, but the "outside" did not exist. In other words, Japan was, in terms of discursive space, confined within quadrant I (see figure 1).

It was only after 1985 that the Japanese began to feel international tension, and, at the same time, the problems of "Shōwa" and of the emperor began to revive. It was not only because the end of Shōwa neared but also because Japan found itself once more in the midst of international tension, which exposed the

Shōwa emperor as a historical problem. This arose not only from within Japan but through external relations with Asia and the West as well. At this point, the discourse on the emperor since the 1970s could only fade quickly away.

Obviously, Shōwa continued even after Mishima put an end to "the spirit of Shōwa." It continued for eighteen more years. After 1970, the emperor aged quietly, like the failed suicide Yasunaga Tōru must have. Faced with the emperor's longevity, supporters and detractors alike were at a loss, because it was a question not of "spirit" but of biological fact. One can say that the very existence of the emperor caused the meaning of Shōwa to fade.

Yet seen in terms of the chronology presented in table 3, this period, after the end of "Meiji," passed through "Taishō" and corresponds precisely to the period extending to Shōwa 5 (1930). In other words, because Shōwa lasted for such a long time, it revolved back around to "Shōwa." In 1989, the binary structure of the United States and Soviet Union came to an end, and a "new world order" is being constructed, one that resembles, in a certain sense, the 1930s; that is, the creation of political and economic blocs is progressing around the world. Take, for example, the creation of the European Union. Even if it was unavoidable in order to counter the economic power of the United States and Japan, how was such a step possible, when the memory of Germany's forcibly carrying out a European unification before the war was still fresh in people's minds? Clearly it was possible because Germany had engaged in a thoroughgoing self-critique and reparations over the past.

Japan, however, has not engaged in such actions. To put it another way, it has been unable to make a break with the past. A major reason for this is the fact that in the postwar period, the emperor was absolved of any war responsibility and survived for many years without having to abdicate his throne. And when Japan revived as a great power, commanding, in effect, a "Greater East Asia Co-Prosperity Sphere" and drawing the scrutiny and caution of other nations, the emperor once more came to serve as its symbol. The same emperor had continued his reincarnation as symbol (sign). No matter how hard they worked in other areas, as long as the emperor was alive, the Japanese were unable to make a reckoning with the past. And with this ambiguous posture toward the past, they found themselves face-to-face with a situation that resembled the prewar period. At a time when America and Europe are forming their own blocs, it is only natural that Japan would be excluded, but at the same time, it is also isolated within Asia. The "aporias" that have existed since Meiji have in no way been resolved.

4

THE ALLEGORY OF ŌE KENZABURŌ

FOOTBALL IN THE YEAR MAN'EN 1

PART I

1

Since Ōe Kenzaburō first debuted in the late 1950s as an epoch-making new writer while still a college student, there have been a number of distinguishing characteristics of his works. One of these hallmarks is that while he repeatedly uses the first-person narrator "I" [*boku*], his works differ from the I-novel, which was then a dominant genre in Japan, meaning that this "I" was distinct from the author. At the same time, this "I" is not an objective narrator and so is not entirely unrelated to the author. Ever since his debut work, "A Strange Job" [*Kimyō na shigoto*, 1957], "I" has pointed to an individual who resembles Ōe, even while it continually signifies something different.

The second characteristic of Ōe's writings, which is closely related to the first, is that there are no proper names. If it is going too far to say that there are no proper names, one can say rather that the names of his characters are the names of *types*. In *Football in the Year Man'en 1* [*Man'en gannen no futtobōru*, 1967], the names Mitsusaburō and Takashi literally reflect their owner's personalities.[1] In contrast to the fact that the elder brother, Mitsu [nectar], is introverted and passive, the younger brother, Taka [hawk], is violent and a man of action. Moreover, each

---

1 *Man'en gannen no futtobōru* has been translated into English by John Bester as *The Silent Cry* (1974). All citations in the text are taken from this translation. However, a more literal translation of the title is used in both this chapter and the one that follows because of its importance in Karatani's analysis. The Man'en era lasted from 1860 to 1861.

one's "character" is unchanging and does not evolve or undergo any reversal in the course of the narrative's progression. Additionally, their family name, Nedokoro [root place], even more clearly points to the novel's theme. It is clear from their very names that these main characters are those who seek their identities or roots.

To take another example, in Ōe's early work "Lavish Are the Dead" [Shisha no ogori, 1957], the story's characters are nameless and are called simply "female student" or "custodian." However, by now it should be clear that these are also the names of certain types. "Lavish Are the Dead" contains the following passages, which clearly reflect the influence of Sartre:

> These dead bodies were different from those cremated immediately after death, I thought. The corpses floating in cisterns had the completely elaborate hardness of a *thing*, a sense of autonomy. Corpses that are cremated right after death never become so completely a thing, I thought....
>
> That is a living human being. And living human beings, human beings with consciousness, have a hot, viscous membrane surrounding their bodies that rejects me, I thought. I had stepped into the world of the dead. And after returning to the midst of the living, everything becomes difficult—this is what I stumbled over first. (Ōe 1996b:26, 31)

Those who are living represent *being-for-itself*, while those who are dead represent *being-in-itself* (a thing). Being-for-itself is never where it is and furthermore is always where it is not. From Sartre's perspective, being-for-itself is essentially nameless, for a name is something pressed upon it by others, something that makes being-for-itself into a thing. One can say that the early Ōe most likely rejected proper names because of the influence of Sartre. Nevertheless, the question of proper names in Ōe actually points to something else, something more serious.

For the moment, what is important is that in Ōe, the types (collectives) such as "female student" or "custodian" have come to function like names. In other words, the specificity of the proper name, which is seen to indicate individuality, has been eliminated. If Ōe's recent novel *Letters to My Sweet Bygone Years* [*Natsukashii toshi e no tegami*, 1987] represents a significant transformation in his writing, it is more than anything because the work marks the recuperation of proper names. In the context of the modern novel and of modernity, what is the significance of the fact that Ōe has consistently, since his earliest writings, placed proper names in brackets? This is the question that I would like to consider here.

The *type* names that I mentioned before were commonplace prior to the advent of the modern novel in both Japan and the West. If anything, one can perhaps say that the distinguishing characteristic of "modern literature" is the appearance of characters with ordinary names. In *The Rise of the Novel*, Ian Watt analyzes the novel's emergence primarily in eighteenth-century Britain and considers it against a philosophical background. That is, he connects the novel's rise to the tendency of nominalism. Unlike realism, which posits the substance of universalism or ideas, nominalism is the thinking that only an individual has substance, from which ideas are abstracted. In this case, it is thought that each individual is indicated by a proper name. What is called realism in literature was born through the rejection of philosophical realism:

> Logically the problem of individual identity is closely related to the epistemological status of proper names; for, in the words of Hobbes: "Proper names bring to mind one thing only; universals recall any one of many." Proper names have exactly the same function in social life: they are the verbal expression of the particular identity of each individual person. In literature, however, this function of proper names was first fully established in the novel.
>
> Characters in previous forms of literature, of course, were usually given proper names; but the kind of names actually used showed that the author was not trying to establish his characters as completely individualized entities. (Watt 1963:19)

The unusual names Mitsusaburō and Takashi are, on one level, proper names; they do not, however, denote "completely individualized entities" but instead signify a certain type. Furthermore, this kind of name was quite common prior to the advent of the modern novel. The protagonist of Futabatei Shimei's *Drifting Clouds* [*Ukigumo*, 1887–1889], considered the first modern novel in Japan, is named Uchimi Bunzō. Yanagita Kunio recorded his surprise, upon reading this novel, that an ordinary character was its hero, but in truth, what is actually surprising is the commonplace name Bunzō. For example, one can compare this with the names of characters in Ozaki Kōyō's *The Golden Demon* [*Konjiki yasha*, 1897], which was written some years after *Drifting Clouds*. The names Kan'ichi and Tomiyama have a certain *typical* meaning, which signals their personalities and actions in advance. Yet it was not only because of its inclusion of ordinary characters and names that *Drifting Clouds* was epoch-making. For such characters also appeared in Edo-period [1600–1867] fiction. What is crucial is that the individuals indicated by such commonplace names are made to bear a certain universality, and it is precisely as the bearer of such universality that the individual appears.

The commonplace proper name indicates an individual, and modern realism focuses on such individuals. The same phenomenon can be seen in the realm of painting; if one can say that previous painters had attempted to give shape to the *concept* of the "pine tree," then modern painters attempt to depict *this* pine or *that* pine—that is, pine trees that could be indicated by proper names (although in practice they are not). In other words, modern realism attempts to grasp individuals that can be potentially (even if they are not actually) called by proper names. It should be noted, however, that the individual thereby always also symbolizes a certain generality (universality). For example, the conviction that by depicting specific, individual pines, one is conversely capturing the universality of the "pine," or that one is thereby able to do so—this is precisely the essence of realism. Needless to say, when I refer to modern realism, I am not referring to any narrowly defined method or school but rather to the posture of modern literature as a whole. The situation is no different in the case of antirealism.

2

This kind of difference is often discussed in terms of the difference between allegory and symbol. Of course, in modern times allegory has had a bad name. This is most typically exemplified by the following words of Goethe, cited by Walter Benjamin:

> There is a great difference between a poet's seeking the particular from the general and his seeing the general in the particular. The former gives rise to allegory, where the particular serves only as an instance or example of the general; the latter, however, is the true nature of poetry: the expression of the particular without any thought of, or reference to, the general. Whoever grasps the particular in all its vitality also grasps the general, without being aware of it, or only becoming aware of it at a late stage. (1977:161)

What I earlier referred to as a conviction is the mechanism whereby "whoever grasps the particular in all its vitality also grasps the general, without being aware of it." This mechanism of symbolic thought exists today in the following manner.

Even while writing about their own specific experiences and their specific selves, writers believe that such narratives maintain a universal significance. Moreover, readers vicariously experience such narratives as their own. But the fact that this practice is based on nothing more than a historical device is clearly shown by the fact that in previous eras people did not write or read in this manner. Modern literature is premised on a certain conviction that the particular "symbolizes" the universal. Otherwise, it would not have been possible for I-novelists to continue to write about such trivial matters ad nauseum.

Even today, the thought of the "symbol" is still powerfully operative among writers, even though it may be expressed in different form. For example, we still find repeated the type of criticism whereby a particular, individual expression is taken to reflect the essence of historical conditions without the author himself being aware of it. This type of criticism considers works that self-consciously point out their own universality to be inferior—such works are rejected as parables or for their "explicitness of theme." To a certain extent, Ōe has been the target of such criticism.

In *The Origin of German Tragic Drama*, Benjamin, writing about seventeenth-century German Baroque tragedy, attempted to extract the significance of allegory, which has been viewed with contempt in modernity. Of course, this was not an attempt to resuscitate a medieval allegorical thought against the symbolic (semiotic) thought of modernity (for, in the first place, he focuses on the Baroque, rather than medieval, period). Rather, Benjamin's work criticized the self-evidence of symbolic thought and tried to demonstrate its historicity. Furthermore, my own interest lies not in literature prior to the modern era but rather in the type of allegorical writers who appear only *after* the self-evidence of symbolic thought is established.

The reason that allegorical works have a bad name is that they appear to shut their eyes to their own particularity while trying to narrate something general. However, it would be a mistake to think that allegorical writers are not concerned with individuality. In fact, precisely the opposite is true. In symbolic novels, the fact that the particular can become general, or that one can sympathize with another's narrative as "one's own," is nothing more than a device. In such works, the kind of unique *singularity* that can never be assimilated to generality (type) is discarded. If it is possible to arrive at the general by way of the individual, it means only that the individual had already belonged to generality to begin with. Furthermore, in such a case the proper name is nothing more than an arbitrary sign attached to an individual entity (substance) that exists prior to it. In a true sense, however, proper names should indicate a singularity that can never be restored to generality or collectivity.

In this sense, modern realism (nominalism), while using proper names in actuality suppresses the proper name.

Those who are concerned with singularity are no doubt unable to enter into this circuit consisting of individual and type. For this reason, they are unable to use proper names as a device of the modern novel. Kafka is one example. While Kafka's works are highly realistic, rather than fantastic, they often lack proper names. Consequently, they are seen as fables rather than as realist works. What Kafka's works eliminate, however, are not proper names per se but the illusion created by proper names; they reflect, paradoxically, a concern for the proper name. On this point, Kafka differs fundamentally from writers of fables.

Another reason that allegory is looked down on, related to what I discussed earlier, is that allegory is based on a thought that the world fundamentally has meaning. Precisely because the world has meaning, "the universal" appears to be given priority. Furthermore, all things appear to possess another, separate world. For example, premodern literature or historical records consider events to have "meaning." History thus becomes a narrative.

Symbolic thought rejects that kind of meaning. Indeed, it was precisely by means of such a negation that modern historiography could be established. Modern historiography first focuses on the truth or falsehood of an individual event, as well as the sequence and causal relationships within which it is situated. It does not question its "meaning." This sort of history rejects the proper name as something that gives birth to narrative and tries to extract a structure without proper names. If a proper name does emerge, it is nothing more than an arbitrary sign entered into one section of the structure. This does not indicate, however, the total elimination of meaning. In fact, this kind of thinking is premised on the idea that individual, particular events are secretly, "without being aware of it," forming a universal meaning, as in Hegel's "the cunning of reason."

For example, historians reject the attempt to read an allegorical meaning into the individual *fact* that "on August 6, 1945, an atomic bomb was dropped on Hiroshima." The same is true for modern novelists. Ibuse Masuji's *Black Rain* [*Kuroi ame*, 1966] is the most esteemed literary work about Hiroshima because it avoids talking about the "meaning" of the atomic bombing while calmly depicting individual "details" and trying thus to arrive at "universality." As I have already noted, however, this merely reflects a certain dominant device, and from this perspective it is inevitable that a writer such as Ōe, who tries to read the "meaning" of the nuclear age, would be given a wide berth.[2]

The view of history as being formed by individual facts, however, is premised upon the tacit conviction that such individual facts connect to generality. This remains the case whether or not the Marxist view of history has collapsed. In such views of history, what is in fact missing is the proper name. That is, what they lack is a *singularity* that resists being dissolved into generality. To put it another way, what they lack is the singular, nonrepeatable event. For example, for Ōe, the fact that his child was born with a handicap must have a "meaning." For him, this event cannot be resolved into any general meaning such as, for example, the problem of handicapped children.

History without proper names is not history. What allegorical writers fix on is the singularity or nonrepeatability of the event. And such an event must bear a universal "meaning." For precisely this reason, however, allegorical works appear to be ahistorical.

3

Of course, proper names not only are those of people but also include place-names and era names. For example, the opening line of *Robinson Crusoe* begins, "I Was born in the Year 1632, in the City of *York*" (Defoe 2007:5). The specificity created by the proper names "1632" and "York" makes the novel seem realistic. Defoe was aware of the fact that the accumulation of

---

[2] Ōe (1996a) has written extensively on Hiroshima and the experience of its survivors as well as the question of nuclear weapons. See also Treat (1995:229–58).

such "details" gives birth to a certain reality. This is the thought that "the devil is in the details," and as I mentioned before, clearly belongs to a kind of symbolic thinking.

These proper names have no meaning outside their referential function. In contrast, in a work such as Bashō's *Narrow Road to the Far North* [*Oku no hosomichi*], the place-names have meanings. If Bashō's work is realistic, it is not realistic in the sense of modern realism. For Bashō, the place-name served as a kind of hinge that connected the landscape before his eyes with previous texts, including the history attached to the place or previous poems. While a certain individual thing [*kobutsu*] is indicated, another is immediately signified. If the meaning of allegory is to say one thing and mean another, then Bashō's text can be considered allegorical.

Symbolic thought rejects the idea that a certain expression would continually signify something else. It is precisely by way of such a rejection that the individual thing could be established as such. In turn, proper names are considered signs that designate such individual things. What Ōe has been resisting is precisely this sort of proper name.

In *Football in the Year Man'en 1*, for example, there are, for the most part, no concrete place-names. This lack of names even gives rise to some awkward passages in the novel. For example, when one character (Takashi) is about to leave the village in the valley to go to the city—which in *Letters to My Sweet Bygone Years* would have been called Matsuyama—he says, "So they came to ask me to go and see the Emperor and discuss what to do with the dead chickens. I can't leave them to their fate. I'm going to the provincial city" (Ōe 1974:81–82; translation modified). Even a resident of Tokyo would never use such a phrase as "provincial city" in conversation. Nonetheless, in his attempt to thoroughly eliminate proper names, Ōe does not hesitate to use such unnatural phrasing. The village in the valley is not given any geographical specificity other than its location on the island of Shikoku. Indeed, his early work *Nip the Buds, Shoot the Kids* [*Memushiri kouchi*, 1958] lacked even the designation of Shikoku, so *Football in the Year Man'en 1* may seem more realistic by comparison.

This clearing out of place-names gives the work an allegorical character. The "village in the valley" is literally a village in a valley, but at the same time it signifies a certain universe. Otherwise, the "small-scale commotion" that Takashi incites in the village could not be compared with or compete with political events such as the Man'en 1 rebellion, not to mention those on the scale and level of Tokyo and America.[3] Furthermore, the present time in the novel begins to signify the time of "one hundred years ago": "Takashi, who as leader of the mob was by now completely identified with great-grandfather's younger brother in 1860, bawled out challenges to mother, myself, and the family spirits as we lurked in the storehouse" (Ōe 1974:102). This statement expresses more than simply Takashi's psychological identification. Ultimately, the narrator "I" and the space-time of the work itself get laid over that of a hundred years ago: "All-pervasive time: Takashi as he ran stark naked was great-grandfather's brother, and my own; every moment of those hundred years was crowded into this one instant in time" (146).

In this way, a transhistorical structure is revealed, one that goes beyond a specific period and that maintains an "all-pervasive time." There appears to exist, within this structure, a concentric correspondence, or harmony, between the microcosmos and the macrocosmos. However, there is actually a decisive disjunction between them. I refer to *Football in the Year Man'en 1* as allegory not because it presents a world in which there is a correspondence between microcosmos and macrocosmos but, conversely, because there is an unbridgeable gap between the two. For example, in his later work *Contemporary Games* [*Dōjidai gēmu*, 1979], Ōe establishes a concentric cosmology between village, nation, and universe.[4] There, history

---

3 In the novel, Takashi is presented as having participated in the 1960 uprising against the renewal of the U.S.-Japan Security Treaty. Ōe juxtaposes this movement with the local peasant rebellion that had taken place a century earlier.

4 As a "belated structuralist" in the 1970s, Ōe studied anthropology and semiotics, using them as the basis of *Contemporary Games*. In *Football in the Year Man'en 1*, however, Ōe had already used such anthropological concepts as scapegoat, freak, and stranger, which he had learned from Japanese ethnologists such as Yanagita Kunio and Orikuchi Shinobu. In the novel, Ōe writes, "I

disappears. Whereas *Football in the Year Man'en 1*, which was written in the 1960s, does indicate such a concentric structure, but at the same time there emerges, from within the disjunctions of this structure, a "history" that cannot be reduced to the structure. *Football in the Year Man'en 1* is, above all, a work that tried to grasp history. The historical setting of this work is indicated only at one point, as follows:

> Takashi had gone to America as a member of a student theater group. Their leader was a Diet member, a woman from the right wing of one of the progressive political parties. The troupe consisted entirely of students who had taken part in the political action of June 1960, but had since thought better of it. Their play was a penitential piece entitled *Ours Was the Shame*, and was followed by an apology to the citizens of America, on behalf of repentant members of the student movement, for having obstructed their President's visit to Japan. (Ōe 1974:12; translation modified)

It would be a mistake, however, to think that Ōe tried to depict the "political action of June 1960" in this novel. If one were to analyze the work along these lines, it would perhaps be more accurate to say that it actually depicts the student movement of the late 1960s, the period *after* it was published. Take, for example, the following words of Takashi:

> I like that—"Taka's riot." Though she's biased, of course. But you know, Mitsu, it isn't just material greed or a sense of deprivation that's got all these people, adults and

learned from an article by Orikuchi Shinobu that these beings who came back from the forest to be greeted with such reverence by the inhabitants were 'spirits' who sometimes exerted a harmful influence from the other world (the forest) on the present world (the valley)" (1974:124; translation modified). Yet there is no need for Ōe to be ashamed of his understanding at this point, even if, from the perspective of anthropology and semiotics, it appears undeveloped. For *Football in the Year Man'en 1* contains a remarkable, intuitive insight that could only belong to this novelist. [Author's note]

> children alike, so worked up. I expect you heard the Nembutsu drums and gongs going at it all today? Well, that's helping to keep the pot boiling—it's the riot's emotional source of energy! The looting doesn't really amount to a riot, Mitsu. It's a piddling little storm in a teacup, as everyone taking part knows perfectly well. Even so, by taking part they're going back a century in time and experiencing vicariously the excitement of the 1860 rising. It's a riot of the *imagination*. Though I don't suppose it ranks as a riot for you, does it? Not if you're unwilling to bring that kind of imagination into play. (197)

In fact, the phrase "revolution of the imagination" would be popularized in 1969. It did not exist in the 1960s prior to this, for the "political action" of the earlier period was carried out in the context of specific objectives and specific dates, and there was no space yet in which small "university liberated zones" could each correspond to a "world." In this sense, one can say that Ōe was prophetic. This foresight arises from the fact that Ōe's work was not directed toward the future but toward the past instead and attempted to overcome a specific temporal setting.

What should be noted, however, is that until the end, Ōe's work does not move away from the specific events that it depicts. Of course, the events continually bear a different meaning. The specific setting of "1960" is laid over Man'en 1 (1860) and over "1945" as well, and thereby stripped of its specificity (individuality). In other words, Ōe eliminates proper names as signs indicating a specific time (individuum). As a result, political struggle comes to appear as a game such as football, or else as a kind of carnival. However, within this allegorical shift, there is a proper place that can never be dissolved: a singular, nonrepeatable "history."

Football in the Year Man'en 1 is not a novel that directly depicts "June 1960," and neither is it a parable that transposes those events onto another setting. It is more parable than realist work in that it veers from the specificity of its time and place, yet it is also more a realist work than parable in that it concentrates until the end on a proper / specific point in time. But this doubleness arises from the fact that Ōe eliminates proper names precisely because he is fixed on the proper name. It is only for this reason that I call him an allegorical writer.

As I mentioned earlier, *Football in the Year Man'en 1* maintains a proper / specific time and space that cannot be reduced to any transhistorical structure. It is the proper name "Man'en 1" itself that serves to anchor this work to "history," as against an anthropological or a mythological structure. If this work had been narrated with the sign "1860" instead, its conception would not have been realized.

I noted earlier that "June 1960" is a proper name indicating a specific point in time. In Ōe's work, however, proper names such as "1960" and "1945" are used to convey a certain meaning. This is clear from the fact that while Ōe uses era names such as "Man'en" and "Meiji," he also avoids the phrasing "Shōwa 35" or "Shōwa 20." In other words, "1960" and "1945" are signs indicating arbitrary points in a global, homogenous time; it is in this sense that they are proper names.

Earlier I wrote that when one says "1960" in the Western calendar, the year is situated within the emergence of a global New Left movement, whereas by contrast, "Shōwa 35" begins to appear as a node gathering together all the questions of Japanese modernity since the Meiji period [1868–1912]. This can, for example, be summarized by the questions that Takeuchi Yoshimi raised at the time, as follows:

> In a way, the "Overcoming Modernity" symposium represented a condensed version of the aporias of modern Japanese history. Faced with the urgent task of interpreting the idea of eternal warfare at a time of total war, the symposium marked the explosion of such traditional oppositions as those of reactionism and restoration, reverence for the Emperor and exclusion of foreigners, isolationism and the opening of the country, ultranationalism and "civilization and enlightenment," and East and West. (2004:145–46)

In fact, the "political action of June 1960" also contained such a "condensation of aporias." If anything, what Ōe tries to reexamine in his work is precisely such questions, those contained within the time and space indicated by proper names such "Man'en" and "Meiji." Despite having "June 1960" as his point of departure, when Takashi returns from America to the village in a valley in Shikoku, he begins to live in the world circumscribed, as it were, by the era names "Man'en" and "Meiji," and as soon as "I" (Mitsusaburō) arrives at the village, he gets drawn into this world as well. In this way, the words "the year Man'en 1" not only are a reference to a hundred-year-old past but also serve to shift people into a space that has been excluded from the discursive space indicated by "1945" or "1960" yet nonetheless continues to exist. This space can be seen to correspond to the left-hand side of the diagram that I introduced earlier [chapter 3, figure 1]. It is a space that has been repressed by postwar discursive space, which is narrated by markers such as "1945" and "1960."

4

I mentioned before that Ōe has consistently used the first-person narrator "I," and I suggested that this usage is closely connected to the question of proper names in Ōe's work. "I" indicates someone like Ōe but continually signifies something else. This "I" itself is allegorical. For example, *Football in the Year Man'en 1* begins with the following lines:

> Awakening in the predawn darkness, I grope among the anguished remnants of dreams that linger in my consciousness, in search of some ardent sense of expectation. Seeking in the tremulous hope of finding eager expectancy reviving in the innermost recesses of my being—unequivocally, with the impact of whisky setting one's guts afire as it goes down—still I find an endless nothing. (Ōe 1974:1)

This sense of "ardent expectation" does not even belong to the narrator. It is a mood that exists at the foundation of this novel and is itself a sense of presence. In fact, in this opening passage, the use of the word "I" is avoided. In this way, "I" metaphorically points to the context. But what does it mean that Ōe does not take the perspective of absolute fiction and always narrates his works by way of "I"?

This is not an attempt to attain generality by committing thoroughly to particularity. Neither is it an abstraction of particularity. His style compels empathy from the reader but simultaneously repels it. Thus, for example, those who try to glean Ōe's personal experience from *A Personal Matter* [*Kojintekina taiken*, 1964] will no doubt be disappointed. At the same time, the work contains a certain raw specificity (singularity) that does not allow for a general reading of it as fable.

In *Letters to My Sweet Bygone Years*, the older brother, Gii, says the following about the early novels written by "I": "It's true that 'I' was just like the author, but it's also true that it's a narrator who embodies the customs of the age." However, even in the later works that were written in a different way, "I" is still not the author himself. Of course I am not talking about the kind of obvious reasoning that there is a difference between the narrating "I" and the author. Ōe's "I," while existing as a specific individual also always veers off to signify something else, thereby accruing a layered meaning, and for this reason, the names of his characters could not be commonplace names. This is different from the posture of the modern novel, which, whether narrated in the first or third person, automatically connects to generality.

Many works have appeared since Ōe—probably written under his influence—that are narrated from the perspective of "I" and from which place-names and personal names have been abstracted. But these works do not maintain the same kind of topology as Ōe's "I," and they also lack internal necessity. For example, their removal of place-names simply reflects the homogenization of contemporary Japan. The same is true in the case of personal names. That is, these works are only "reflections of the times." For Ōe, however, the elimination of proper names is fundamentally a fixing on the proper name. This also cannot be separated from the perspective that takes the world to have meaning, one that in effect gives precedence to the "universal."

PART II

1

In *Football in the Year Man'en 1*, "I" is Mitsusaburō, but it is also the context, a sense of presence, and even the domain of consciousness. This can also be said of the name Mitsusaburō itself. He is also referred to as "Rat." On the other hand, Takashi is that which "I" fears most, something violent, or the domain of the unconscious. Takashi is initially introduced as a leftist activist who had undergone ideological conversion and who had taken the "role of a regretful student activist" in America. As soon as he arrives in the village in the valley, however, he takes on the role of "violent criminal" in the rioting and the looting of the supermarket owned by a Korean man. For "I," this is incomprehensible and strange.

Gradually it becomes clear that this violence has a deeper source. It is not only that Takashi is violent but that he is enveloped by violence, which is the source of his actions and oscillations. What is this violence that he continually confronts and tries to escape from yet conversely becomes immersed in—a violence that he continually tries to affirm but also must condemn?

This violence exists at the foundation of Takashi's "politics." In his *Reflections on Violence*, Georges Sorel distinguishes between "the *force* that aims at authority, endeavouring to bring about an automatic obedience," and "the *violence* that would smash that authority" (1999:170). The latter form of violence is an affirmation of life. The two cannot, however, be easily separated. A left wing without violence would merely fall into force, but a left wing that affirms violence would also fall into force. In truth, Sorel's theory, which proclaimed revolutionary syndicalism, was taken up by Mussolini. But there is no easy path, as evidenced by Takashi's oscillation. Is he a right-winger inside a left-winger or else violence within force? Such distinctions are not easily drawn. "I"'s question of who Takashi is represents nothing other than the question of what life is—life that manifests itself as violence.

The "truth" that Takashi confesses is not political but consists rather of his having impregnated his mentally handicapped sister and having caused her to commit suicide. However, this too is connected to the doubleness (ambivalence) of the violence of life / sexuality (eroticism). Faced with this violence, Takashi seeks a violent resolution. Ultimately, Takashi gathers upon his body all the violence of life and dies, thus emerging as a savior. He no doubt will recall for readers the figure of Christ. In fact, the theme of "atonement" is discussed repeatedly in the novel. In some sense, this work foregrounds a certain catholic "meaning," although in a negative form.

Such meaning, however, belongs to the allegorical framework of the novel. What is narrated *within* this frame is, conversely, a nonrepeatable historicity. What I would like to focus on in my analysis of *Football in the Year Man'en 1* is that which is situated within a certain historical specificity. Takashi states at one point, "You know, it may be naive of me, but I've always wondered at the way my ancestors managed to survive the violence all around them and hand on life to me, their descendant. After all, they lived in a savage age. It's incredible to think of the massive violence that the people leading to me had to fight against just so that I could be alive now" (Ōe 1974:143). This violence is not merely a metaphysical violence that inheres in life. Neither is it what René Girard (1977) has described as that which exists generally in the structure of the community, whereby a scapegoat is excluded in order to rejuvenate the community. Ahistorical theorists of "culture" may point out the pervasiveness of this kind of violence. But it is only puerile to point out that modern politics contains the same elements as carnival. The real question is more fundamental.

Our question is: Why do the elements that appear in carnival as an "affirmation of life" or "dissipation of life" invariably turn into fascism? It gets us nowhere to point out that Nietzsche and Bergson were not fascists. Just as there can no longer be anything like pure carnival, a pure "philosophy of life" is also impossible. As soon as such things exist in a historical context, they are subject to unimagined reversals and transpositions. In truth, one can say that *violence* is something that appears in modernity. The "ancestors" that Takashi refers to at most go back to the late Edo period.

2

In *Football in the Year Man'en 1*, violence appears as a historical specificity. For example, the genealogy of the Nedokoro family is seen as follows from the perspective of "I":

> [Great-grandfather's] younger brother, as central figure in the group of young men incited to action by the crafty older farmers of the valley, had preempted the title of "boss" of the whole valley, and had not only gone personally to negotiate the loan from the lord of the clan but had actually headed the violence when it was refused. Thus, at least in the eyes of other members of the Nedokoro family, he was a madman of the worst kind, who had broken up and set fire to his own home. Father, who had lost his life and property for the sake of some mysterious and profitless work in China, had inherited the same family streak of madness. As for my brothers, the eldest—who, however briefly, had taken a job on graduating from the Law Department—wasn't so bad, since he hadn't gone into the army voluntarily, but S, who had gone out of his way to volunteer, had inherited from his father the same blood as great-grandfather's younger brother. (Ōe 1974:105)

Of course, this "blood" does not refer only to a biological genealogy. The bloodline of violence simultaneously contains within itself the "aporias of modern Japanese history." What should be noted is that the members of this bloodline are all connected in some way with Asia. First, there is the father who had gone to Manchuria:

> My father was in northeast China doing work of an unspecified nature that remained a mystery not only to us children but to grandmother, who was still alive then, and to mother as well. For the sake of that work, he would sell enough fields to provide the money to cross the straits and spend more than half every year in China. . . .
>
> At the outbreak of the war, father had let us know that he was abandoning his work in China and coming home, but had then disappeared without trace until three months later, when his body was handed over to my mother by the Shimonoseki police. (94, 96)

In addition, the eldest brother, who had been conscripted and sent to the Philippines, where he died in combat, left a journal that includes the following passage:

> "Take a look at Japan today," he writes. "Utter chaos. Utterly unscientific, utterly unprepared. And half-baked into the bargain. Now look at Germany—the coupons for the rationing system actually in force at the moment were printed way back in 1933 when Hitler first came to power. I pray to God that the Soviet Union rains bombs on us. The Japanese have been poisoned by the dream of peace and got themselves in an unholy mess, but they're still rushing round and round in circles." (119)

It also describes the execution of a native man: "The unit commander who captured him apparently said at first that he'd have a recruit bayonet him, but then he took over himself and, wielding a Japanese sword for the first time in his life, cut off the native's head" (119).

Furthermore, the older brother S, who had been in the special forces, had taken part in the assault on the Korean settlement in the village following the war and had been killed. Finally,

Takashi organizes the youths of the valley and, using their prejudice against the Korean community, attacks the supermarket owned by the Korean man referred to as the Emperor. Seen in this way, it is clear that the entire bloodline of violence relates in some way to Asia. On the other hand, from Takashi's perspective, the bloodline relating to "I" (Mitsusaburō) appears as follows: "Great-grandfather and grandfather—and their wives too—were the same type as Mitsu. Almost all the other people in our family died prematurely, but they lived on comfortably and peacefully into old age" (Ōe 1974:100).

These characters can be situated in the quadrants of the diagram I introduced earlier (figure 2). "I"-Mitsusaburō of course exists in the first quadrant. Takashi originated in the fourth quadrant but then shifted into the discursive space represented by the left-hand side of the diagram. It remains unclear, however, whether he exists in the second or third quadrant—whether he represents, in Sorel's words, violence or force or, in Takeuchi's formulation, whether he represents imperialism or Asianism. To be involved with "Asia" is to be involved with precisely such ambivalence.

For example, Takashi says the following about his eldest brother, who actively executed natives: "It means I've found

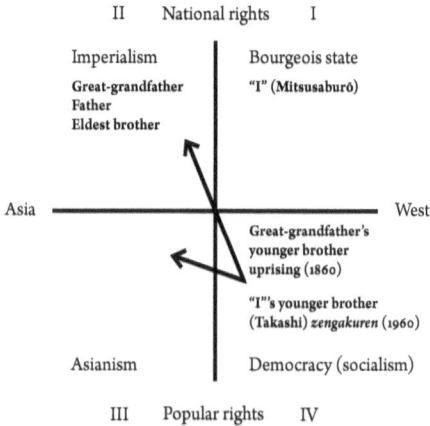

FIGURE 2 The discursive space of *Football in the Year Man'en 1*.

one close relative at least who maintained his ordinary approach to life even on the battlefield, yet was an effective perpetrator of evil. Why—if I'd lived through the same times as him, this might have been my own diary. The idea seems to open up a whole new perspective in my view of things" (Ōe 1974:119–20). Furthermore, he says the following about his older brother S, who died after attacking the Korean ghetto: "It's just that he was the leader. I know even without Mitsu telling me that this is a dream memory, but I seem to remember a splendid scene—S in the winter uniform of a naval air cadet, standing at the head of a group from the valley doing battle with the pick of the men from the Korean village" (75).

Ōe would never even attempt to recount such words in an essay or another public statement. The discursive space of postwar Japan has, in effect, been confined to the first and fourth quadrants of the diagram, and one can say that the left-hand side of the diagram is taboo. And, in general, Ōe is seen as a faithful flag bearer of this type of postwar discursive space. Or rather, we might say that for this very reason in his novels he is focused solely on the left-hand side of the diagram. Not only in *Football in the Year Man'en 1* but in his other works as well, the narrating "I" is situated in the first quadrant. "I" represents the conditions of postwar Japan itself. It is sexually impotent, passive, and closed off. And the younger brother figure of whom "I" is terrified even as he is drawn to him exists in the third quadrant.

What should be noted is that this third space is not verbal but rather always exists as something "insane and dark and terrifying." In other words, if "I" represents consciousness, the younger brother is id (the unconscious). And if the latter is verbalized, or made conscious, it frequently takes the form of the second quadrant.

One can say that if anything, "I" is a device to liberate the discursive space represented by the left-hand side of the diagram. It is for this reason that Ōe refers to the novel as "self-salvation." "I" is not the self. The overall movement within these coordinates is what constitutes "salvation of the self." Yet in my analysis of *Football in the Year Man'en 1*, what I would like to concentrate on is the fact that this "salvation of the self" is, simultaneously, an attempted salvation of modern Japanese history.

3

At the *root* [*nedokoro*] of this violent bloodline is the younger brother of the great-grandfather, who led the uprising of Man'en 1 (1860). After the uprising, he alone survived, but his subsequent fate is unclear. According to legend, he changed his name and became a top government official. He is also said to have become a "spirit" of the village. What is his true identity? The characters of the novel continually ask this question as they act. Of course, the younger brother, Taka, who has identified with the younger brother of his great-grandfather, likens the attack on the supermarket to the uprising of Man'en 1.

On the other hand, "I" speaks as follows:

> Among the various human types found in the Nedokoro family, I'm the kind that refuses to be inspired to heroic thoughts by the Man'en 1 business. It's the same even in my sleep: far from identifying with great-grandfather's intrepid brother, I have wretched dreams in which I'm a bystander cowering in the storehouse, incapable even of firing a gun like great-grandfather. (Ōe 1974:117; translation modified)

This is not, however, merely a question of "character" but rather one that involves modern Japanese history. As long as the actions of the great-grandfather's younger brother are in question, the "valley" is not a general cosmos but instead signifies the discursive space of modern Japan. As I mentioned earlier, "I," who says, "I no longer had any roots there [in the valley] nor made any attempt to put down new ones" (Ōe 1974:134–35), belongs to the diagram's first quadrant; in other words, he exists in the space that is cut off from "Asia," a space where he locates his own identity:

> But on the other hand I'd been released from the feeling of guilt, which had pursued me ever since I came back to the valley, at losing the identity that should have been mine since childhood.
>
> Now, even if the whole valley should charge me with being a rat, I could retort with hostility, "And who are you, to insult a stranger whose affairs are none of yours?" Now I was just a transient in the valley, a one-eyed passerby too fat for his years, and life there had the power to summon up neither the memory nor the illusion of any other, truer self. As a passerby I had a right to insist on my identity. Even a rat has its identity as a rat. If I was a rat, then I had no need to be disturbed at being called one. (135)

The "village as a whole" can be seen to represent the whole of modern Japanese history, good and bad. Against this totality, "I" claims to be nothing more than a "passerby." From this position, he tries to fight against Takashi and the image of the great-grandfather's younger brother, with whom Takashi has identified:

> I read the letters he [great-grandfather's brother] wrote. They show that he stopped being a man of violence. What's more, even in his own mind he lost the enthusiasm he'd had as a rebel leader. Nor was it a case of self-punishment. He simply forgot his experiences in the rising and spent his last years as a perfectly ordinary citizen.... In practice he died a mere sheep of a man, absolutely unqualified to become any kind of "spirit." (242)

To put it in other words, "I" also places his great-grandfather's brother in the category of the rat. And he says that Takashi will end up the same way. (If we here substitute the emperor as living god for "leader of the uprising," then it begins to resemble Mishima Yukio's condemnation of the "living emperor" in *Voices of the Heroic Dead* [*Eirei no koe*, 1966]. In this sense, the fact that "I" belongs precisely to postwar space should become clear.) In response, Takashi says only the following: "Mitsu, why do you resent me so much? Why have you always disliked me? We two brothers are all that's left of the Nedokoros, aren't we?" (242).

However, what Takashi is talking about is more than familial love. Their "root place" contains a pair of siblings—their great-grandfather and his younger brother. The younger brother assaulted the Nedokoro family estate. In effect, their root identity was divided from the beginning. Moreover, this assault was undertaken to hide the fact that both the great-grandfather and his brother had conspired together to bring about the uprising. In other words, the enmity of the two brothers is collaborative, while, conversely, their association is itself a form of division. That is, when Mitsu and Taka seek their own identities, they cannot help but arrive at enmity and collaboration.

Yet this collaboration and enmity represent modern Japanese history itself. For example, in the Seinan War, Saigō Takamori struggled against the government, but because of his self-destructive rebellion, he ended up contributing to the consolidation of the institution of the modern state aimed at by Ōkubo Toshimichi. If Saigō truly had had the intention of winning, he would not have started a rebellion limited only to the samurai class. And Ōkubo, who had previously rejected Saigō's plan to conquer Korea, ended up putting this plan into action after Saigō's death. The Satsuma revolutionaries Ōkubo and Saigō were, in effect, siblings. Ōkubo would become a symbol of national rights and imperialism, whereas Saigō would become a symbol of Asianism and the Shōwa Restoration who furthered the Meiji Restoration and tried to spread it to Asia.

This opposition, however, may have been secretly collaborative. In fact, the later Asianists and young officers of the Shōwa Restoration ultimately contributed only to imperialist state power. Such relationships of opposition and collaboration make the previously mentioned coordinate space rather complicated. Takashi's dizzying "conversions" reveal that the entire discursive space emerges from the same "root."

According to the letter written by the great-grandfather's brother, which is discovered in the course of the narrative, he countered his older brother's rejoicing at the news of the constitution's promulgation in Meiji 22: "Wasn't it somewhat hasty— the letter inquired rather depressingly—to become infatuated with the word 'Constitution' without even finding out what its actual provisions were?" (Ōe 1974:206). This constitution was imposed "from above" and did not emerge in any way "from below": "As this letter showed, he [the younger brother] viewed the political regime following the Restoration with the eyes of a man with a 'cause,' in his case the cause of popular rights. It seemed likely, therefore, that the legend that he became a high official in the Restoration government was the exact reverse of the truth" (206; translation modified).

In the Meiji 10s, the great-grandfather's younger brother had been an advocate of "people's rights" and had apparently maintained this cause into the Meiji 20s. Historically, however, many of the advocates of "people's rights" converted to "national rights" during this period, or else converted to Asianism. The "violent" lineage of the Nedokoro family can be seen to demonstrate this process. As I pointed out earlier, the members of this lineage are each connected in some way to Asia.

Regarding the 1960 Ampo struggle, the critic Isoda Kōichi claimed that the Kishi cabinet actually welcomed the intensification of protests as a means to strengthen its hand in negotiations with the United States (1983:150–51). I usually don't take to "shrewd observations" of this type, but I believe that such a thing was possible. Such a perspective, however, can already be found in *Football in the Year Man'en 1*.

The work presents myriad interpretations of the Man'en rebellion. The interpretation of the head priest, a local historian, is as follows. The unavoidably disruptive conditions of the uprising were caused by the agitation of infiltrators from Tosa beyond the forest:

> I imagine that the priest and your great-grandfather shared the view that only a rising could bring any relief

> to the valley peasants. The priest took neither side, while the overseer was on the side of the establishment—but ruin for the masses would have meant their both going under too. So the real question plaguing them was what kind of rising to instigate and where. The easiest course, you see, would be to provide some outlet for the violent energies building up to a rising before things got so bad that the attack was concentrated on the overseer himself, and to keep violence in the valley to a minimum while diverting the rest to the castle town. (Ōe 1974:113–14)

In other words, the great-grandfather's brother was used for this purpose. Therefore, as compensation for his role, he alone was allowed to escape, and he changed his name and became a top government official.

This represents, in effect, the interpretation of advocates of "national rights." In contrast, according to Takashi's interpretation the great-grandfather and his younger brother were used by the peasants who desired the uprising. They pushed to the front the juvenile delinquents organized by the great-grandfather's younger brother, the "revolutionary youth" and "young officers": "You see, whenever it became necessary to injure or kill the enemy of the moment, they could always leave it to the young men without dirtying their own hands. The arrangement meant that the rank and file of the farmers could take part in the rising without any fear of being charged with arson or murder afterward" (Ōe 1974:150). For this reason, the young men, who tried to survive even after the uprising, were ostracized by the villagers and betrayed, and finally holed up in the storehouse to continue their resistance.

Although it is not explicitly mentioned, the Bund faction of the 1960s, to which Takashi most likely belonged, can be said to represent this type of "revolutionary youth." In fact, Bund produced converts to "national rights" (of whom Shimizu Ikutarō is representative), as well as those who, like "I"'s description of his great-grandfather's younger brother, abandoned or at least concealed their passion for criminal acts, achieving thereby a maturity with which they endured everyday life. This does not, however, represent a new form. The political struggle of 1960 / Shōwa 35 contains within it the political and ideological dynamics of Japan since the end of the Tokugawa [Edo] period. And, apart from *Football in the Year Man'en 1*, there is no work that tries to grasp the "totality" or fragmented "root place" of these dynamics. By linking together the "political action of June 1960" and the "uprising of Man'en 1," this work was able to grasp the parallax between 1960 and Shōwa 35.

Incidentally, the image of the great-grandfather's younger brother that "I" ultimately discovers differs from those mentioned above. He did not escape from the valley but rather confined himself for life in a cellar beneath the storehouse. The letters to his older brother were written from this place: "Though he'd been unable to prevent the tragedy of the others' decapitation, he himself had carried out his own punishment. On the day of the final annihilation, he'd shut himself up in the cellar and there maintained his integrity as leader of the rising, albeit in a passive way, without ever going back on his beliefs" (Ōe 1974:257; translation modified).

Just once, however, he did come out into the open. The *Account of the Ōkubo Village Peasant Revolt*, which the grandfather had recorded concerning an uprising in Meiji 4 [1871], notes that a tall, hunched-over man with superior leadership ability suddenly appeared and then disappeared after the incident was over. "I" believes that this man was his great-grandfather's younger brother: "He'd invested everything won during more than ten long years of self-criticism in a second and successful rising utterly different from the first. The first rising had been bloody and doubtful in its achievement. In the second, no one was killed or injured either among the rioters or the bystanders" (Ōe 1974:263). Afterward, he once more confined himself to the cellar of the storehouse, where he lived on for another twenty years.

This "self-confinement" can be seen to exist at the foundation of Japan's modern literature. In "The Discursive Space of Modern Japan," I wrote that the character K in Natsume Sōseki's *Kokoro* contains something that connects him to Kitamura Tōkoku and Nishida Kitarō, who confined themselves in a kind of self-punishment in the Meiji 10s. It was nothing other than this identity as a self-confined person that was recalled for Sōseki as the "spirit of Meiji" in Meiji 45. The character Sensei in *Kokoro* thinks as follows about K's suicide: "Finally, I became aware of the possibility that K had experienced loneliness as terrible as mine, and wishing to escape quickly from it, had killed himself. Once more, fear gripped my heart. From then on, like a gust of winter wind, the premonition that I was treading the same path as K had done would rush at me from time to time, and chill me to the bone" (Natsume 1957:240–41). The relationship between "I" and his younger brother in Ōe's novel resembles the relationship between Sensei and K. "I" too discovers a "terrifying" sight in Takashi, who commits suicide. Moreover, they are eminently connected to the identity of the self-confined person in the Meiji 10s.

In 1970 / Shōwa 45, Mishima completed *The Sea of Fertility*, depicting, through the form of reincarnation, the repetition of the "spirit of Meiji." The person most antagonistic to this attempt was Ōe. For in fact, in *Football in the Year Man'en 1*, Ōe had himself evoked the "totality" of modern Japanese history and attempted to "save" it—not by way of the device of reincarnation but rather through the device of allegory. Furthermore, clearly Ōe was oriented in the direction of popular rights instead of toward national rights. But the reason that Ōe opposed Mishima to the utmost extent was that Ōe was, in some sense, closest to Mishima. Between the two was precisely the type of older brother–younger brother relationship that Ōe depicted in his novel. And after these two writers grasped the discursive space of modern Japan as a totality, what was left for Japan's modern literature?

5

THE LANDSCAPE OF MURAKAMI HARUKI

PINBALL IN THE YEAR 1973

PART I

1

In Murakami Haruki's *Pinball in the Year 1973* [*1973-nen no pinbōru*, 1980], there is an absence of proper names.¹ This is common to Murakami's works from *Hear the Wind Sing* [*Kaze no uta o kike*, 1979], his first novel, to *Hard-Boiled Wonderland and the End of the World* [*Sekai no owari to hādoboirudo wandārando*, 1985]. Yet *Pinball in the Year 1973* is worth noting in that there is one exception: the appearance of the name Naoko. Naoko is the name of the woman who commits suicide. Attentive readers may notice that the name Naoko also appears as the name of the heroine in *Norwegian Wood* [*Noruwei no mori*, 1987]. Needless to say, *Norwegian Wood* is a work in which ordinary proper names appear, and, fittingly, the novel gained a level of readership on a completely different scale from that of Murakami's previous works.

It is not clear whether Murakami offered up the name Naoko having already planned future works at the time of writing *Pinball in the Year 1973*, and delving into this matter is not important. For now, it is enough to simply look at the fact that ordinary proper names were excluded from *Pinball in the Year 1973* to such an extent that the appearance of the name Naoko becomes extremely conspicuous. The same applies to the title, *Pinball in the Year 1973*. It is of no importance whether or not

1   *1973-nen no pinbōru* has been translated into English by Alfred Birnbaum as *Pinball, 1973* (1985). All citations in the text are taken from this translation. However, a more literal translation of the title is used in this chapter in order to reflect its close resemblance to Ōe Kenzaburō's *Football in the Year Man'en 1*.

Murakami deliberately titled his work as a parody of Ōe Kenzaburō's *Football in the Year Man'en 1* [*Man'en gannen no futtobōru*, 1967]. Rather, we should pay attention to the fact that it effectively *is* a parody, and to what is brought to light through a comparison of the two works.

For example, the absence of proper names in Ōe's works has a completely different meaning than in Murakami's works. The names Takashi and Mitsusaburō in *Football in the Year Man'en 1*, as well as Mitsusaburō's nickname, Rat, are type names. However, the name Rat that appears in Murakami's first three works has no relation to the appearance or personality of the character with this name:

> "You can call me 'Rat,'" he said.
> "How'd you get a name like that?"
> "I forget. Goes a long way back. At first I really hated being called that, but now I don't even think about it. You get used to anything." (1987:17)

In contrast to the fact that Rat in *Football in the Year Man'en 1* dwells on his name and even takes the tactic of discovering in himself a rat identity, for the Rat in *Hear the Wind Sing*, the name is merely a sign to tell one thing from another and has no meaning whatsoever. The same is essentially true for the names given to the female twins in *Pinball in the Year 1973*. They are called "208" and "209" by "I" [*boku*]: "Even so, when I was desperate to distinguish the two of them, I had no recourse but to rely on the numbers. I just couldn't come up with any other way to tell them apart" (Murakami 1985:37).

Names here are nothing more than differential signs for distinguishing things that are completely indistinguishable. In other words, proper names are dissolved into language in general. This kind of thinking is common in post-Saussurian linguistics. An object is recognized as such only when articulated via a differential system; it is not that a preexisting object is given a name. This articulation / differentiation is not merely spatial but also applies to the dimension of time. "I," who lives with the twin sisters, begins to lose his "sense of time":

> The whole situation was beyond me; my imagination couldn't cope with what it must be like to be a twin. I mean, I'm sure that if I had a twin brother, and we were alike in every detail, I'd be really mixed up. Because I'm mixed up enough as it is.
>
> Still, all things being equal, the two girls went about their affairs with the utmost equanimity. As a matter of fact, the girls were shocked when they found out I couldn't tell them apart. They were furious, in fact.
>
> "Why, we're completely different!"
>
> "Total opposites!"
>
> Which shut me up. So I just shrugged.
>
> I can't even begin to guess how much time has gone by since they moved into my apartment. The only thing I know for certain is that ever since they'd begun living with me, my internal clock has been running perceptibly behind. It occurs to me that this must be how organisms that multiply by cell-division experience time. (Murakami 1985:30–31; translation modified)

Rather than being Saussurian, however, this represents cognition according to Kant's *Critique of Pure Reason*, the book in which "I" is ardently absorbed. According to Kant, we are unable to know the world-in-itself (things-in-themselves). The world is given to us through our senses, but in order to recognize the world as object, we must organize it through a priori forms. To rephrase this in contemporary terms, we grasp the world though the arbitrary differential system that is language; this applies not only to time but to "I" as well. It is not that there is a subject, which is then labeled "I," but rather, the subject comes into existence through the word "I."

In this way, Murakami's "I" speaks as if there were no such thing as "I." If Ōe's "I" belongs to this world (the world of the work), or rather, *is* the state of the world itself, Murakami's "I" is continually saying that "I" itself is arbitrary—that is to say, that the state of the world itself is arbitrary.

"I" does not judge anything and does not assert anything. At the same time, there are judgments and assertions everywhere.

These judgments and assertions are mostly those having to do with judgments of taste. As for Kant's "critique," it is seen as a "transcendental" critique of metaphysical dogma that created the foundation for cognition. The *Critique of Judgment*, which is a transcendental critique of judgments of taste, so to speak, was written last and is viewed as if it were a secondary work. Yet we should keep in mind that originally the word "critique" comes from the domain of judgments of taste. In the domain of taste, there are no certain standards. After all, no matter what the opinion, it is nothing more than "dogma and bias." Kant considered the domains of truth and the good to be nothing more than the domain of judgments of taste, and he made an attempt to see all judgments as judgments of taste. This is Kant's "critique." This being the case, it is not surprising that German Romanticism, which regards everything as aesthetic judgments of taste, emerged from there.

In this sense, it could be said that Murakami's "I" is reading Kant's *Critique of Pure Reason* "correctly." "I" is a transcendental subject that considers all judgments as a matter of taste, and accordingly nothing more than "dogma and bias." This is not an empirical subject (self). Murakami's works impart an extremely "private" impression, but they are not I-novels. The empirical "I" on which the I-novel is premised is denied; "I" is in a state of dispersal. There is, however, a transcendental self that coldly gazes at the dispersed "I."

Whereas Ōe's "I" is a device that brings about allegorical crossings or disjunctions in language, in Murakami's works, language is always governed by this transcendental subject. Although it appears as if language were in a state of dispersal, this is only for the purpose of conversely proving the certainty of the transcendental subject.

2

Earlier, I argued that the emergence of ordinary names in Futabatei's *Drifting Clouds* is a symptom of the modern novel.

However, this is not yet a negation of proper names as such. Perhaps the first time that the negation of proper names as such may be seen is in Kunikida Doppo's "Those Unforgettable People" [Wasureenu hitobito, 1898]. In this story, the protagonist Ōtsu talks about "unforgettable people" to a man named Akiyama, whom he met at an inn called Kameya. "Unforgettable people" refers not to important people whom one should not forget, but to people who are unforgettable despite their meaninglessness and irrelevance. They are "landscapes" rather than people. The work has the following denouement:

> Two years passed. Ōtsu was living in a part of Tōhoku. He never again saw or had any communication with Akiyama whom he had met for the first and only time in the Mizonokuchi inn. One rainy evening in the same season of the year as when he had stayed at that inn, Ōtsu was sitting along at a table, deep in thought. He had in front of him the manuscript "Those Unforgettable People" which he had shown to Akiyama those two years ago. The latest entry was under the heading "The Kameya innkeeper."
>
> Of Akiyama there was no mention. (Kunikida 1982: 46)

The name Akiyama is rejected, while the nameless "master of Kameya," who was nothing more than mere landscape, has become one of the "unforgettable people." We must note the fact that there resides here an instance of spite. Previously, I described this as the "discovery of landscape": contrary to what might be expected, it is the "internal human being," one who turns away from exterior landscapes, who discovers landscape as landscape; hidden there is a "fundamental inversion."[2]

Along the same lines, I would like to rethink this question in terms of proper names. In "landscape," there are no proper

---

2   For an analysis of the inversion involved in the modern discovery of landscape, see Karatani (1993b:11–44).

names. To be certain, Doppo depicted a landscape having the name "Musashi Plain." Yet he did this because he tried to depict, for the first time, a nameless landscape as opposed to a named landscape [*meisho*, or "famous place"]. In other words, he did not depict the Musashi Plain because it was a place called Musashi Plain. Readers who enjoy reading "The Musashi Plain" [Musashino, 1898] are already blind to Doppo's inversion or his perverse intent. The self-evident status of "modern Japanese literature" is thus established.

Doppo is a Romantic not because he depicts landscapes or throws himself into nature, but because he does so within an ironic consciousness. When one says Romantic irony, most anyone would think of Yasuda Yojūrō. Although Yasuda, who theorized about Meiji-period [1868–1912] Romanticism, did not realize it himself, Doppo already had this ironic consciousness inside him. What I have called "fundamental inversion" or "spite" is this ironic consciousness. This is the transcendental self (consciousness) that coldly gazes at the empirical self.

This self-consciousness is never wounded, nor is it defeated. For this self-consciousness despises the empirical self and its objects. Needless to say, this kind of victory of "interiority" is merely the evasion of "struggle." Because Sōseki did not accept this kind of evasion, he continued to have a sense of estrangement with respect to "modern literature." The type of defeat and delimitation belonging to the second decade of the Meiji period, to which Sōseki adhered, are transcended in the kind of irony represented by Doppo. For all limitations are overcome in "interiority." What we need to be mindful of is the fact that in Doppo, the kind of "history" that has proper names is transcended. It is precisely at this point that "landscape" emerges.[3]

What Murakami discovered is also "landscape" in this sense. Admittedly, his works lack the kind of depictions of nature emblematized by Doppo. Murakami's works are inundated with proper names, of the type found in the following

---

3   For a discussion of Doppo's work, see Karatani (1993b:65–72). For the English translation of "Musashino," see Kunikida (1982:97–112).

examples from *Pinball in the Year 1973*: "The dogs were sopping wet, right down to their buttocks; some looked like waifs from a Balzac novel, others like pensive Buddhist priests" (1985:100). "The whole time, the rain poured down relentlessly and silently over the reservoir. The sound was something like shredded newspaper falling on a thick pile carpet. It was like the rain that falls in Claude Lelouche movies" (101).

It is likely that very few readers know about "waifs from a Balzac novel" or "rain that falls in Claude Lelouche movies," and there is no need for such knowledge. It is precisely for this reason that these similes are being used. In other words, they are "unforgettable" things. Murakami discovers (creates) landscape of this kind. Product names, avoided by modern novelists, spill out of the text. This has the appearance of new scenery. Just as ardent readers of Doppo did not see the spite of the transcendental self-consciousness hidden in his landscape, ardent readers of Murakami merely receive the impression of a stylish, of-the-moment landscape. Furthermore, this has led to new "landscape" novels by naive writers being produced one after the other.

As I explain later, however, it would be a mistake to label this as merely postmodern. This is because the "inversion" hidden in Murakami's "landscape" is of the same mold as that in Doppo—in, that is to say, "modern literature."

3

Doppo's "The Musashi Plain" is not a novel. In the same way, Murakami's *Hear the Wind Sing* and *Pinball in the Year 1973* are not novels. In *Hear the Wind Sing*, Murakami writes: "What I can set down here in writing only amounts to a catalogue. Not a novel, not literature, not even art" (1987:10). This is merely "landscape." Murakami's power to influence lies in making this landscape self-evident. This is by no means an external landscape. In other words, it is not that the world began to manifest the conditions of a postindustrial capitalist consumer society, which Murakami grasped more quickly than others. This "landscape," just as in Doppo's landscape, comes into existence only through a kind of *écriture* or a kind of internal "inversion."

It is not as though Murakami remained confined to this "landscape." In his third work, *A Wild Sheep Chase* [*Hitsuji o meguru bōken*, 1982], a story—as Hasumi Shigehiko (1989) has discussed, a commonplace storytelling structure—is introduced. Yet we cannot help but recognize that Murakami's "newness" lay in a certain posture whereby "landscape" is discovered. Needless to say, this is an inversion of value in which something meaningless is placed above something with meaning. The overflowing numbers in Murakami's works plainly demonstrate this inversion: "I waited for the compressed-air hiss of the elevator doors shutting behind me before closing my eyes. Then, gathering up the pieces of my mind, I started off on the sixteen steps down the hall to my apartment door. Eyes closed, exactly sixteen steps. No more, no less" (1989:13).

What meaning does the exactness of the number, "sixteen steps," have? In some cases, an extreme sense of reality may impart a dreamlike sense of unreality. When Dostoyevsky writes, "it was exactly three steps," the extreme exactitude imparts a sense of reality that is so real that it becomes unreal. On the other hand, Murakami's "sixteen steps" are merely arbitrary and impart the sense that events are arbitrary. This number is the same as saying that the names of the twin sisters are 208 and 209. Murakami writes as follows:

> The third girl I slept with used to call my penis my raison d'être.
>
> ...
>
> I once tried to write a novella on people's raisons d'être. It never got off the ground, but for a while there I kept thinking about people's reasons for doing anything at all, which put me in a strange frame of mind. I was habitually reducing everything to numbers. For about eight months, I was a driven man. I'd board a train and first thing count the passengers in the car. I'd add up all

the steps in staircases. If I had a spare second, I'd take my pulse. According to my records at the time, between August 15, 1969, and April 3 of the following year, I attended three hundred fifty-eight classes, had sex fifty-four times, smoked six thousand, nine hundred and twenty-one cigarettes.

All that time, it seems I seriously believed that putting a numerical value on everything would enable me to transmit something to others. And as long as I had something to transmit, my existence would be assured. But, of course, no one showed the slightest interest in the number of cigarettes I smoked or the number of steps I climbed, or the size of my penis. Hence I lost sight of my own raison d'être, leaving me the odd man out.

...

So it was that when I learned of her death, I was smoking my six thousand, nine hundred and twenty-second cigarette. (1987:77; translation modified)

Numbers are an extreme manifestation of the act of reducing the meaning of words and regarding them as differential signs. They merely indicate difference or sequence. Here, the woman who commits suicide is nothing more than "the third girl I slept with." In the moment that this woman is called, for example, "Naoko," irreplaceable singularity / historicity would no doubt be recovered. Numbers are put to frequent use in order to reject such singularity / historicity. In Murakami's works up to *Dance, Dance, Dance*, there is a great proliferation of dates, which function in the same way:

This story begins on August 8, 1970, and ends eighteen days later, on August 26 of the same year. (1987:11)

September 1973, that's where this novel begins. That's the entrance. We'll just hope there's an exit. If there isn't one, there wouldn't be any point in writing anything. (1985:25)

Most writers try to "generalize" their works by omitting dates. Murakami, however, constantly positions his works in a specific date and time. This is not a manifestation of historical consciousness, however, but rather an attempt at its evacuation. At first glance, the dates appear as if they would evoke a nostalgic, shared generational sense in those readers who experienced them. Yet this is not the case. The dates are entirely private and meaningless:

> "What were you doing when you were twenty?"
> "I was crazy about a girl." Back in 1969, *our* year.
> "So what happened to her?"
> "Things came between us." (Murakami 1985:107)

The shared generational sense that, for a moment, the phrasing "1969, *our* year" seems as though it may evoke is completely negated in this context. Needless to say, the fact that 1969 was the time of the student movement is not hidden; rather, Murakami refers to the student movement so frequently it is almost provocative. He writes, for example, "Any number of people were cutting their lives short, going out of their heads, burying their hearts in the sludge of time, burning up their bodies with pointless thinking, making trouble for one another. Nineteen seventy was that kind of year" (Murakami 1985:60). But at the moment that "1969" or "1970" is about to take on some meaning, Murakami inverts it. "1960," a privileged point of time in Ōe's *Football in the Year Man'en 1*, is described in *Pinball in the Year 1973* in the following way:

> Naoko had moved to the area when she was twelve. 1961. The year Ricky Nelson sang "Hello Mary Lou." (16)

> That was in 1960, the year Bobby Vee sang "Red Rubber Ball." (17)

Of course, Murakami is fully aware of what "1960" means, but he acts as if he were unaware. This is irony in the original sense of the word. Murakami erases important matters that should not be forgotten and emphasizes the "unforgettable" landscape of Ricky Nelson's "Hello Mary Lou" and Bobby Vee's "Red Rubber Ball." The reason that Murakami overuses proper names is in fact to deny proper names. The overuse of numerals has the same intention.

4

As I stated earlier, this excess of dates is not the manifestation of historical consciousness but, on the contrary, an attempt to evacuate historical consciousness. Alternatively, it asserts the "end of history." The fact that the repetition of such gestures is actually an attachment toward something, however, is transparent. This is clear from the fact that Naoko, the sole character given an ordinary proper name, is described as follows: "On the train ride back, I told myself over and over again, it's all over with now, you got it out of your system, forget it. Isn't that why you came here? Yet I couldn't get it out of mind, that place. Nor the fact that I loved Naoko. Nor that she was dead. After all, I still hadn't closed the book on anything" (Murakami 1985:23; translation modified).

Yet Murakami must create the appearance that everything has ended and nothing will occur. The "love" that Murakami writes of in this work is directed not at "Naoko" but at the pinball machine encountered in "the winter of 1970." "I" refers to it as "she" [*kanojo*]: "She was great, though. That three-flipper 'Spaceship'... only I understood her, and only she understood me. Whenever I pressed her replay button, she'd perk up with a little hum, click the six digits on the board to zero, then smile at me" (Murakami 1985:118–19).

The only positive action that "I" takes in this work is locating this "phantom machine" that ceased to be manufactured after a mere three units were imported into Japan. "This is a novel about pinball" (Murakami 1985:27). This search not only has as its object a machine for play but also is itself play. It is nonetheless pursued seriously—in this work, meaningful things are looked down upon, while meaningless things are engaged seriously. This attitude is also seen in the following description of "historical fact": "To be sure, it's a historical fact that by this man's very hands the first prototype of the pinball machine was brought unto this realm of defilement in 1934 from out of the great, golden cloud of technology. Which is again the very year that, across that giant puddle called the Atlantic, Adolf Hitler was getting his hands on the first rung of the Weimar ladder" (27).

Here, Murakami places mainstream culture and subculture, political events and matters of custom on the same level. This attitude should not, however, be misunderstood as some kind of historically new attitude. For it is the same as the ironic consciousness seen earlier in Doppo. "In irony, everything should be playful and everything serious, everything naively exposed and everything deeply disguised" (Schlegel, quoted in Hartmann 1960:175). What, then, is secured through this kind of irony? The answer is a transcendental self that exceeds all kinds of limitations.

"I" finally manages to reunite with the machine, which had been stored in a warehouse, and he has a conversation with it:

> We fell silent. What we shared was nothing more than a fragment of time that had died long ago. Even so, a faint glimmer of that warm memory still claimed a part of my heart. And when death claimed me, no doubt I would walk along by that faint light in the brief instant before being flung once again into the abyss of nothingness.
>
> You'd better be going, she said.
>
> The chill was getting unbearable, to be sure. I shook all over as I stomped out my cigarette.
>
> Thanks for coming to see me, she said. We may not meet again, but take care.
>
> Thanks, I said, farewell. (Murakami 1985:163; translation modified)

This "conversation" is, obviously, a conversation with oneself (monologue). "She" is not an other like "Naoko." That is, she does not place limits on "I." The love that "I" has for the machine is nothing but self-love.

This dialogue in one sense seems similar to the dialogue between "I" and the dead in Ōe's "Lavish Are the Dead" [Shisha no ogori, 1957]. Following this dialogue, "I" says the following: "I had stepped into the world of the dead. And after returning to the midst of the living, everything becomes difficult—this is what I stumbled over first" (Ōe 1996b:31). We might say that Murakami has also "stepped into the world of the dead," since neither "I" nor "Rat" can return to the world of "the living." At the very least, however, the dead are not machines. What Murakami's "I" is attached to is an arbitrary world that does not accept any limitation whatsoever.

Murakami's "I" is completely different from Ōe's "I." It is an "I" that pretends as if there were no "I" and that never stumbles. Ōe's "I" is an allegory that is constantly replaced with another "meaning." In contrast, Murakami's "I" is the consciousness of a transcendental self that, by flaunting its baseless absorption with something meaningless, looks down on those who hold on to meaning or goals and avidly pursue something.

As I mentioned earlier, this is the repetition of something that belongs to the lineage of "modern literature" brought about by Doppo. In other words, it is the reemergence of the sleight of hand in which real "struggles" are abandoned and, through this abandonment, made into an internal victory. Murakami appears to have negated the "interiority" and "landscape" of modern literature. But what he actually brought about is "interiority" and "landscape" in a new dimension, and the solipsistic world of this dimension has become a self-evident foundation for the young authors of today.

PART II

1

I have stated that *Pinball in the Year 1973* is a kind of parody of *Football in the Year Man'en 1*. This is seen not only in the contrast between "the year 1973" and "the year Man'en 1" but even more clearly in the contrast between "pinball" and "football."

Claude Lévi-Strauss, after comparing games and rituals, wrote as follows:

> Games thus appear to have a *disjunctive* effect: they end in the establishment of a difference between individual players or teams where originally there was no indication of inequality. And at the end of the game they are distinguished into winners and losers. Ritual, on the other hand, is the exact inverse; it *conjoins*, for it brings about a union (one might even say communion in this context) or in any case an organic relation between two initially separate groups, one ideally merging with the person of the officiant and the other with the collectivity of the faithful. In the case of games the symmetry is therefore preordained and it is of a structural kind since it follows from the principle that the rules are the same for both sides. Asymmetry is engendered: it follows inevitably from the contingent nature of events, themselves due to intention, chance, or talent. The reverse is true of ritual. There is an asymmetry which is postulated in advance between profane and sacred, faithful and officiating, dead and living, initiated and uninitiated, etc., and the "game" consists in making all the participants pass to the winning side by means of events, the nature and ordering of which is genuinely structural. Like science (though here again on both the theoretical and the practical plane) the game produces events by means of a structure; and we can therefore understand why competitive games should flourish in our industrial societies. Rites and myths, on the other hand, like "bricolage" (which these same societies only tolerate as a hobby or pastime), take to pieces and reconstruct sets of events (on a psychical, socio-historical or technical plane) and use them as so many indestructible pieces for structural patterns in which they serve alternatively as ends or means. (1966:32–33)

Of course, I did not quote the above passage with the intention of saying that Murakami is retrieving the kind of "savage mind" of myths and ritual, but rather in order to indicate the extent of the difference between "football" and "pinball."

"Football" in *Football in the Year Man'en 1* is the kind of game talked about by Lévi-Strauss. Ōe incorporated football into his work in order to view history as events created "from structure." Lacking this viewpoint, the kind of themes in *Football in the Year Man'en 1* would have constituted a run-of-the-mill historical novel (story). Yet if this novel had been written merely as events created by structure, "history" would likely disappear.

"History" exists outside of structure. To put it another way, it comes into being as intercourse within asymmetrical relationships. In actuality, most so-called events are created from structure. However, there is an *eventness* [*dekigotosei*] that in no way can be reduced to structure, and only this should be called history. The union of "the year Man'en 1" and "football" signifies, as it were, a plan to see history within structure, and structure within history. But what about the union of "the year 1973" and "pinball"? "1973" is merely a number: "September 1973 . . . more like some dream it was . . . 1973, who'd have thought such a year would *really* exist. And for some reason, that thought was funny beyond measure" (Murakami 1985:52; translation modified). "1973" exists as nothing more than a mere sign (difference).

On the one hand, pinball appears to create the outcome of asymmetrical relationships of winner and loser, in the same way as football. However, the idea of a machine as victor is odd. It is also odd for the player to be the loser. Victory and defeat do not become events (it is another matter if one is competing against another player). In one sense, the player always loses. Yet this does not constitute an event, for players need only to replay. They act only within the rules of this machine, and what is tested is nothing more than the extent to which they have (physically) mastered those rules.

What Murakami wants to say with this pinball metaphor is not just that history is events created from structure (a system of rules) but also that history no longer exists. The union of

"1973" and "pinball" only emphasizes repetition as replay in this way: "It was another rerun of the same old day. One you almost had to dog-ear to keep from getting it mixed up with the rest" (Murakami 1985:85). At the end of this work as well, there is the following passage: "The bus door banged shut, the twins waved from the window. Everything was repeating itself" (179). This is narrated as follows with regard to pinball:

> Pinball machines, however, won't lead you anywhere. Just the replay light. Replay, replay, replay. . . . So persistently you'd swear a game of pinball aspired to perpetuity.
> We ourselves will never know much of perpetuity. But we can get a faint inkling of what it's like.
> The object of pinball lies not in self-expression, but in self-revolt. Not in the expansion of the ego, but in its compression. Not in extractive analysis, but in inclusive subsumption.
> So if it's self-expression or ego-expansion or analysis you're after, you'll only be subjected to the merciless retaliation of the tilt lamps. (28)

To be sure, the expansion of the ego and self-expression in the ordinary sense are likely to be denied in this game. After all, the player merely submits to the rules, and even if the score rises, this is not "self development." Yet this game comes about via a single human being, and the world of the game exists for only that person. The world depends on the arbitrary will of the player playing the game. The player—that is, the transcendental subject—is the agent that enables this game to come into being. As I explain later, *Hard-Boiled Wonderland and the End of the World* is a product of this sort of subjectivity. In short, when it seems as though it is absorbed in this kind of game, the empirical self is reduced, but the transcendental self viewing the empirical self swells to an extreme.

It is hardly necessary to point out that today's computer games are the descendants of pinball. One should nevertheless be alert to the fact that romance (story) close to "myth or ritual" is being brazenly revived in computer games. Of course, science fiction, too, is a contemporary form of myth. In this sense, it is not at all strange that *A Wild Sheep Chase* and *Hard-Boiled Wonderland and the End of the World* revive this kind of story.

2

This type of consciousness has already been narrated in *Hear the Wind Sing*, as the "idea of the universe" or the "song of the wind":

> "In another two hundred and fifty thousand years the sun will explode," the breeze whispered to him. "Click... Off. Two hundred and fifty thousand years. Hardly much time now, is it?" (Murakami 1987:103)

> For, in his conception, the novel had to be a medium of information like any graph or chart, its accuracy increasing in direct proportion to its volume.
> He was consistently critical of Tolstoy's *War and Peace*. Not, of course, on the volume criterion, but because it lacked any idea of the universe, so the resultant work struck him as really rather patchy. The words "idea of the universe" by and large equate the concept of "barrenness" in his usage. (100)

This sort of consciousness belongs, in a word, to information theory. Needless to say, "information" is being used in contrast to "meaning" or "matter." Information is difference, to which meaning or matter is reduced. Information theory is regarded as having brought about a new point of view that existed in neither idealism nor materialism, one that furthermore runs throughout natural history (including cultural history) in a unified manner. According to Bateson, this was the most important intellectual revolution of this century.

When Murakami gives the twin sisters the names 208 and 209, for example, it could have been 0 and 1 (on and off); that is to say, the only issue is difference (binary opposition). Their faces, their thoughts—indeed, even whether the twins "exist" to begin with—do not matter. This is because in order for us to recognize that something exists, we must grasp it as some kind of difference. Frogs do not recognize insects as insects but only recognize them when they move. In other words, for frogs, there is only the movement of insects (difference, i.e., information); it is not that insects exist. Even less does the idea (meaning) of insects exist. What Murakami is talking about in these works is this kind of information theory, and he ties it to the absence and barrenness of history. However, there lurks here an illusion, or perhaps an intentional misapprehension.

For example, both meaning and matter can be reduced (bracketed) only after being experienced. As an example, say we took the letters on this page and scattered them about so that they produce no meaning whatsoever. At this point, it could be said that information is zero, and entropy (the degree of randomness, as it were) is infinite. Next, if we rearrange them, they start to produce meaning in various places. If we say that one way of arrangement has meaning, the calculation of the probability of this arrangement being formed (strictly speaking, the reciprocal number of the probability) in comparison with the initial chaos is the quantity of information. This being the case, saying that meaning can be reduced to information is clearly mistaken. For, unless there is an agent that recognizes meaning, the amount of information cannot be calculated.

The same applies when Saussure says that language is no more than a system of differences. Saussure started out from the "speaking subject's" experience of meaning but bracketed it phenomenologically in order to discover form (difference). To put it another way, what is called structure or system is premised on a subject that brings it into being: namely, the transcendental subject.

This can be asserted for cases where matter is reduced to information as well. Those who explain the world through information theory are "transcendental subjects," but this is constantly being concealed or forgotten. The subjectivity of scientists thinking about the origin and age of the universe transcends this natural history. Whether it be the sun exploding in

250,000 years or the galaxy's life span ending in some number of years—the self that points out such things transcends this kind of finitude. Those who talk about the extinction of the universe emphasize the finitude and meaninglessness of the empirical self but in fact thereby confirm the unlimited nature of the transcendental self. Needless to say, scientists make their calculations only within an agreed-upon area. When they go beyond this area to begin talking about history or culture, they are already no longer scientists but nothing more than commonplace philosophers.

To repeat, information and structures do not exist "objectively" but are actually discovered within consciousness and through the bracketing of consciousness (phenomenological reduction). They are, however, seen as existing outside of consciousness, and in fact "consciousness" is subsequently attacked from that external position. This is an illusion. Yet in this illusion, or more appropriately in the case of Murakami, in this *intentional* misapprehension, the transcendental self-consciousness secretly confirms its supremacy:

> "People go through changes, sure. But up to now, I never did get what those changes were supposed to mean." The Rat bit his lip and looked down at the table pensively. "Then it came to me. Whatever step forward, whatever the change, it's really only a stage of decay. Does that sound so off target?"
>
> "No, not so very off."
>
> "That's why I never felt the least scrap of love or goodwill toward the run-of-the-mill people who go merrily about their way to oblivion . . . not even in this town."
> (1985:142; translation modified)

"The run-of-the-mill people who go merrily about their way to oblivion" refers to the run-of-the-mill people who go merrily about their way toward *meaning*. However, those who say that "whatever the change, it's really only a stage of decay" secure the superiority of the transcendental self by saying so. The previously mentioned Romantic irony can be seen here.

Along with information theory and structuralism, theories stating that history is nothing more than the transmutation of something structural have spread since the 1970s. For example, it is from this position that Michel Foucault's statement about the "death of Man" arises. We should note, however, that this sort of thought is based on a transcendental consciousness with respect to history. "Man" is certainly dead in this context—for he is no more than the result (effect) of various structures—yet the consciousness that "Man is dead" or that "history has ended" is itself secured. In its contempt toward those still clinging to meaning in the form of "Man" or "history," this consciousness manages to confirm its own superiority. In this way, postmodernism recalls, in a certain form, the Romantic irony that it has supposedly long since buried.

3

Earlier I stated that *Pinball in the Year 1973* is a type of parody of *Football in the Year Man'en 1*. Yet this is not in the sense that *Don Quixote* and *Madame Bovary* are parodies of chivalric tales and romances. Rather, it should more precisely be called a pastiche. Fredric Jameson has found the characteristics of postmodern literature in pastiche:

> This is the moment at which pastiche appears and parody has become impossible. Pastiche is, like parody, the imitation of a peculiar or unique style, the wearing of a stylistic mask, speech in a dead language: but it is a neutral practice of such mimicry, without parody's ulterior motive, without the satirical impulse, without laughter, without that still latent feeling that there exists something *normal* compared to which what is being imitated is rather comic. Pastiche is blank parody, parody that has lost its sense of humor: pastiche is to parody what that curious thing, the modern practice of a kind of blank irony, is to what Wayne Booth calls the stable and comic ironies of, say, the 18th century. (1983:114)

In fact, Murakami writes in his debut work *Hear the Wind Sing*: "What I can set down here in writing only amounts to a catalogue. Not a novel, not literature, not even art" (1987:10). To put it another way, this is pastiche. Yet while *Pinball in the Year 1973* and *A Wild Sheep Chase* may appear to be examples of "the modern practice of a kind of blank irony," what the works indicate is the strong attachment and will to inversion that this conceals.

This "hidden motive" is not present in Murakamiesque writers after Murakami. Their works are pastiche in a literal sense. This is precisely what happened when, for writers after Doppo, "landscape" was no longer inversion but rather something self-evident. What we should note is an irony different from the irony that exists in the historical forms called parody or pastiche: namely, Romantic irony. Romantic irony, more than anything else, should not be overlooked when considering Japanese postmodernism.

In *A Wild Sheep Chase*, for example, a certain right-wing political power broker's organization requests that "I" search for a "sheep." This power broker in 1936 suddenly had "risen to the top, in every sense of the word, of the right wing" (Murakami 1989:117), in the next year crossed over to the Chinese mainland, and after the war built a "powerful underground kingdom" (118). "From the establishment to the anti-establishment, everything" (118) was subsumed. Furthermore, it was a sophisticated organization in which "very few if any of them even noticed they had been co-opted" (118). This power broker is on the verge of death, and the organization is in danger of dissolution. After all, if this "Boss" dies, the "Will" supporting the organization will be lost:

> "... The Boss has been in a coma for two weeks now. Very probably he will never regain consciousness. And if the Boss dies, the mystery of the sheep with the star on its back will be buried with him forever. I, for one, am not about to stand by and let that happen. Not for reasons of my own personal loss, but for the greater good of all."

> I cocked open the lid of the lighter, struck the flint to light the flame, and closed the lid.
>
> "I am sure you think that all I am saying is a load of nonsense. And perhaps it is. It might well turn out to *be* total nonsense. But just consider, this may be the sum total of all that is left to us. The Boss will die. That one Will shall die. Then everything around that Will shall perish. All that shall remain will be what can be counted in numbers. Nothing else will be left. That is why I want to find that sheep."
>
> He closed his eyes a few seconds for the first time, saying nothing for a moment. Then: "If I might offer my hypothesis—a hypothesis and nothing more, forget I ever said a thing if it does nothing for you—I cannot help but feel that our sheep here formed the basic mold of the Boss's Will."
>
> "Sounds like animal crackers," I said.
>
> The man ignored my comment.
>
> "Very probably the sheep found its way into the Boss. That would have been in 1936. And for the next forty years or so, the sheep remained lodged in the Boss." (121–22)

The concept called "sheep" seems to stand in opposition to "those two pillars of Western humanism, individual cognition and evolutionary continuity" (Murakami 1989:120). With regard to Western humanism, only "a world of uniformity and certainty" (119) and "what can be counted in numbers" (122) will remain. In other words, the world is made out in terms of information theory: "The expansion of consciousness your generation underwent or at least sought to undergo at the end of the sixties ended in complete and utter failure because it was still rooted in the individual. That is, the attempt to expand consciousness alone, without any quantitative or qualitative change in the individual, was ultimately doomed. That is what I meant by your mediocrity" (120). In contrast, the concept of "sheep" denies thought rooted in the individual and guarantees "meaning" as opposed to the "world of uniformity and certainty."

What does this concept of "sheep" mean, in concrete terms? Of this, Murakami never speaks. Yet one could also say that he speaks of it everywhere.

The story of the right wing appearing in this novel would certainly bring to mind the fact that amid the flourishing student movement "at the end of the sixties" that was "rooted in the individual," there was a man who opposed the student movement and advocated an emperor system–based "cultural defense," launching an incident imitating the February 26 Incident of 1936 (Shōwa 11) and then killing himself. Despite the fact that Murakami is clearly alluding to this event, he denies it. That is, at the same time that Mishima Yukio's name is not casually but rather ostentatiously presented as in the passage below, it is denied as something that "didn't matter one way or the other." This, truly, is the "practice of a kind of blank irony" "We walked through the woods to the ICU campus, sat down in the student lounge, and munched on hot dogs. It was two in the afternoon, and Yukio Mishima's picture kept flashing on the lounge TV. The volume control was broken so we could hardly make out what was being said, but it didn't matter to us one way or the other" (Murakami 1989:8).

At the end of *A Wild Sheep Chase*, "Rat" kills himself after pinning down the "sheep." This is because the "sheep" had entered him: " 'What happened was this,' said the Rat. 'I died with the sheep in me. . . . If I had waited, the sheep would have controlled me absolutely. It was my last chance' " (Murakami 1989:281). "Rat" says that by committing suicide, he killed the "sheep" that had entered his body. With regard to this point, as I have discussed previously, what Takashi, one of the characters in Ōe's *Football in the Year Man'en 1*, calls forth and further tries to reject through suicide is the third quadrant in the discursive space of modern Japan: namely, the domain of "violence" that exists in the axis of Asia and popular rights. It could be said that what Murakami calls the "sheep" is this kind of domain.

Mishima's attempted coup d'état and suicide should not, however, be described as *propagation* of the "sheep" concept but rather as an attempt to bring it to an end. In an interview one week before his death, Mishima stated that his actions were "final" and that it was inconceivable that there could be someone "continuing afterward." While flamboyantly exhibiting the "sheep" concept to the extreme, Mishima killed it with his own hand, so to speak. For Mishima, suicide was confirmation of the "transcendental self" that despises the empirical self to the utmost degree.

If "in irony, everything should be playful and everything serious" (Schlegel), then describing Mishima's actions as intentional fakery or kitsch would be off target. Furthermore, if in irony "everything [should be] naively exposed and everything deeply disguised," then inquiring into Mishima's "motive" or "reasons" would be the height of foolishness. For irony is a question that belongs not to psychology but to thought.

Mishima's incident does not indicate that the "sheep" concept still lives on today. Rather, by demonstrating the ultimate enactment of the individual-negating "sheep" concept, the "will" of the individual that assumes itself to be the "final" person (transcendental self) lives on. Murakami is aware of this. Yet the "final" person must be Murakami himself, rather than Mishima. That is, the person who shows that "1970 / Shōwa 45" has completely ended has to be Murakami himself.

Murakami is also the type of writer for whom "everything is naively exposed and everything deeply disguised." To find a psychological "puzzle" here or to mystify it would be foolish. What *A Wild Sheep Chase* indicates is not resistance against the "world of uniformity and certainty" but rather the superiority of the self-consciousness that actively chooses it. It is here, or within "blankness," that Romantic irony "lives on."

4

The transcendental self that has transcended everything, however, is confined within solipsism. For, as Kant stated, even if reality (things-in-themselves) other than what is constructed through a priori "forms" exists, we are unable to know such a reality. Murakami holds that the world depends upon arbitrary "forms":

On the whole, I think of myself as one of those people who take a convenience-sake view of prevailing world conditions, events, existence in general. Not that I'm such a blasé, convenience-sake sort of guy—although I do have tendencies in that direction—but because more often than not I've observed that convenient approximations bring you closest to comprehending the true nature of things....

So I try to look at things from the perspective of convenience as much as possible. I think of the world as being made up of truly various—actually, infinite— possibilities. The choice within the possibilities must be to some degree up to the individuals making up the world. The world is a coffee table made up of condensed possibilities. (1991:4; translation modified)

The "possibilities" mentioned here are not related to modality, as I discuss later. Instead, they are close to the theory of possible worlds one finds in science fiction. It is no more than saying that since the world is formed of a certain axiomatic system, if another axiomatic system is chosen, then another world becomes "possible," so to speak. For example, if we choose an axiomatic system where there are unicorns, then that kind of "world" exists.

Needless to say, this kind of debate arose in the context of the emergence of non-Euclidean geometry. The formalist David Hilbert, for example, stated that geometry can be done with coffee tables.[4] This is because mathematics does

---

4 See the explanation in Corry:

> Hilbert's main achievement concerning the foundations of geometry was— according to a widely-held view—to present this mathematical domain as an axiomatic system devoid of any specific intuitive meaning, in which the central concepts (points, lines, planes) could well be replaced by tables, chairs and beer-mugs, on condition that the latter are postulated to satisfy the relations established by the axioms. (1997:84)

For more on Hilbert and Gödel, see Karatani (1995:54–56).

not depend on its object but on a formal axiomatic system. If you choose one axiomatic system, it becomes Euclidean geometry; if you choose another axiomatic system, it becomes non-Euclidean geometry. However, this sort of thinking en-counters a fundamental difficulty, as Gödel later indicated. This is, to put it in other words, the paradox encountered when one views the self, who already belongs to this world (history), as being able transcendentally to lay the foundation of that world. In *Hard-Boiled Wonderland and the End of the World*, Murakami creates an arbitrary world. However, at the end of this lengthy work, "I" says the following:

> "No, that is not it at all, not all of it," I say. "I have discovered what created this Town. That is why I have an obligation to remain here, a responsibility. Don't you want to know what created this Town?"
>
> "I don't want to know," the Shadow says, "Because I already know. You yourself created this Town. You made everything here. The Wall, the River, the Woods, the Library, the Gate, Winter, everything. Even this Pool, and this snow." (Murakami 1991:398–99; translation modified)

We didn't need to be told—we knew from the beginning that the person who created this "world" was "I." Murakami cannot escape from this solipsism, no matter how many possible, multiple worlds he hypothesizes—so long as they themselves are products of a transcendental self. However, he has no intention of escaping. What is the "responsibility" that Murakami speaks of here? "'I have responsibilities,' I say. 'I cannot forsake the people and places and things I created as I pleased.... This is my world. The Wall is here to hold *me* in, the River flows through *me*, the smoke is *me* burning'" (Murakami 1991:399; translation modified).

This is the same thing as "I" seeking out and meeting a certain pinball machine in *Pinball in the Year 1973*. "Responsibility" with respect to something irrelevant that "I created as I pleased" is another name for "irresponsibility." Emphasizing responsibility toward something meaningless makes responsibility meaningless. In this way, "irresponsibility" is actively spoken of in terms of "ethics." That is to say, everything is playful and, at the same time, everything is serious.

However, that this is an escape from this world to which we already belong, or an escape from alterity, is announced by Murakami himself. For example, we should be mindful of the name Naoko, which appears at the beginning of *Pinball in the Year 1973*. Contrasting the fact that all the other names are arbitrary signs—and accordingly the world is nothing more than something that "I" "created as I pleased"—this ordinary name alone is something different that resists arbitrariness.

For example, in Saussure's linguistics, names are rejected. This is because names enforce the way of thinking that regards language as something connected to objects. Although we say general names as opposed to proper names, strictly speaking, general names are not names. In saying "general names," one is made to think that words are the names of things. By rejecting names, Saussure was able to draw out language not as something that is tied to objects but as something that, on the contrary, articulates and structures objects. Yet the result was to discard the problem of names in their original sense—that is, of proper names. Furthermore, it causes one to fundamentally lose sight of the link between language and the external world. The result is the kind of thinking where arbitrary differentiations in language are regarded as freely transforming the external world. This is parallel to the birth of idealism after Kant, when, that is to say, the "ego" (Fichte) or "spirit" (Hegel) that give birth to the world made their appearance. Today, this is called "text."

To be sure, this type of thinking has a certain reality in consumer society. In the 1980s, an advertisement copywriter or its theorist could indeed have nonchalantly flung out the following words: "Dull translation jobs or fraudulent copy about margarine, it's basically the same. Sure we're tossing out fluff, but tell me, where are the words with substance? C'mon now, there's no honest work anymore. Just like there's no honest breathing or honest pissing" (Murakami 1989:49; translation modified).

However, thinking that advertising copy sells products is a misapprehension produced during prosperous times, and the seller eventually confronts the "reality" of not being able to sell no matter what the copy. This "reality" is not an issue of the relationship between things and language. In the first place, whether something sells or doesn't sell is a question of the relationship with the other. It is exteriority as other—and not the exterior as object—that causes the collapse of the kind of thinking that the world can be arbitrarily structured.

Proper names are important not because they are tied to their objects but because they are always already given by others. In other words, proper names indicate the exteriority of the world, an exteriority that the transcendental subject cannot overcome. For example, when the "spirit," which creates the world and brings it to its completion, is called by the name Hegel, it has no choice but to become part of history.

Accordingly, Murakami is fixated on names (proper names). The question of what names are is ceaselessly asked in his works:

> "Nice kitty-kitty," said the chauffeur, hand not outstretched. "What's his name?"
>
> "He doesn't have a name."
>
> "So what do you call the fella?"
>
> "I don't call it," I said. "It's just there."
>
> "But he's not a lump just sitting there. He moves about by his own will, no? Seems mighty strange that something that moves by its own will doesn't have a name."
>
> "Herring swim around of their own will, but nobody gives them names."
>
> "Well, first of all, there's no emotional bond between herring and people, and besides, they wouldn't know their name if they heard it. Of course, giving a name is up to the person."
>
> "Which is to say that animals that not only move by their own will and share feelings with people but also can hear qualify as deserving of names then?"

"There, you've got it." The chauffer nodded repeatedly, satisfied. "How about it? What say I go ahead and give the little guy a name?"

"Don't mind in the least. But what name?"

"How about 'Kipper'? I mean you were treating him like a herring after all."

"Not bad," I said.

"You see?" said the chauffeur.

"What do you think?" I asked my girlfriend.

"Not bad," she said. "It's like being witness to the creation of heaven and earth."

"Let there be Kipper," I said.

"C'mere, Kipper," said the chauffeur, picking up the cat. The cat got frightened, bit the chauffeur's thumb, then farted. (Murakami 1989:152–53; translation modified)

Yet here the myth that God gives out names is simply replaced with the myth that the transcendental subject structures everything. In arguments of this kind, general names and proper names are always confused. Fundamentally speaking, infantile arguments of the above type can be called nominalist. Nominalists have asserted that individual objects are existing entities and can be represented by proper names. (In this case, individual objects do not signify just things. For example, events such as the 1969 campus riots are also included. Individual objects refer to things or units of reality that would disappear if they were taken apart any further.) This kind of thought was brought to its extreme by Bertrand Russell (1905). According to Russell, it must be possible to reject so-called proper names. Russell maintained that proper names that denote true subjects / existing entities are words such as "this" or "that," while ordinary proper names could be dissolved into a bundle of predicates, just as, for example, the name Mount Fuji could be replaced by the definite description, "the tallest mountain in Japan." In this way, Russell dissolved proper names in a different way than did Saussure.

It is not strange for a cat to have the name Kipper. If instead it were to be named Cat, that would not be objectionable either. This is because proper names do not serve as proper names because of the qualities of the individual object or of the name itself. Names have to do with people's attitude toward the individual object. This is tied to seeing the individual object not merely as "this," or as one thing of a certain type, but as "this thing that is none other." Canceling proper names with a definite description is to dissolve them in a bundle of predicates, or in a bundle of general concepts (assemblage). What Murakami is assiduously attempting is to erase proper names, or in other words to make this world out to be arbitrary.

Incidentally, Kripke (1980) has criticized the kind of thought expounded by Russell and revived the issue of proper names by introducing the modal logic of possible worlds. For example, in a counterfactual possible world, it would be possible to say, "Mount Fuji is not the tallest mountain in Japan." Yet it would not be possible to say, "The tallest mountain in Japan is not the tallest mountain in Japan." Thinking about possible worlds depends on proper names. In this way, Kripke maintains that proper names do not merely refer to things—they stabilize the reference.

Since I have examined these issues in detail elsewhere, here I will merely point out the fact that "reality" in terms of epistemology, and "reality" in terms of modal logic (possibilities, inevitabilities, and chance) are completely different (Karatani 1995). The world or reality described by Saussure or Russell is seen entirely in terms of epistemology. Murakami's question, "Does the year 1973 exist?" for example, is also epistemological. The answer is that 1973 is merely something that we arbitrarily structured. Yet "1973" as a proper name refers to the reality that a certain event occurred, which could have been otherwise but in actuality was that way. This cannot be dissolved into arbitrariness.

For example, Kobayashi Hideo writes as follows: "A person comes into the world embracing various possibilities. He may wish to become a scientist, a soldier, or a novelist, but he can never become other than who he is—a marvelous human fact" (1995:21).

Reality [*genjitsusei*] is something that exists within the possibility that it could have been otherwise, and yet is not. Romanticism is an escape from this kind of delimitation: for example, "I" in *Hard-Boiled Wonderland and the End of the World* sees reality as an arbitrary instance among limitless possibilities. But this in itself indicates his limitation.

"History" is "reality" in the sense mentioned above. However, Kobayashi attempts to understand this astonishing "reality" as "necessity" (fate). In the end, however, this is nothing more than another strategy for securing the superiority (freedom) of the transcendental subject. From that standpoint, "history" itself eventually disappears.

5

Murakami's information theory–based worldview—or his view of "the end of the world"—is an escape from "reality" in the sense explained above and is a Romantic rejection of it. To put it another way, it is a rejection of proper names. As I have already mentioned, however, despite this attempt to replace proper names with differential signs—with, in this sense, typical numerals—Murakami informs us of its very impossibility from the beginning of *Pinball in the Year 1973*. The mark of this impossibility is the name Naoko. "Naoko" is not an arbitrary name given by "I." Rather, it indicates that Naoko is the sole, irreplaceable *this thing*. The same could be said for "1969."

In *Norwegian Wood*, Naoko makes a reappearance. At the same time, "1969" is historically reviewed. With respect to the recovery of proper names, or the relationship with "1969," Murakami's *Norwegian Wood* should be compared with Ōe's *Letters to My Sweet Bygone Years* [*Natsukashii toshi e no tegami*, 1987], which was written in about the same period. Just as Ōe looks back on *Football in the Year Man'en 1* from the middle of the 1980s in *Letters to My Sweet Bygone Years*, Murakami looks back on the world of *Pinball in the Year 1973* from the middle of the 1980s in *Norwegian Wood*. If we are to view *Pinball in the Year 1973* as a parody of *Football in the Year Man'en 1*, then these two authors confronted the same issues at the same time.

But what happened in the 1980s? The object to which Ōe and Murakami had been attached, whether it be from a negative stance or an escapist stance, abruptly vanished in this period. Concretely speaking, in the mid-1980s, it was claimed that Japan's capitalist economy had surpassed that of the United States and gained control of the world. At that time, the word "postmodern" began to gain fashion in Japan, but in the Japanese context, this signified the realization of the slogan "Overcoming Modernity." What had been planned in the Konoe cabinet's "new order" (1940) was realized during this period. It appeared as if the "aporias" with which Japanese society had struggled since the Meiji period (as Takeuchi Yoshimi wrote) had vanished. However, this was also the vanishing of what had enabled Japan's modern literature (novel) to exist.

The vanishing of these aporias led authors to look back to the period when they still existed. In contrast to the way in which Ōe's *Letters to My Sweet Bygone Years* is brimming with emotions of loss and grief, however, Murakami's *Norwegian Wood* is nonchalant. Murakami takes up the world from which he had escaped through irony in *Pinball in the Year 1973*. In a word, he had been released from the history indicated by the name Naoko. If irony is removed from Romantic irony, "Romantic" remains. That is to say, Murakami simply wrote a romance (love story) in *Norwegian Wood*.

Since he had been released from the history from which he had continually fled via irony, irony was no longer necessary or meaningful:

> That was in 1960, the year Bobby Vee sang "Red Rubber Ball." (Murakami 1985:17)

There is no need to "feign ignorance" in this way. By now, only a few people know about "1960." Moreover, the majority of people take Murakami's irony literally. The "landscape" that Murakami discovered in the past through an inversion of value is now a landscape that has become self-evident on a global scale.

Translated by Hisayo Suzuki

6
THE END OF THE MODERN NOVEL

1

As I read Ōe Kenzaburō's *Letters to My Sweet Bygone Years* [*Natsukashii toshi e no tegami*, 1987], I was reminded of Lawrence Durrell's *Alexandria Quartet*.[1] The initial volume in the latter has as its first-person narrator "I," the novelist who is supposed to have written it, while the second volume takes the form of a revision of that novel by the same "I" in a moment of critical self-reflection. The third volume is written as an objective third-person novel, so that the "I" appearing in it is thoroughly relativized, merely one character among others. The world that in the first two volumes centered on male–female relations is seen here from a bird's-eye view and becomes a political world. The fourth volume is written once again from the perspective of "I." Guided by a woman named Clea, "I" achieves a degree of self-awareness and in the end manages to shake free from the consciousness of writing a novel. The work

---

This chapter was originally titled "Kindai bungaku no owari" (The End of Modern Literature). Since Karatani subsequently published a separate, widely cited essay and book by the same title, the chapter's title has been changed in consultation with the author to avoid confusion between them.

1 I previously discussed these issues and Durrell in my master's thesis, "The Dialectic of the *Alexandria Quartet*" [*Arekusandoria karutetto no benshōhō*], reprinted in *Collected Early Essays by Karatani Kōjin* [*Karatani Kōjin shoki ronbunshū*]. The year I submitted my thesis was also the year that *Football in the Year Man'en 1* was published. When I read Ōe's *Letters to My Sweet Bygone Years*, which looks back nostalgically at that year, I couldn't help but recall what I, too, had written then. [Author's note]

concludes with the words "Once upon a time": the beginning of a story [*monogatari*].[2]

The Alexandria Quartet is a romance novel, a political novel, and—seen from a different viewpoint—a bildungsroman and even a metafictional novel. It is a "total novel," albeit in a different sense from the way that Marxists use that term. It is not total in that it synthesizes a variety of perspectives but rather in that it presents perspective (subjectivity) itself in the form of absolute subjectivity—or, to say the same thing in different words, in that it represents the extinguishing of perspective. In its final stage, "I" has already given up writing novels. What emerges at the end is the "story."

Looked at in this way, it is clear that its structure corresponds to that of Hegel's *Phenomenology of Spirit*. That is, the four volumes of the quartet parallel Hegel's chapters on natural consciousness, self-consciousness, reason, and absolute knowledge. In other words, the quartet traces the process by which "I" moves from "natural consciousness" to absolute knowledge as a novelist. At the same time, this is the process by which the novel reaches its own ending: the end of the novel as a genre. Durrell himself thought of the structure of the quartet in terms of the "time–space continuum" from the theory of relativity. He wasn't thinking of Hegel as he wrote—in fact, he probably hadn't even read Hegel. But what the theory of relativity brings to mind here is merely the structural equation of the four dimensions with the four volumes of the quartet. It in fact provides no necessary reason for structuring it along the lines of the *Phenomenology*. The reason it comes to resemble Hegel here derives from the fact that in it, it is impossible to separate the novel from the act of writing that novel, or to distinguish the novel from the one who writes that novel. Hegel's phenomenology of spirit is "the Science of the *experience of consciousness*" (1977:56), which includes simultaneously both the experience of the object of consciousness

---

[2] Karatani here and throughout the essay contrasts two genres of fictional narration: the *shōsetsu* (novel), which he associates with linear time, modernity, and enlightenment, and the *monogatari* (story), which he associates with cyclical time, as well as with both premodernity (as in *The Tale of Genji*) and postmodern critiques of modernity, as in the works of Nakagami Kenji.

and the consciousness of this experience—that is, the experience of self-consciousness. Accordingly, this is a forward-looking movement of the subject (both the subject of consciousness and the subject of perception) and, at the same time, a backward-looking, retrospective movement from the perspective of the "ending," in which "spirit" returns to itself.

When a novel appears in which it is difficult to distinguish that novel from the consciousness of it, from the consciousness of the act of writing that novel, it already amounts to a prophesy of the end of the novel as a genre. What Durrell was opposing was Proust's *Remembrance of Things Past*, or alternatively perhaps the form of temporality found in Judaism that, since it always has its sights on the ending, is forever postponing that ending. Durrell tried to set Irish laughter in opposition to this. This is a matter of "living within an eternally repeating time" (Ōe 1997:308). On this point, Durrell may have received a hint from Einstein's notion of the time–space continuum, one he took beyond its meaning in physics to help him transcend the concept of "time" as a linear unfolding. Nonetheless, the structure of his actual work bears a much stronger resemblance to Hegel.

In *Letters to My Sweet Bygone Years*, on the other hand, we find the key to the work's structure and meaning in Dante's *Divine Comedy*. The *Divine Comedy* is a record of the "experience" by which the soul (spirit) achieves purification. In this sense, we might say that Hegel, too, wrote his own version of the *Divine Comedy*. But nowhere in the *Divine Comedy* do we find the "experience" of existing within a duality: the inseparability of the novel and the one who writes the novel. To push this further, the perspective of *Letters to My Sweet Bygone Years* is a counterfeit version of a Japanese I-novelist's "gaze from the deathbed." This "gaze from the deathbed" is one type of "old age," but it is nothing more than an ordinary psychological subject.[3]

---

3 The I-novel (*watakushi shōsetsu* or *shishōsetsu*) is a prominent genre of fiction in modern Japan. Although its stories are conventionally understood to be autobiographical in origin, they are typically narrated in third-person voice and with a fair degree of narrative distance, as if the author were narrating from his deathbed. Hence, in Hegelian terms, they are not written in dialectical fashion from a perspective of absolute subjectivity.

For example, the subject that Kant refers to is in fact the subject of the "labor" that gives shape to the world. Accordingly, it lays the foundation for modern science, which pursues truth through a process of hypothesis and experimentation. In Hegel, too, spirit is posited as the labor that gives birth to and shapes the world. The "experience of consciousness" discussed in *The Phenomenology of Spirit* is nothing other than the "labor of spirit." In the same way, the "experience" written about in *Letters to My Sweet Bygone Years* is above all *work* (in the sense both of the work one does and of a literary work). This is not simply the experience that "I" encounters in the external world but rather the experience acquired as an author attempting to give form to it. There is one other reason *Letters to My Sweet Bygone Years* unintentionally comes to resemble Hegel, just as did Durrell: in it, the "experience of consciousness" occurs only through so-called labor. In fact, Ōe is the sole author (with the exception of Mishima Yukio) to realize and admit to others that novel writing is not the work of genius or a mystical happening but rather a form of "labor."

Having said that, the *work* I am quoting here is known as the work of one "Ōe Kenzaburō." Therefore, people might read it as an I-novel or as autobiography. They might read out of it Ōe's own painful "self-criticism," or again his skillful "self-defense." At the same time, however, we must note here that the characters in it, beginning with Brother Gii, are all entities produced and raised within the body of texts under discussion here. For example, *Football in the Year Man'en 1* [*Man'en gannen no futtobōru*, 1967] is mentioned in it as one of the works that "I" has previously written, yet in fact the materials for *Letters to My Sweet Bygone Years* originally derive from that earlier work. For example, in *Letters to My Sweet Bygone Years*, Brother Gii is described as being the model for the character Takashi in *Football in the Year Man'en 1*, but in fact the opposite is true. To put this another way, the text that is *Letters to My Sweet Bygone Years* may appear to be trying to write about the extratextual world and history, yet it remains wholly within the interior of this textual corpus.

In sum, while "I" here might appear to be "Ōe Kenzaburō," in fact he is not. The work may appear to be something like an autobiography written by the author "Ōe Kenzaburō," yet everything in it is woven out from the text itself. It gives the experience of "I," but at the same time it is also the self-realization of the text as subject. In Hegel's case, we have the individual "experience of consciousness," which is also on the other hand one moment in the self-realization of "spirit." It is in this sense that we can say that *Letters to My Sweet Bygone Years* takes a Hegelian form. At its ending, the following scene appears:

> My dear Brother Gii! I return again and again to this scene, the view from the island with the Tenkubo cypress. Brother Gii is lying in the grass. A little way off, Oset-chan and our younger sister are picking grass. Then I find myself sprawled out in the grass next to Brother Gii, and Hikari and Oyū-san have joined in the grass picking. The sun makes the pale green of the new buds on the willow trees sparkle brilliantly, the dark green of the cypress too has been washed clean by the nighttime rains, and the white flowers of the *yamazakura* cherry trees on the opposite shore flutter in the breeze. Time passes ever so slowly. Then a dignified old man appears and scolds us: *What are you doing, stopping here? Run up the mountain and cleanse yourself of your impurities! If you don't, the gods won't appear!* In great haste, all of us rush in the direction of the great cypress, running up the mountain. . . . Time returns in a cycle, and once again Brother Gii and I are lying on the grass, Oset-chan and our younger sister are picking the green grass, and the child-like Oyū-san and Hikari—who is so young and pure, whose handicap ends up actually giving him a sense of charming frankness—join in the circle to pick grass. The sun makes the pale green of the new buds on the willow trees sparkle brilliantly, the green of the cypress is an even deeper shade, and the white flowers of the *yamazakura* cherry trees on the opposite shore flutter without pause. At this

point a dignified old man should appear again and yell at us, but let us just remain here, we who have clamored up the hill, within this cyclical time, as if it were all a quiet, earnest game, frolicking in the grass on the island of the great cypress tree....

My dear Brother Gii! I have written countless letter after letter to the "we" who go on living within the eternally repeating time of that sweet, beloved year. These letters are a beginning: in the real world where you no longer exist, I will keep on writing until the end of my life, the life's work that lies ahead of me. (Ōe 1997:307–8)

In this pastoral scene, a scene of affirmation that is reached only after passing through the negation of everything, we hear the sort of voice that says "Once upon a time . . ." Here, everything will return again, everything becomes "a quiet, earnest game" played out "within this cyclical time." This, of course, is what Hegel would call "absolute knowledge."

2

In anthropological terms, "absolute knowledge" means "old age." In fact, Hegel describes this as follows:

The old man lives without any definite interest, for he has abandoned the hope of realizing the ideals which he cherished when he was young and the future seems to hold no promise of anything new at all; on the contrary, he believes that he already knows what is universal and substantial in anything he may yet encounter. The mind of the old man is thus turned only towards this universal and to the past to which he owes the knowledge of this universal. But in thus dwelling in the memory of the past and of the substantial element, he loses his memory for details of the present and for arbitrary things, names, for example, in the same measure that, conversely, he firmly retains in his mind the maxims of experience and feels obliged to preach to those younger than himself. But this wisdom, this lifeless, complete coincidence of the subject's activity with its world, leads back to the childhood in which there is no opposition, in the same way that the reduction of his physical functions to a process-less habit leads on to the abstract negation of the living individuality, to death.

The sequence of ages in man's life is thus rounded into a notionally determined totality of alterations which are produced by the process of the genus with the individual. (1971:64)

In this way, old age returns to its youth, and the cycle comes round to completion. Of course, this view is not unique to Hegel. In a sense, it parallels the view of the Romantic poets (Wordsworth, for example, and Coleridge) and marks the fundamental problem taken up by Romanticism. Here, the unfolding of spirit occurs by way of internal reflection, in opposition to immediate, sensible experience. But this process of maturation also means the loss of immediacy. Hegel puts it this way: "The more educated a man is, the less he lives in immediate intuition, but, in all his intuitions, at the same time lives in recollections; so that for him there is little that is altogether new but, on the contrary, the substantial import of most new things is something already familiar to him" (206). And yet aren't, for example, persons approaching old age more apt to envy the blind, reckless actions of youth than to feel pride in their own self-reflective insight? Mishima in his last years provides a clear example of this.

In Ōe's *Letters to My Sweet Bygone Years*, the following passage appears, attributed to Brother Gii:

> *Even when I was young, I had this feeling of grief that was at times violent.*[4] I couldn't agree more with your observation. Yes, I sometimes remember it, mine, yours—it all

---

4 The words in italics are Brother Gii's quotations from published transcripts of talks given by K.

comes back to me, together with the image of our youthful faces. When we talk about those days, it's all a little vague, but I think you can sense what I mean. Back then, K-chan, you were worried that your forehead looked too narrow. I happened to see you talking on TV this spring; my eyes went to your forehead, and this feeling just hit me.

Well, what did you say next? *I grew older, and I came to realize that the grief I felt had become something very quiet.* I have to agree with this, at least at a certain stage, up to a certain step. After all, I remember that I too until quite recently felt the same thing. But I am five years older than you, and so there is no way I can agree with your next comment: *From now on, as I grow older, this feeling (what I might call my very quiet grief) will simply grow deeper, I suppose.*

When you get older, you sometimes undergo a sudden reversal. A terrible, violent grief might be lying in wait for you—K-chan, do you ever think that? It may be a waste of time to point this out to you, who shows no sign of ever wanting to really read Dante, but his hell and purgatory are filled with old people tormented by violent grief. I looked at the transcript of your remarks, and it set me off to write this, a report of my recent state of being. Anyhow, I pray for your health—yours, Oyū-san's, the children's. (1997:10)

It is clear that when he wrote this work, Ōe was conscious of "old age"—and also that Mishima was at the back of his mind. It seems likely that Ōe felt pressured to make a certain choice.

The notion that in the midst of a deepening, quiet grief one achieves "absolute knowledge" characterizes Hegel—as well as the Romantic poet Wordsworth. They thought that the immediacy that had been lost could be recovered through internal recollection. In other words, they thought that the individual thing was absorbed into the general, the contingent into the necessary. Hegel's philosophy proclaims the triumph of this sort of "internalization." Alexandre Kojève explains this as follows:

> Proceeding in this fashion, Hegel finally comes to a point that is none other than his point of departure: the *final* synthesis is also the *initial* thesis. Thus he establishes that he has gone around or described a *circle*, and that if he wants to continue, he can only *go around again*: it is impossible to *extend* his description; one can only *make it again* as it has already been made once.
>
> This means that Hegel's discourse exhausts *all* the *possibilities* of thought. One cannot bring up any discourse in opposition to him which would not already be a part of his own discourse, which would not be reproduced in a paragraph of the System as a constituent element (*Moment*) of the whole. Thus we see that Hegel's discourse sets forth an *absolute* truth, which cannot be negated by anyone. (1980:194; italics in original)

Certainly, Hegel's system encompasses everything. For example, the Young Hegelian school (to which Marx belonged early on) criticized Hegel—and yet they were quite literally Young Hegelians; likewise, Kierkegaard ended up in a position of subjective existence, unable to achieve objectivity, which is to say he ended up a Young Hegelian. If "absolute knowledge" consists of the perfect repetition of the entire process by which it has been achieved, then in a sense even Nietzsche's "eternal return" is anticipated here. We must note, however, that this circularity becomes possible only through an "internalization" that sacrifices all contingency and all immediacy. Moreover, we can say that Hegel's system is all encompassing only because it is a form of pure speculation—or, to put it the other way around, only because everything has been lost in it. For example, note that in Hegel's *Phenomenology of Spirit*, not a single proper name appears. As in the passage I quoted above, Hegel wrote that an old man "loses his memory for details of the present and for arbitrary things, names." In this sense, "absolute knowledge" is "old age."

3

The "grief" of old age lies in the fact that the more fully one attains the stage of the general, the more one loses the immediate and the singular: the more one attains clarity of vision, the more one loses the ability to act blindly. But one also comes to realize that there exist singularities and contingencies that can never be subsumed under the general and the necessary. For example, let us suppose there is a cat named Blackie. It is an individual belonging to the category of "cat." Of course, none of us has ever seen the concept "cat"; what we have seen are a number of individual cats, from which we arrive at the generality of "cat." Blackie is that sort of individual. Cognition, even though it starts out from various individuals, eventually attains to generality. In this case, Hegel would say that each individual cat already harbored within itself the general category of "cat." But Blackie is also this specific cat, one that cannot simply be dissolved into the general category of "cat." For its owner, it is not interchangeable with any other cat. The very existence of a proper name here is connected to the notion of something irreplaceable and unlike any other. For example, when this cat dies, how will its owner overcome his or her "grief"? The "grief" arises precisely because it is a matter of this specific cat Blackie.

In Hegel, it is "old age" and "absolute knowledge" that forget names and move toward the general. Accordingly, for him, the individual known by the name Napoléon is simply a manifestation of a world historical idea (concept): that individual in himself already harbored the idea. For Hegel, the name Napoléon is merely something that indicates particularity and for that reason can be subsumed within a generality. And yet, as soon as we abandon the proper name Napoléon, history as such disappears. This is precisely what Hegel means when he discusses the end of history. It means the subsumption of all particular and contingent events, the subsumption, that is, of everything that makes history history.

In the deepening of our "grief," however, we come to realize the necessity of individual, contingent events, we realize that they cannot possibly be otherwise. Hegel's "absolute knowledge" arises with this sort of resolution. Ōe, too, seems to feel pressured to reach such a resolution. For example, Brother Gii says the following:

> The novel you're writing now seems to be still at the rough-draft stage, so what I'm about to say is by no means a final verdict.... But K-chan, you're using a first-person narrator to write about your family, especially Hikari-san, right? Reading it, I found myself wondering whether that was best. Up until now, K-chan, you've used the informal pronoun "I" [*boku*] for the first-person narrator in your novels, and in those novels where you wrote about your memories of childhood during the war or about the anxieties a youth feels in a new big city, it felt like it really worked for you. That "I" was clearly somebody close to the author, but it was also clearly a narrator who embodied the customs and mores of the age. The work was one social phenomenon, but so too was the author himself—the author who made ends meet by working as a home tutor and who ate his meals at cheap cafeterias, he was also a social phenomenon. There was a certain meaning that arose from this.
>
> But now, K-chan, now you're writing a novel about your real family, and you're using the more formal pronoun "I" [*watashi*] for your first-person narrator. That's how you're trying to write the story of how "I" has lived up until now, how "I" is living today, now that you are past the age of forty. It's just like that line from one of Sōseki's sad characters you quoted in a lecture once: "Please remember: this is how I lived." But if you're going to do it that way, as a person writing a novel, you really have to throw yourself into it. K-chan, are you fully conscious of this: have you really steeled yourself to do it? (Ōe 1997:270)

Previously, K-chan had written in a style in which "I" indicated something particular and, at the same time, a general category. But at some point, he changed to a style in which "I" takes on a strong sense of the particular. For example, in *A Personal Matter* [*Kojintekina taiken*, 1964], "I" is simultaneously something specific and something general. But in the novels in which Hikari appears, this is no longer always the case. In this series of novels, accordingly, proper names are repeated. What Brother Gii is asking about here is whether it is possible to bestow a universal meaning on a world of events that are so closely linked with specific proper names.

In *Letters to My Sweet Bygone Years*, unlike *Football in the Year Man'en 1*, we encounter actual, concrete place-names and dates. These are, as I noted before, nearly all autobiographical in nature. Yet these words of Brother Gii's, while being a comment on this novel, are also themselves something that belongs to the interior of the work. Brother Gii is critical of "I." However, this dialogue with Brother Gii is nothing more than an internal self-reflection by "I"—a conversation with his own self, an internal monologue.

For example, with regard to the happy ending in *A Personal Matter*, Brother Gii proposes that it should be revised. "I," after giving this serious consideration, ultimately rejects it. But Brother Gii's criticism in fact is simply an "internalization" of "Mishima Yukio's review of the book" (Ōe 1997:242). The abrupt appearance of the name "Mishima Yukio" here represents an attempt to insert this work into "history." But this is immediately internalized in the form of Brother Gii's words or, to put it another way, in the form of "I"'s internal monologue. In sum, *Letters to My Sweet Bygone Years* takes on a Hegelian form: it manifests the personal (that is, events associated with specific proper names) but then subsumes it into the general through a process of "internalization."

4

And yet the name "Mishima Yukio" that appears here, albeit only momentarily, is in fact connected with the question of ending, and therefore persists as a kind of exteriority that the work is unable to absorb into itself. This work is written almost entirely as a criticism of Mishima. It is interesting to note, incidentally, that Mishima's *Sea of Fertility* also parallels the form of Hegel's *Phenomenology of Spirit*. It depicts the "experience of consciousness" of Honda Shigekuni in the form of a tetralogy, a quartet of novels. The three active protagonists—that is, Matsugae Kiyoaki in *Spring Snow* [*Haru no yuki*, 1965–1967], Iinuma Isao in *Runaway Horses* [*Honba*, 1967–1968], and Princess Chantrapa in *The Temple of Dawn* [*Akatsuki no tera*, 1968–1970]—are all different in terms of external appearance and other aspects, but in the form taken by their lives they are identical. Moreover, only Honda Shigekuni is able to perceive this identity. Honda believes them all to be reincarnations of a single spirit.

In this way, *The Sea of Fertility* is, on the one hand, the "repetition of identity" of the protagonists and, on the other, the "experience of consciousness" of Honda Shigekuni, who seeks identity. Honda lacks the sort of naturalness and immediacy that the other characters possess. It is precisely by being cut off from these that he can exist in the form of "self-consciousness." What remains possible for him is to repeat that naturalness and directness in an ultimate cognition. But Honda never achieves that sort of "absolute knowledge." To the contrary, he is betrayed and left trapped in the barrenness and humiliations of old age.

In *The Decay of the Angel* [*Tennin gosui*, 1970–1971], the final volume, the protagonist Yasunaga Hideo is different from the characters in the preceding three volumes. Whereas each of them was able to live out freely his or her destiny, Yasunaga is conscious of being a reincarnation and strives to prove his identity with the earlier characters. In sum, Yasunaga represents the moment of "self-consciousness." What makes Yasunaga nothing more than a fake are precisely his attempts to become the real thing. Honda dislikes Yasunaga because they are the same type of person. *The Sea of Fertility* (the title refers to the surface of the moon) falls far short of reaching happy "absolute knowledge"; far from it, it reaches its conclusion in what is literally a barren wasteland.

Hence, whereas Mishima follows Hegel up to a point, in the end he rejects him. What Hegel was fighting against was

Romantic irony, as seen in Schlegel. It attempted to stop at and thereby preserve forever the moment of "possibility." In contrast, Hegel's stance was to accept all that had happened as having been inevitable and necessary. But Mishima—who made his authorial debut as the youngest member of the Japanese Romantic school, which during the war trumpeted its own brand of Romantic irony—once he reached his forties found himself decisively rejecting that version of maturity. He heaps barrenness and scorn on those who would think rather than act. He had already decided this before he wrote the tetralogy. On the day he finished writing the final volume, Mishima committed suicide after urging the Self-Defense Forces to mount a coup d'état.

Nonetheless, his actions then were counterfeit actions, on the same level as those of Yasunaga Hideo. In other words, when he tried to "identify" himself with the young officers who mounted the February 26, 1936, coup d'état, Mishima was already operating not in the manner of Iinuma Isao from *Runaway Horses* but rather in that of Yasunaga Hideo from *The Decay of the Angel*. Mishima himself was fully aware of this. According to Schlegel, seriousness is the highest form of irony. Mishima's actions were a game played to the death. Here we should recall Freud's words: "The opposite of play is not seriousness but—reality" (1957:174; translation modified). This "reality" means, of course, "history."

5

Looked at in this way, it becomes apparent that Mishima and Ōe are linked by their opposing stances toward the problem of Romanticism. Simply put, Mishima refuses "old age," while Ōe embraces it. Of course, this is not merely a problem of Romanticism in the narrow sense, nor is it a problem of relative age. For example, Mishima was unable to find any meaning in being alive after World War II, which was supposed to be the world's final war. But that same war was also the first nuclear war, which subsequently made total war impossible. What Ōe calls the "atomic age" was a product of that war. Their stances here—one that sees no meaning in living on after the final war, the other that trembles in fear at the coming final war (total nuclear war)—are two sides of the same coin. In the way their consciousnesses are fixated on the problem of "ending," the two are linked as if by an umbilical cord. Moreover, this cannot be detached from "history."

Ōe tries with all his might to negate Mishima, just as Hegel tried with all his might to negate Schlegel. But this is not a unilateral gesture on his part. In short, it is not simply a matter of Ōe, who comes from a later generation, rejecting the older Mishima. After all, Mishima began writing *The Sea of Fertility* around the same time that Ōe published *Football in the Year Man'en 1*. Mishima's criticism of the "ending" in *A Personal Matter* applies equally well to *Football in the Year Man'en 1*. It is an "ending" in which "I," who would rather think, admits his defeat at the hands of Takashi, who would rather act—and yet still tries to recuperate and repossess this within his consciousness (through internalization). This is not simply a question of whether or not it is a happy ending. It seems likely that Mishima, when he wrote *The Sea of Fertility*, deliberately intended to reject an Ōe-style ending.

But I cannot complete my discussion here by just speaking about Mishima, Ōe, and Murakami. I would like to introduce a writer who, while sharing many points in common with these others, is qualitatively different from them: Nakagami Kenji, who in 1983 published *The End of the Earth, the Supreme Time* [*Chi no hate shijō no toki*]. Since *Football in the Year Man'en 1*, Ōe has used as the basis for his works the "remote forest village" on the island of Shikoku, and Nakagami has similarly used as the setting for a series of works the "alley" [*roji*] in southern Kishū. This was not necessarily because of the influence of his predecessor, Ōe. Ōe's "remote forest village" was suggested to him by Faulkner's use of the fictional Yoknapatawpha County as the setting for a multivolume saga. Nakagami was similarly influenced by Faulkner. This fictional place (the "alley") is connected to actual historical space (the outcaste *buraku* districts), but it also maintains an existence as an independent, symbolic space.

The End of the Earth, the Supreme Time was written as a continuation of *The Cape* [*Misaki*, 1975] and *The Sea of Withered Trees* [*Karekinada*, 1978]. This trilogy is clearly linked by a strong Oedipal motif: the hero, Akiyuki, is driven by a desire to kill his real father, Hamamura Ryūzō. But in *The End of the Earth, the Supreme Time*, the protagonist Akiyuki vaguely senses that he is losing his urge to kill his father, that the act is losing its meaning; nevertheless, out of inertia he still plots to kill him. It is at this point that the father, Hamamura Ryūzō, takes matters into his own hands and commits suicide. Upon seeing his father's corpse, Akiyuki mutters, "That's not it."

What does this mean? To kill the father is to take a step beyond the preceding generation, to initiate ceaseless forward progress. Moreover, to have a father worthy of being killed gives rise to a "subject" that takes shape by internalizing the father's repression. Modernity is a world ruled by this sort of Oedipal motif, as is the modern novel. In that sense, the work *The Sea of Withered Trees* preserves in itself the core of a modern novel, no matter how hard it tries to negate this. By contrast, what appears in *The End of the Earth, the Supreme Time* is the self-destruction of the norm that one was supposed to overcome.

The End of the Earth, the Supreme Time was written after the disappearance of the Shingū special *buraku* district, the symbolic setting that Nakagami in his works calls the "alley"; it was torn down as part of a redevelopment project in the early 1980s. This redevelopment project did not solve the problem of discrimination. In terms of external appearances, however, it erased it from view. Moreover, it also extinguished the cultural base that had fostered resistance against discrimination—the "alley" itself. Of course, the primary focus in Nakagami's works is not on this sort of localized event. In fact, what takes place in Nakagami's "alley" was at that time taking place everywhere in Japan, as it floated on the economic bubble of the 1980s.

I have previously argued that in the 1980s, the aporias of modern Japan disappeared. This does not mean that they were somehow resolved, but rather that in terms of external appearances they were erased from view. Moreover, we did not bring about this change: it was brought about through the workings of capitalism. It is as if, before we were able to kill our father, the father killed himself. It is at such a moment that the hero Akiyuki thinks, "That's not it." This utterance likewise describes Nakagami's reaction to Japanese postmodernism. In the end, his protagonist Akiyuki sets fire to the grass fields that sit on the former site of the alley.

But in the wake of the trilogy, Nakagami, who together with his protagonist Akiyuki had burned up the space that had grounded his works up until then, now encountered an unprecedented difficulty. After this, the works Nakagami wrote were no longer novels but rather stories [*monogatari*]. For example, in *A Thousand Years of Pleasure* [*Sennen no yuraku*, 1984], two transcendental perspectives appear: that of the midwife Oryū no Oba, who equates and affirms all things from the viewpoint of life (birth), and the priest Reijo-san, who equates and affirms all things from the viewpoint of death. In it, Hanzō and all the other various protagonists are essentially identical, so that for Oryū no Oba it makes no difference which comes first and which comes last. They are all repetitions of the identical "noble, stagnant Nakamoto bloodline." In this world, there is no such thing as history. All events and occurrences are absorbed into a formal identity. The deaths of the protagonists are already foretold by destiny. That is to say, they are viewed from the perspective of the "ending." The world of *A Thousand Years of Pleasure* is not a premodern world, nor is it a legendary world. It is a posthistorical world. Following *The End of the Earth, the Supreme Time*, it seems, it was no longer possible to write "novels."

If *A Thousand Years of Pleasure* depicts a world of reminiscence, driven by a deep sense of loss following the disappearance of the "alley," *Different Tribes* [*Izoku*, 1984–1991] depicts the subsequent world of the youths who have lost the symbolic space of the "alley." They become emperor worshippers, mobilized under the lead of a man who has been a behind-the-scenes leader of the right wing since before the war and who is now plotting a new "Greater East Asia Co-Prosperity Sphere"; they recruit Ainu, Korean, and Taiwanese youths into this scheme. But the protagonists who manage to get out of Japan gradually come to reject emperor worship and instead form alliances based on an antirightist pan-Asianism, even joining in to fight alongside communist guerrillas in the Philippines. It is worth noting that what I elsewhere—in reference to Ōe's *Football in the Year Man'en 1*—have called "the discursive space of modern Japan" is repeated in its entirety here. But in this work, what the youths are able to rally together transcends ethnic differences and is based on an identity rooted in the "bruises" they all bear on their bodies. In sum, this is a story along the same lines as Bakin's *Tale of the Eight Dogs* [*Nansō Satomi hakkenden*, 1814–1842]; the work is less a novel than a kind of comic-book world.

Nonetheless, after *The End of the Earth, the Supreme Time*, Nakagami did write at least one additional "novel": *Miracles* [*Kiseki*, 1989]. It was written around the same time as Ōe's *Letters to My Sweet Bygone Years* and Murakami's *Norwegian Wood* [*Noruwei no mori*, 1987]. I want to focus on this work because in it, "history" once again appears. In *Miracles*, as in *A Thousand Years of Pleasure*, we find the transcendental, all-encompassing perspectives of the midwife Oryū no Oba, representing the assimilation of all life (a lack of discrimination), and the priest Reijo-san, representing the assimilation of all death (again, a lack of discrimination). But in *Miracles*, there is one additional perspective, one that in fact probably provides the work's dominant viewpoint: that of Tomo no Oji, the alcoholic mental patient who is haunted by the fantasy that he has become a fish. Not only does the work begin and end with his hallucinations, but each chapter begins with his reminiscences, together with his hallucinations.

In *A Thousand Years of Pleasure*, from the perspective of Oryū no Oba, who seems to have lived in the "alley" for thousands, perhaps tens of thousands, of years, the various protagonists reach a kind of salvation within a greater, absolute sadness. But in *Miracles*, Tomo no Oji is nothing more than an old man, a pathetic, alcoholic ex-gangster of the sort who should be watched over by Oryū no Oba and Reijo-san. His sadness is perhaps best called "remorse." This feeling of "remorse" is on display over the course of the entire work, as if to eat away at any possible sense of absolute sadness and affirmation:

Tomo no Oji, like one tracing through the lineages of the gods and buddhas, recalled to mind Taichi of the noble, stagnant Nakamoto bloodline in the alley: that was how it was that time, this is how it was that other time. At the psychiatric hospital in Miwasaki, what went on speaking from morning to night, day after day to Oryū no Oba, whose appearance hovered somewhere indistinctly between illusion and reality, was nothing other than the profound lamentation of the alcoholic Tomo no Oji. (Nakagami 1996:191)

To feel "remorse" is to think that things could have been otherwise. It is to be conscious of the ineffaceable differences that arise between the various characters, of the singularity of events that cannot be absorbed within the "identity" represented by Oryū no Oba and Reijo-san. In this way, in *Miracles* we are presented with a temporality that cannot be absorbed into any sort of structural identity. The same is true for spatiality in the work. For example, in *A Thousand Years of Pleasure*, the "alley" functions as a complete universe. But here the "alley" is given a proper name: Shingū. It is no longer a self-enclosed world surrounded by an absolute exteriority (the other world) but rather a world surrounded by a relative exteriority. In fact, the local Shingū *yakuza* are mere subordinates to a vast organization headquartered in Osaka that "aims at complete nationwide domination." The "world" [*tenka*] that Taichi wants to conquer has lost all cosmological significance, as the following passage demonstrates: "Hey, Oryū no Oba, when I rule the world and become the boss of this whole area, I'll build me a house that's just like a castle on top of this mountain" (418).

In *Miracles*, there is no longer any apparatus functioning that is capable of switching back and forth between the noble and the vulgar, the abject and the sacred, pain and pleasure. Despite numerous interjections made from Oryū no Oba's vantage point, Tomo no Oji finds himself "starting to think that all living things, the grass and trees, the beasts and fowls, fish and insects, all of them are cut into by a sharp ray of light so that they mistake pain for pleasure, confuse pleasure with pain—that heaven and earth, that this world and the underworld, that all of creation is nothing more than a dream seen by a single person" (Nakagami 1996:430). This is not, however, "the decay of angels." What appears here is instead the fatal flaw of a circuit that would try to connect heaven and earth, the sacred and the profane. "Heaven" now exists only in the fantasies of Tomo no Oji, who considers himself the alcoholic reincarnation of an angel. The world that presented itself as an actuality in *A Thousand Years of Pleasure* here appears in the form of nothing more than the hallucination of an aging alcoholic.

Tomo no Oji sees everything from the perspective of the "ending." He tries to accept all things, but this is possible only from within madness. He becomes an enormous grouper fish, swimming through the ocean, and eats the flesh of Taichi, who was killed by being wrapped up in a reed screen and then drowned in the ocean. But it is also stressed several times that this endless cycle (eternal return) is madness, that it is a hallucination that attracts the laughter and scorn of the local youths.

But if one rejects the sort of play advocated by Schlegel, and also the Hegelian notion of reconciliation, what else is left? Earlier, I noted Nietzsche's "eternal return" not only failed to transcend Hegel, it was actually anticipated by him. This may be true in the ordinary sense. But yet, in the following letters, Nietzsche writes some very strange things:

> I am Prado, I am also Prado's father, I venture to say that I am also Lesseps . . . at root every name in history is I.

> My beloved Princess Ariadne . . . In India I was Buddha. In Greece, I was Dionysius. Alexander and Caesar were incarnations of me. . . . Finally, I was Voltaire and Napoléon. I may even have been Wagner. . . . I was crucified on the cross.[5]

---

5 The first passage is from Nietzsche's letter to Jakob Burkhardt, January 6, 1889 (1969:346–48). The second passage is from Nietzsche's letter to Cosima Wagner, January 3, 1889; the text of the letter is missing from this English-language edition of Nietzsche's letters, and the translation is by Michael K. Bourdaghs.

For Nietzsche, the eternal return meant the repetition of individualities (singularities) that could never be internalized or reduced to generalities; it meant the recuperation of proper names. It is also true, however, that Nietzsche wrote these letters in the year that he went mad. Three years after writing *Miracles*, Nakagami died of liver cancer. His final wish was to live longer, even if just one day longer, than Mishima, who committed suicide at the age of forty-five.

Translated by Michael K. Bourdaghs

7

BUDDHISM AND FASCISM

1. Buddhism and Modern Japan

Buddhism, which is said to have entered Japan in the sixth century, was established as a state religion in the seventh and eighth centuries because the Yamato court, which at the time had achieved unification through the conquest of disparate clans, made use of it as a world religion that would transcend the gods of the multiple clans. For this reason, it was at the time no more than an esoteric religion centered on the pacification and protection of the realm by way of prayer and ritual [*chingo kokka*]. If it had remained as such, no matter its theoretical profundity, it would undoubtedly have been absorbed into native religions. Thus one can only truly say that Buddhism took root in Japan at the stage of Kamakura Buddhism, which was produced by monks such as Hōnen, Shinran, Dōgen, and Nichiren. They had originally studied at the state-sanctioned monastic center on Mount Hiei, but they discarded this training and began to proselytize directly to the people.

Philosopher Watsuji Tetsurō (1962) argued that Buddhism in Japan had already been given its unique interpretation in the seventh and eighth centuries, and that this interpretation blossomed in thirteenth-century Kamakura Buddhism. In addition, Suzuki Daisetsu (1968) wrote that Kamakura Buddhism gave expression to the "Japanese spirit." In other words, they saw the

An earlier version of this chapter was translated by Joseph A. Murphy as "Buddhism, Marxism and Fascism in Japanese Intellectual Discourse in the 1930's and 1940's: Sakaguchi Ango and Takeda Taijun" (Karatani 2001). I also consulted James Dorsey's translation of "The Irrational Will to Reason: The Praxis of Sakaguchi Ango" (Karatani 2010).

revolutionary aspect of Kamakura Buddhism as the Japanization of Buddhism. In my view, however, Kamakura Buddhism was epoch-making because in it the radical thought that Buddhist texts originally contained was read anew.[1] The question, then, is: Why did it occur at this historical moment in Japan?

The city of Kamakura, which served as the site of the first military government, is located at a distance from the centers of the old order, Kyoto and Nara. During the transitional period from clan society (aristocratic rule) to the feudal system (military rule), Buddhism was reborn when it was read outside the framework of its traditional interpretation. What may appear as the Japanization of Buddhism was, if anything, a return to origins. Shinran, Dōgen, and Nichiren each selected a Buddhist text and purified its logic. For example, whereas Shinran (Jōdo Shinshū, or True Pure Land sect) thoroughly rejected the will to seek salvation on one's own and advocated devout faith in a transcendent being (Amida), Dōgen (Sōtō school of Zen Buddhism) posited the transcendent as nothingness and advocated fervent Zen meditation, while Nichiren (Nichirenshū, or Nichiren sect) advocated national reform based on Buddhist teachings. These are not as different as they appear on the surface. In China, in fact, they formed a unity, existing within the same temple as expedient measures, with Zen being directed at intellectuals and Pure Land teachings at the masses. But in Kamakura Buddhism, such teachings were separated and emerged as different religious sects.

As a result, Zen was generally accepted in the new ruling classes—the warrior and intellectual classes—but did not spread among the masses. To the extent that "culture" means

---

1 However, this is not something that contradicts the "Japanization" of Buddhism. For example, in Germany Luther's movement to return to the Bible was carried out by way of his translation of the Bible into German. Furthermore, this translation helped to create the national language of Germany. In other words, from a certain perspective, in Germany the Protestant Reformation was nothing other than the Germanization of Christianity. In fact, Shinran, Nichiren, and Dōgen wrote in a style mixing Chinese characters and the phonetic *kana* syllabary, directed at the masses. It would have been impossible for Buddhism to "take root" without such a language. [Author's note]

the culture of the ruling classes, it is no stretch to say that Zen came to shape what today goes under the name of "Japanese culture." However, it does not represent the full extent of Japanese Buddhism. What is of greater importance in Kamakura Buddhism are the True Pure Land and Nichiren sects, which gradually spread among the populace and even led to the creation of peasant nations and self-governing city-states as the feudal order collapsed leading into the Warring States period of the fifteenth to sixteenth centuries. In histories of Buddhism, such phenomena are often described as marking the politicization and decline of Buddhism. But that is a thoroughly modern view, which sees religion as a question of individual, internal faith. Furthermore, it is nothing more than a kind of false advertising that presents Buddhism as particularly apolitical and nonmilitant.

In Europe, the Reformation led directly to peasant wars and citizen revolts. This signifies less the power of religion than that the Reformation itself emerged in a period of social transformation. The fact that in the fifteenth and sixteenth centuries Buddhism created such self-governing cities as Sakai (True Pure Land sect) and Kyoto (Lotus sect), or independent states such as Kaga, far from being a sign of Buddhism's degradation, simply demonstrates that Buddhism was a universal religion. Furthermore, if we situate the phenomena that arose in Japan in the context of post-Columbian "world capitalism," its global synchronicity becomes apparent (Inamura 1937 [author's note]).

In the latter half of the sixteenth century, the Society of Jesus spread throughout western Japan. Yet its significance in relation to the people was virtually the same as that held by the True Pure Land and Nichiren sects in relation to those living in eastern Japan. The Society of Jesus represented a religious reformation on the Catholic side to counter the Protestant Reformation. And one of its founders, Francis Xavier, himself came to Japan, devoting himself to missionary work. As I elaborate later, there were not a few monks and warriors associated with Zen Buddhism who converted to Christianity, but no such phenomenon arose among the monks and believers of the True Pure Land sect. In other words, the Jesuits were unable to encroach upon the might of True Pure Land Buddhism [commonly referred to as the Ikkō, or "single-minded" sect], which was spreading throughout eastern Japan.

The reason that Oda Nobunaga—who most fully utilized the guns and cannons that had spread throughout the country in his attempt to establish absolute power—protected and supported the Society of Jesus is that he had his sights set on the Ikkō sect as his greatest target. In actuality, it was the Christian daimyo who suppressed the Ikkō sect. Without realizing that they might be next to fall, these Christian daimyo suppressed the social revolution that took the form of this religious movement.

It appears as though Nobunaga, colluding with the urban bourgeoisie of Sakai, was aspiring to become a European-style absolute sovereign who annihilates the feudal lords. In truth, he was aware of such circumstances existing overseas (Ruiz de Medina 1988 [author's note]). Nevertheless, it was precisely this iconoclastic posture that led to Nobunaga's death at the hands of someone with ties to the established order. Toyotomi Hideyoshi, who became Nobunaga's successor, turned to the suppression of Christianity after the surrender of the True Pure Land sect. The period of social upheaval and mobility [*gekokujō*] that had spread beginning in the fifteenth century was brought to an end by someone (Hideyoshi) who had literally embodied it himself.

After Hideyoshi's death, Tokugawa Ieyasu, who had gained control over the entire country, took a variety of measures to ensure the longevity of his regime. This included, of course, the policy of national seclusion [*sakoku*], which meant a withdrawal from the world market. Instead of becoming an absolute sovereign who destroyed the feudal lords as Nobunaga had intended, Ieyasu left the various daimyo in their domains while prohibiting their military and economic growth, following policies such as the daimyo's alternate-year residence in Edo [*sankin kōtai*] to consume and exhaust their financial power. This was also a system that formally revered the emperor and utilized his authority while in actuality keeping him confined in Kyoto.

These characteristics of the Tokugawa order can most typically be seen in relation to religion. The Tokugawa regime persecuted not only Christianity but the Nichiren sect as well, while at the same time using the True Pure Land sect as a means to suppress such other heretical sects and religions.[2] The entire populace was required to belong to "patron households" [*danka*] affiliated with Buddhist temples, many of them Pure Land or True Pure Land temples.[3] Buddhism, which had given rise to peasant-led revolutionary wars in the sixteenth century because of its emphasis on the transcendence and equality of the individual, became an administrative tool binding people to the land. In this way, True Pure Land Buddhism expanded to the point where it included a large proportion of Buddhist adherents in Japan. At the same time, it lost its significance as a religion. Even today, the majority of Japanese belong to patron households dating to the Tokugawa [Edo] period [1600–1867], but they do not see themselves as Buddhists.

The "prohibition against transcendence," enacted in all areas in order to protect the pax Tokugawa, was precisely what allowed the Tokugawa regime to last for 250 years. Alexandre Kojève referred to Japan after the Battle of Sekigahara in 1600 as "posthistorical" and called human existence there a kind of "snobbery" (1980:161n.6); whatever one may call it, it was something formed by the Tokugawa order, which maintained its longevity by deliberately avoiding "transcendence." It is no exaggeration to say that what is currently considered Japanese culture or the Japanese way of life was created during this period. It was something fundamentally different from what had existed in antiquity, the feudal period, or the Renaissance-like period of the fifteenth and sixteenth centuries.

In *The Peasant War in Germany*, Engels writes that Luther's betrayal, the defeat of the peasants, and the profusion of competing nobles set Germany back by two hundred years; a similar statement can be made about Japan. It was the defeat and conversion of the True Pure Land sect (Honganji) in the sixteenth century that gave rise to the Tokugawa order. It was in 1867 that

---

2 The Fujufuse branch of Nichiren Buddhism was outlawed by the Tokugawa government in the seventeenth century. See Ooms (1985:190–92).

3 On the *danka* system, see Hur (2007).

this Tokugawa order collapsed at the hands of the anti-*bakufu* movement that emerged from domains in the west such as Satsuma and Chōshū. Incidentally, it was four years later that the federation of states governed by semifeudal lords that was the legacy of the peasant war was unified by Prussia. Furthermore, it was on the model of Prussia that the Meiji government built its regime.

In modern Japan, Buddhism was never able to recover the type of social significance it had held until the sixteenth century. After Meiji, Buddhism was able to live on as an old custom and system—that is, one centered on funeral rites. Therefore, it did not even have an active need to recuperate itself as a religion. As a result, after the Meiji period [1868–1912], it was only the new religions arising from Shinto, as well as those arising from the Nichiren sect—which was subject to persecution during the Tokugawa period—that were able to have vitality as religions among the people.

In modern Japan, Buddhism came to be privileged only among intellectuals, for whom Buddhism was seen as a principle to be used to counter the modern West. Yet this understanding was itself something derived from the West. After the Meiji period, it was thought that in order to establish Buddhism as a scholarly discipline, it would be necessary to go back to the original Sanskrit texts instead of the Chinese translations that had been previously used. Therefore, scholars went to study in England and Germany. In other words, they drifted away from established Buddhist tradition and encountered a Buddhism that had been routed through Europe. In addition, Japanese philosophers became aware of the movement in Europe, exemplified by Schopenhauer, to discover in Buddhism a key to overcoming the limits of modern Western thought. Consequently, Buddhism was seen as having the capacity to counter the modern West. Zen Buddhism in particular was seen as suitable for this task. For Zen, in contrast to the popular True Pure Land sect, had spread only among the intellectual elite, and in particular within the warrior class. Furthermore, Zen most explicitly named the transcendent being as emptiness and therefore could appear as the sole principle to rival Christianity and Western philosophy.

At the same time, some True Pure Land monks, such as Kiyozawa Manshi, returned to the teachings of the founding father, Shinran, to attempt religious reformation, but this was a response to the perceived threat posed by the spread of Christianity among intellectuals. Furthermore, this religious reformation was itself something that had been learned from Christianity. The most telling example was the attempt to spread the text *Tannishō* [*Notes Lamenting Differences*], which transmitted the words of Shinran in an easily comprehensible form.[4] In other words, the *Tannishō* was "discovered" as a text that would be equivalent to the Bible. In some ways, it was not a forced analogy. In fact, the Jesuit missionaries of the sixteenth century had recognized similarities between True Pure Land Buddhism and Christianity. Nonetheless, the sudden emergence of the *Tannishō*, which had not been widely read until then, as the Bible of True Pure Land Buddhism can only be understood as an effect of the influence of Christianity as well as the attempt to counter it.

Generally speaking, however, religion in the Meiji period, whether Christianity or Buddhism, did not have widespread influence. Christianity, which spread among the intelligentsia of the time, was unable to respond to the social contradictions exposed by the rapid development of industrial capitalism. Many Christians therefore felt dissatisfaction with internal "faith" and converted to socialism. In the 1930s, however, there was a revival of Christianity and Buddhism among intellectuals. Differing from the Meiji period, this was a phenomenon produced by the collapse of the socialist movement. For example,

---

4 Chikazumi Jōkan [1870–1941], a monk of the Ōtani school of True Pure Land Buddhism, worked toward the reformation of True Pure Land Buddhism along with Kiyozawa Manshi. He opened a religious learning center and founded the journal *Kyūdō* [*Seeking After Truth*] and widely introduced Shinran's *Tannishō* to society; he is said to have exerted a strong influence on college students in particular. See Ikeda (1987). [Author's note]

the Kyoto school philosopher Miki Kiyoshi wrote a study of Pascal after studying with Heidegger in Germany; upon his return to Japan, he was active as a Marxist. However, upon falling away from Marxism, he turned to Shinran—in other words, to the Japanese Pascal (Miki 1966, 1968). That is to say, "Shinran" signified not only salvation from the sense of guilt and nihilism that was a result of the conversion away from Marxism but also a certain type of "return to Japan."

To repeat, Buddhism was discovered as a principle of Eastern or Japanese culture that would counter the modern West. It was Okakura Kakuzō who advanced this kind of perspective. Okakura found in Buddhism a principle to unify the arts of the East, but this principle was, in effect, unrelated to religion. What was important to him was art, and Buddhism was nothing more than a logic to explain it. Nevertheless, Okakura's writings were aimed at foreign readers and had virtually no influence in Japan in his time. It was Watsuji who, after World War I, spread the type of perspective associated with Okakura. As a student, Watsuji had audited Okakura's lectures on "The History of Far Eastern Art" at Tokyo Imperial University, which are said to have made a profound impression on him.[5]

Among Watsuji's writings, *A Pilgrimage to Ancient Temples* [*Koji junrei*, 1919] had the broadest popular influence. There were many who "discovered" Buddhism or ancient Japanese culture by way of this book. However, the Buddhism that Watsuji discerned was nothing other than art. What he admired above all were the old temples. The ethnologist Yanagita Kunio claimed that ancient temples should be colorful and gaudy, but Watsuji and those influenced by him loved dilapidated, somber temples. This is similar to the European Romantics' discovery of the Middle Ages in the desolate ruins of old castles. Just as they discovered Catholicism, Japanese intellectuals discovered Buddhism. What they found, however, was an aesthetic object of the imagination, completely unrelated to the Buddhism of the past.

5 For the transcriptions of these lectures, see Okakura (1980).

Romanticism represented the first critique of modernity in the West, and subsequent critiques would tacitly return to it. A similar situation existed in Japan. What is typically cited as the tradition of Buddhism is nothing more than a discovery of the modern consciousness, by way of an aesthetic imagination. The kind of turn experienced by Watsuji after World War I would come to the fore in the late 1930s under the rubric of "overcoming modernity." For example, a symposium under this title was held in early 1942, soon after the beginning of the Pacific War. This conference was convened by the group affiliated with the journal *Literary World* [*Bungakukai*], led by literary critic Kobayashi Hideo, but its participants also included representatives of the Kyoto school such as Nishitani Keiji, as well as of the Japanese Romantic school. The participants are frequently lumped together with fanatical reactionaries, emperorists, xenophobes, and imperialists, yet they not only differed from those types but were, if anything, opposed to them. As an illustration of this, we should note the participation of the Catholic theologian Yoshimitsu Yoshihiko. Yoshimitsu sought the overcoming of modernity in a "new Middle Ages," which he distinguished from both a Romantic nostalgia and a Eurocentric perspective:

> More precisely, the "new Middle Ages" must be sought less in the individual moments of the Middle Ages than in the more internal and subjective form of a *"new order,"* whereby the idea of metaphysical unity as sought but unrealized during the Middle Ages comes to be discussed and explored as a task of the new era. It is not to be found in any impossible and meaningless return to the historic Middle Ages....
>
> Hence, for this author, the problem of the West as a mere "culture" of human society located on the European peninsula is, apart from its religious and metaphysical significance, a matter of indifference, regardless of its intrinsic value. Just as, before God, both East and West face the *one source of love and truth*, so too are they given

their own *immediate existential tasks*. With the utmost earnestness, we must live the path of man—that is, the path to God—within the spiritual history and tradition of our homeland. Yet this standpoint does not, as some believe, lead to a kind of humanism or relativism of the truth, since *existence*, which is concretely grasped and realized as a singe *truth* (logos), is determined *providentially*, as it were, in each of its historic and social forms. (2008:88, 91)

While other speakers presented a "Japanese-style" thought based on Buddhism or Shinto, Yoshimitsu in this way argued in favor of Catholicism. Although Japan's alliance with Germany may have played a part in making possible such an assertion from a Catholic theologian at a time when deification of the emperor had reached an extreme level, the more significant reason is that Buddhism and Christianity, despite their differences as religions, maintain essentially similar structures. In effect, both Christianity and Buddhism were "discovered" by Romanticism.

In this way, what is presented as Eastern or Buddhist discourse in modern Japan was in fact always Romanticist and aesthetic. One can say the same of philosopher Nishida Kitarō, a central figure in the Kyoto school. The Marxist Tosaka Jun, a student of Nishida's who died in prison in 1945, pointed this out incisively:

It is true that recently Nishida's philosophy seems to have somewhat lost its outer Romantic and aesthetic coloring, but that is only because the Romantic, aestheticist method has been fully established, which is, namely, precisely what Professor Sōda began to call "Nishida philosophy."[6] . . . To repeat, Nishida's philosophy is by

---

6 Economist and philosopher Sōda Kiichirō (1881–1927) coined the phrase "Nishida tetsugaku" in his essay "On the Method of Nishida Philosophy" (Nishida Tetsugaku no hōhō ni tsuite). See Sōda (1930).

no means based on a feudal, Gothic method. Rather, its essence is modern and Romantic. It would be impossible to find anything that more fully substantiates the cultural consciousness of the contemporary man of culture. The modern, capitalist cultivation of the contemporary person will find in this philosophy a proxy for his own consciousness of cultural freedom. And in this sense, it functions as representative of the philosophy of cultural liberalism, as opposed to economic and political liberalism. This is the basis for the popularity of Nishida philosophy. (1935:230–31)

In the same way, to call Nishida's philosophy Buddhist is a meaningless assertion that ignores the historicity of Buddhism itself. It is true that from around 1934 Nishida began to call his own perspective "Eastern" or "Buddhist," but that fact itself demonstrates that his thought belonged to a particular historical context. Until then, he had attempted to articulate his thought via the terms of Western philosophy; in truth, what he refers to as the "place of nothingness" corresponds to the Kantian transcendental apperception. Kant argues that this is empirically nothing, but he grasps it as a "function" that serves to bring about the unification of consciousness. Like Fichte, Nishida perceives this transcendental self as a practical entity and tries to structure the world from that perspective, but in contrast to Fichte, he continually tried to see it as the "place of nothingness" or the "work of nothingness." One cannot say, however, that this is particularly Buddhist. For example, what Heidegger called the "ontological difference" between entities and being was, in essence, derived from Kant's distinction between the empirical and the transcendental. Thus for Heidegger, the being that is lost sight of in its positing as an entity is precisely a kind of nothingness that exists as a function. Nishida articulated this as the "place of nothingness" or as "absolute nothingness."

Still, after 1934 Nishida began to refer to his own thought as "Eastern." This was the period when Japan thrust itself into war with China and constructed a fascist order, while in Germany

Heidegger actively committed to the Nazi Party. Just as Heidegger supported the Left faction of the Nazi Party, Nishida supported the comparatively liberal navy as opposed to the militarist army. He tried to provide a philosophical basis for showing that Japan's Greater East Asia Co-Prosperity Sphere represented the liberation of Asia from Western colonial rule rather than a form of imperialism. In comparison with his Kyoto-school disciples, who jockeyed about much more spectacularly and opportunistically, Nishida himself appears rather reticent and passive, but there is no doubt that his disciples were supported by his way of thinking.

For example, Nishida defines the emperor as follows: "In our nation's history, the imperial household has always been a being of nothingness, a contradictory self-identity" (2004b:49). Concepts such as "being of nothingness" (the work of nothingness) and "contradictory self-identity" had somehow come to signify the emperor system. There is perhaps no starker example of Althusser's statement that philosophy itself is a form without content to which historical context gives meaning. According to Nishida's thinking, the imperial household is not itself a political power and, for that reason, continues to exist as a "being of nothingness" in the background of shifting political power. Although the Meiji constitution designated the emperor as sovereign, he is essentially a "being of nothingness"; similarly, in the context of the Greater East Asia Co-Prosperity Sphere, he does not rule over all from above, as in the case of the Soviet Union, but rather exists at the foundation as a "transcendental apperception" (zero sign) that unifies the various autonomous countries of Asia. Of course, this was, as Marx might say, simply changing an interpretation of the reality that Japan had taken the place of the Western powers in ruling over Asia.

Furthermore, Nishida presented a lecture addressed to the emperor in which he stated: "Today, individualism and totalitarianism are thought to be in opposition to each other; needless to say, what is called individualism is behind the times, but a totalitarianism that rejects the individual is also nothing more than a relic of the past." And: "In our nation's history, the totality has not been set in opposition to the individual, and the individual has not been set in opposition to the totality, but rather the totality and the individual have been in a relation of mutual negation, enjoying vigorous and steady growth with the imperial household at the center" (2004a:436).[7]

This is not a type of dialectics in which the contradictions between individualism and totalitarianism are sublated. There is no need for sublation, since the opposing terms are already essentially the same. Previously, Okakura had referred to this logic as "Advaitism," which is recast by Nishida as "absolute contradictory identity."[8] If, however, one were to insist that this logic is somehow Buddhist, then one would have to assert that politically Buddhism worked precisely as the logic of fascism. For the type of thinking that avoids both individualism and totalitarianism, both capitalism and socialism, is nothing other than the counterrevolutionary thought of fascism, which demanded this kind of logic. Miki Kiyoshi, who was Nishida's disciple, referred to this thought as "cooperatism" [*kyōdōshugi*], which served as the philosophy of the "Konoe New Order" (1940). According to such logic, the Kyoto school deconstructed all binary oppositions of the modern West. This was for them the "overcoming of modernity."

In the postwar period, however, the philosophers of the Kyoto school, particularly Nishitani, erased this type of political commitment on Nishida's part, thereby also erasing their own political participation. And when that history was obscured, Nishida's philosophy was also naturally dehistoricized and reborn as though belonging to Eastern thought or to Zen Buddhism. In the case of Heidegger, no matter the assessment of his work, there is no one who ignores his involvement in Nazism,

---

7 Nishida delivered the address to the emperor on January 23, 1941. For a complete English translation, see Yusa (2002:314–18).
8 In *The Ideals of the East*, Okakura wrote: "Thus Japan is a museum of Asiatic civilization; and yet more than a museum, because the singular genius of the race leads it to dwell on all phases of the ideals of the past, in that spirit of living Advaitism which welcomes the new without losing the old" (1970:7–8).

but Nishida's work is often presented as a completely depoliticized, profound "Eastern philosophy" and circulates within this circumscribed area in both Japan and the West.[9]

2. Sakaguchi Ango

I would like to turn to a number of writings—including "A Personal View of Japanese Culture" [Nihon bunka shikan, 1942], by Sakaguchi Ango, and *Sima Qian: The World of the "Historical Records"* [*Shiba Sen: Shiki no sekai*, 1943], by Takeda Taijun— that were published roughly contemporaneously with the overcoming modernity debate and that pose a fundamental critique of the latter, even though it is not an explicit target. What is of interest is that these most severe and essential critiques of the discourse of overcoming modernity emerged from those who had experienced institutional and popular forms of Buddhism. One can say that the radical core of Buddhist thought can be seen in these two antitraditionalists.

Ango's "Personal View of Japanese Culture" critiques the book *The Rediscovery of Japanese Beauty* [*Nihonbi no saihakken*, 1939], by Bruno Taut, a modernist architect who lived in Japan for three years beginning in 1933. The German-Jewish Taut, born in Königsberg, was an expressionist who turned to socialism, and he fled Nazi Germany, arriving in Japan as a quasi-refugee.

---

9   Suzuki Daisetsu is well known internationally because of his English-language introduction of Zen Buddhism. Less known, however, is the fact that he was a close acquaintance of Nishida's and that both of them withdrew from high school together. Unlike Nishida, Suzuki was a man of religion, and furthermore did not comment on actual political and social issues. However, in his book *The Japanese Spirit* [*Nihonteki reisei*], which he wrote during the war, he asserts that Zen, True Pure Land Buddhism, and Shinto are all embodiments of the "Japanese spirit." There is no question but that he conformed to the emperor-system fascism of his day. After the war, though, this fact was entirely overlooked. In the case of Zen, which argues for the renunciation of subjectivity, the question of responsibility is not raised. The Zen monk Ichikawa Hakugen (1902–1986) pointed out the lack of the consciousness of responsibility and ethics in the philosophy of both Zen and Nishida. See Ichikawa (1970). [Author's note]

He had been invited by a group of modernist architects, but when he arrived he devoted himself more to writing than to design, and his texts exerted a broad influence during an era sliding toward emperor-system fascism. For example, he described Ise Shrine, which was a symbol of the nationalist emperor-system ideology, as being characterized by a purity of structure, an extreme lucidity, immaculate materials, and a beautiful symmetry, while denouncing the Nikkō Tōshōgū Shrine, dedicated to Ieyasu, as the kitsch of a dictator and representing an "unassimilated, imported" style (Taut 1962:17–29). Even if one grants the possibility of seeing architecture as ahistorical art, there is no chance that Taut was unaware of the clear political connotations that such monuments held.

Taut differed from typical Orientalists in that he did not compare Japan and the West but simply made a distinction between things that were native and things that came from abroad. In this sense, as opposed to the Nikkō Tōshōgū Shrine, in which imported and native elements were mixed, he praised the Katsura Detached Palace and Ise Shrine as examples of "original Japanese culture" (Taut 1962:17). Nonetheless, the 1930s was a time when the National Learning scholar Motoori Norinaga, who tried to find the original contours of Japan in the ancient culture that existed prior to the arrival of Chinese civilization, was held in highest esteem. Furthermore, in Germany, this was a time in which the original Germanic culture prior to the process of Latinization was praised. In that sense, one must say that it is strange that Taut, who had fled from Germany at this time, made similar assertions in the Japanese context.

He most likely had a separate political strategy, however. His intention was to criticize the imperial crown style [*teikan yōshiki*], which mixed together nineteenth-century European architecture and traditional Japanese elements, and which symbolized Japanese imperialism. This was also the expectation of those architects who had invited him to Japan. Taut adopted the strategy of taking on the "traditionalism" of the imperial crown style by praising another form of "tradition." In that sense, one can say that this was the strategy of a modernist driven into a corner. Yet the end result was to give a universal meaning to

Japanese tradition, as something that could be valued even by foreigners. Consequently, he was welcomed by the dominant discourse of the day, which touted the "fall of the West" and the "overcoming of modernity." In a certain sense, this is similar to the fate of Roland Barthes's *Empire of Signs*, which was taken out of its original French context and read by Japanese postmodernists as a new version of overcoming modernity. Ango criticizes Taut in the following manner:

> There exists a gap greater than Taut ever imagined between his discovering Japan with all its traditional beauty and our actually being Japanese, though we may have lost sight of the traditions of Japan. In other words, whereas Taut had to discover Japan, we have no such need, for we *are* Japanese. Even though we may have lost sight of our ancient culture, surely we have not lost sight of Japan itself. "What is the essence of the Japanese spirit?" We, of all people, do not need to theorize that. Japan does not arise from some explication of its spirit, nor can something like the Japanese spirit be explained. If the everyday life of the Japanese is healthy, Japan itself is in good health. We yank trousers over our stubby bowlegs, deck ourselves out in Western clothes, waddle about, dance the jitterbug, toss out the *tatami*, and strike our affected poses amid tacky chairs and tables. That this appears completely absurd to the Western eye has no bearing on the fact that we ourselves are satisfied with the convenience of it all. There is a fundamental difference between their standpoint, from which they chuckle pitifully at us, and ours, from which we go on with our everyday lives. As long as our day-to-day lives are rooted in proper desires, their condescending smiles don't mean a damn thing. (Sakaguchi 2005:825)

Of course, Ango's point is not that Taut had discovered a false Japan, or that Japan is comprehensible only to us Japanese. His true target is not Taut himself—who by then had already left Japan for Turkey, where he died in 1938—but rather the type of

Japanese intellectual who was then busy proclaiming "ancient Japanese culture" and the "overcoming of modernity." To begin with, such things as a nation's "culture" or "tradition" are always "discovered" by foreigners or else by people who have drifted away from their own countries. It is nothing more than an empty image found at a remove from our actual lives, which, whether we like it or not, are being transformed by the modern capitalist order.

Ango writes that "beauty" is not what appears beautiful, for there is no beauty where one is conscious of it. Instead, beauty is a form in which only what is necessary is situated in the necessary place: "It is only 'necessity' from beginning to end, it is all 'necessity.' And the unique form that responds to this ceaseless essence is what gives birth to beauty":

> What really matters is substance. Beauty for beauty's sake is not sincere; it is not, in the end, authentic. Such beauty is essentially empty and has no truth capable of moving people. When all is said and done, we can just as well do without such items. I couldn't care less if both the Hōryūji and the Byōdōin burned to the ground. If the need should arise, we'd do well to tear down Hōryūji and put in a parking lot. (Sakaguchi 2005:834)

What Ango refers to as necessity does not merely indicate practical utility. As examples of architecture that generated a powerful emotional pull for him, Ango lists some buildings that he happened to see, such as Kosuge prison, a dry-ice factory, and a destroyer. He writes,

> What makes these three things—the prison, the factory, and the destroyer—so beautiful? It is the fact that no frills have been added for the sake of beautifying them. Not a single pillar or sheet of steel has been added in the interest of beauty; not a single pillar or sheet of steel has been removed because it is not aesthetically pleasing. What is needed, and only that, has been placed precisely where it is needed. With the superfluous removed,

the unique form demanded by necessity emerges. (834; translation modified)

According to architectural historians, however, at the very least Kosuge prison (which is no longer standing) was at the time highly valued as an example of modernist architecture. Ango, who was completely ignorant of architecture, was nonetheless intuitively responding to the famous words of Walter Gropius, the leader of Bauhaus: "We want to create a clear, organic architecture, whose inner logic will be radiant and naked, unencumbered by lying façades and trickeries; we want . . . an architecture whose function is clearly recognizable in the relation of its forms" (1938:27).

In the same way, Taut, himself a prominent member of Bauhaus, can be said to have found in the Katsura Detached Palace and Ise Shrine a "unique form demanded by necessity," "with the superfluous removed." In that sense Ango, in criticizing Taut, may have unwittingly adopted a position surprisingly close to his. The historical conditions that gave meaning to their discourse, however, left them far apart. The distance separating them was by no means that of "Japan" and the "West." Responding to Taut's praise of the rock garden at Ryōanji and the garden at the Shūgakuin Detached Palace, Ango wrote as follows:

> What is the rock garden of Ryōanji trying to express? What sorts of concepts is it attempting to weave together? Taut, for his part, showered praise on the black-and-white checked wallpaper in the library of the Shūgakuin Detached Palace, claiming that it represented the sound of a waterfall. Forcing an appreciation to the point of such tortured explanations is downright embarrassing. Landscape gardens and tearooms, like the enlightenment of a Zen monk, are castles in the air. They have nothing but Zen-like hypotheses to support them. "Wherein lies the Buddha nature?" one asks. The answer: "In a shit scoop." Someone puts a rock in a garden and says, "This is indeed a shit scoop, but it also

has the Buddha nature." That works just fine as long as people are willing to cooperate and consider the thing to be Buddha-like. But the minute somebody sees the shit scoop as just a shit scoop, well, that's the end of that. The obvious, self-evident observation that a shit scoop is just a shit scoop and nothing more makes for a more persuasive argument than any following the conventions of the Zen dialogue. (Sakaguchi 2005:829–30)

I would add two points to supplement the passage above. At the time he wrote this essay, Ango was researching sixteenth-century Christians in Japan. Or rather, he was studying the overall history of the fifteenth to sixteenth centuries. It was a general phenomenon of this age, a time when the overcoming of modernity was being proclaimed, that left-wing intellectuals discovered the possibility of an alternative overcoming of the modern in the Renaissance, which at once belongs to modernity yet remains free of the enclosed space of modern knowledge. Around the time that Antonio Gramsci was writing *The Modern Prince* in an Italian prison and Mikhail Bakhtin was writing about François Rabelais under Stalinism, in Japan Hanada Kiyoteru (1946)[10] and Watanabe Kazuo (1943) were writing about the European Renaissance. Furthermore, the Marxist Fukumoto Kazuo was conceiving his *On the History of the Japanese Renaissance* [*Nihon runessansu shiron*, 1985] in prison.[11] For his part, Ango found a certain type of Renaissance in fifteenth- and sixteenth-century Japan. This era marked a fundamental overturning of the value system of the feudal order since the Kamakura period [1185–1333], as well as that of aristocratic culture since antiquity, but Japanese historical accounts were marked by a lack of proper historical sources. It is only natural that Ango, with his knowledge of multiple languages, from

---

10 The majority of essays collected in Hanada's volume were written between 1941 and 1943.
11 Fukumoto notes in the afterword that he first conceived of the book in 1936 while he was in prison (1985:824); the book was first published in 1967.

Sanskrit to Latin, turned to the historical sources on the Christian side, an attempt that, prior to Ango, no historian had made.

For example, the Jesuit missionary Luís Fróis left a number of records about Japan at the time, including his *History of Japan*; one of his writings, a treatise contrasting Japanese and European customs completed in 1585, contains observations of some interest:

> In Europe, the supreme honor and treasure of an unmarried woman is her chastity and her unsullied purity. Japanese women place no weight on virginal purity. Even if it is lost, a woman will not face dishonor or be unable to marry.
>
> In Europe, property is held in common by husband and wife. In Japan, each keeps his own. At times, the wife will lend money to her own husband at high interest.
>
> In Europe, to divorce one's wife is not only a sin but also the highest dishonor. In Japan, one divorces at will, any number of times. The wife thereby loses no honor, and is able to remarry.
>
> In Europe, it is usual for the husband to divorce the wife. In Japan, it is frequently the wife who divorces the husband.
>
> In Europe it is of utmost importance to confine young women, and this is carried out religiously. In Japan, maidens will go off on their own whim for days at a time without even getting permission from their parents.
>
> In Europe, a wife needs her husband's permission to leave the house. Japanese women have the freedom to go where they will without even telling their husbands.
>
> In our society, it is rare for women to be able to write. Among Japanese upper-class women, it is thought that if they do not know this, their value will drop.

In Europe, women usually prepare the meals. In Japan, it is the men who do so.

In Europe, it is considered impolite for women to drink wine. In Japan, this is a common occurrence, and during times of festival, they will frequently drink until inebriated. (1991:39–57)[12]

As a missionary, Fróis no doubt encountered people of all different social classes, so the women of Japan whom he describes here are not limited to a particular class. Yet, as in the case of the "Europe" to which he refers, his "Japan" also belongs to a specific historical context. Not only did this type of Japan disappear after the seventeenth century—in other words, after the formation of the Tokugawa order—but it was even forgotten that such a Japan had ever existed. For example, early-twentieth-century Japanese feminists, in seeking an earlier time when Japanese women had exalted status, turned to the matriarchal age of antiquity, much like the National Learning scholars; as a result, they would lapse into emperor-system fascism during the 1930s, whereas awareness of the kind of history described above may have helped them to avoid such a trap. One can infer from the observations of Fróis that what is considered in today's Japan to be "traditional" was in fact constructed after the Tokugawa period and in modernity. The discourse of overcoming modernity tends to invoke the distant Middle Ages or ancient periods. But is the sixteenth century modern or premodern? It is both, and neither. I therefore refer to it by the term "renaissance," but this is not simply a question of analogy with European history. In point of fact, Japan was at that point connected to contemporary Europe. In other words, the Japan of this period cannot be considered in isolation from post-Columbian world intercourse. The internal social transformations in Japan existed in the context of what Wallerstein

---

12 This is a Japanese translation of Fróis's manuscript "Tratado em que se contem muito susintae abreviadamente algumas contradições e diferenças de custumes antre a gente de Europa e esta provincia de Japão" (1585).

(1980) calls the world system. One can say that Ango, in his research into this period, was seeking an alternative form of the overcoming of modernity, one that would stand apart from what was popular at the time.

Ango refers to the record of a debate between Francis Xavier and a Zen monk. His commentary contains further explanation of a passage cited earlier:

> In other words, in Zen there are conventions belonging only to the world of Zen, and [the monks] simply play with a logic based on this type of convention. It is a world in which everything is based on an understanding agreed upon in advance. For example, if one asks, "What is the Buddha?" they might answer, "Nothing" or, "It is a shit scoop." Everyone pretends to understand, based on convention, but this understanding is no more than pretense. They don't even know whether or not they understand.
>
> For this reason, when actually faced with the kind of straightforward logic that the Buddha is the Buddha, or a shit scoop is a shit scoop, their own logic is useless. What kind of power has the capacity to thoroughly overturn this most matter-of-fact logic? One can find such power only where practice and thought are unified.
>
> But for Zen monks this way of living is exceptionally difficult. They only think about things according to convention; what they lack is practice. They are merely groping for enlightenment in the world of concepts; relying only on intellectual power, they have no way to know their true strength. Faced, then, with men of religion such the Catholic priests, who put everything on the line in their practice, the Zen monks felt a tremendous threat. They were made to feel their own miserable lack of real strength. And in this way, it became very popular for those believing in Zen, even monks, to convert to Catholicism. The numbers were far greater than we imagine today. (Sakaguchi 1991:472–73)

Ango here is not criticizing Zen from the perspective of modern rationalism. Even less is he saying that Christianity is more rational than Zen. For the logic that "the Buddha is the Buddha, a shit scoop is a shit scoop" can also be aimed at the Holy Trinity. That is to say, if God is God and man is man, how can the human Jesus be God? The Christian missionaries of this time overwhelmed the Zen sect not through the theoretical rationalism of its doctrine but rather through the irrationality of their coming so many thousands of miles away to the Far East in order to spread their religion. However, is it not the case that to be rational itself requires an irrational will and passion? In the 1930s, when an antimodern "irrationalism" had run rampant, Ango strove to be thoroughly rational. This should be distinguished from "rationalism." For example, in the same time period Edmund Husserl wrote *The Crisis of European Sciences and Transcendental Phenomenology*, in which he stated that human beings can be rational only by way of a will to be rational. Obviously this "will" itself is not rational.

In effect, the issue here is not any opposition between Christianity and Buddhism. For Ango, any type of thinking that did not in practice involve itself with the other was without meaning. Ango is not deriding Zen monks who were defeated in public debates and converted to Catholicism. Far from it. For it was only during this period that such things were possible. It was only in this period—when one of its very founders, Xavier, would have traveled all the way to Japan—that the Society of Jesus would have such power. Thereafter, it would become an established religious order that colluded with the state's colonial policy. But from another angle, one can say that Buddhism too, at a certain historical moment, maintained such a power of theory and practice.

Ango's indifference to Zen enlightenment also derives from another, more personal reason. When he was around twenty years old, Ango himself aspired to become a Buddhist monk, and he put himself through a rigorous period of study and training. As a result, he suffered a nervous breakdown and abandoned Buddhism. Later, he would look back on this experience with derision, but based on recently uncovered materials it is clear that such self-effacement cannot be taken at face value. At the age of twenty, he worked on a journal with other students who aimed for a new life through Buddhism; one issue included a column in which all the members expressed their opinions on the future of temple life. Contrary to other comments, which included such statements as "There is nothing worth valuing among the rotten-to-the-core Buddhist clergy," or "The motto of temple life is 'faith first,'" Ango wrote as follows:

> If there is a life unique to the temple, it is none other than a life of abstinence. However, one cannot forget that there is a life that follows the ordinary human being; in other words, a life that follows passion and desire. The people of the temple are prone to overvalue the ascetic life while forgetting that a life that, as it were, follows the earthly passions also contains the power of the moral code and knowledge. There is no reason that the ascetic life is morally superior, nor any reason it should lead more quickly to enlightenment. Life is something that should follow each person's principles and can essentially take any form, but I cannot abandon the bonds of sexual desire. The wish to maintain even the appearance of the ascetic life seems rather shallow. If anything, the true path is to start a new life that follows common desires. (Sakaguchi 1999:10)

Although Ango claimed to have grown disillusioned with Buddhism, this does not necessarily appear to be the case. Even at the time that he aspired to be a monk, he was already writing about "starting a new life that follows common desires." From the perspective of the monastic order, moving away from an ascetic life appears to be a "fall" [*daraku*]. But if one considers that the Buddha himself had broken the long tradition of using abstinence and ascetic practices to seek emancipation from the cycle of reincarnation, then one can also say that the Buddha had "fallen." In that sense, Ango, at the moment when he left the world of Buddhism, can be said to have become truly Buddhist.

He never wrote positively about Buddhism. In particular, he was extremely vitriolic against anything with pretensions to a Zen-like enlightenment or subdued refinement. Yet, paradoxical as it may seem, his criticism is eminently Buddhist.

In this way, "fallenness" would become Ango's key word. In truth, it was his postwar best seller, *On Fallenness* [*Darakuron*], in which he encourages his readers to continue to fall, that made him famous.[13] Nonetheless, his term *daraku* does not contain the usual sense of "decadence," and it maintains no connection to the currents of postwar culture. For Ango, fallenness meant existing in a state of exposure and opening to the other. For example, he scathingly criticized Nagai Kafū, at a time when the latter was considered one of the great masters, as a "popular novelist." After the High Treason Incident of 1910, Kafū had proclaimed that since he was powerless and ineffectual as an intellectual, he would henceforth live as a Tokugawa-period popular writer, and he spent his days enjoying the company of courtesans in the pleasure quarters of Asakusa, which provided the material for his fiction. It was this posture of "decadence" that was praised after the collapse of the Marxist literary movement in the 1930s, and that allowed Kafū to be revived as a great master. Ango writes,

> From the moment of his birth, Kafū was blessed with his family's reputation and modest fortune. And hatred of having his own personal circumstances threatened by another became the decisive element of his morality; at no time did he ever give himself over to any good-faith questioning of the nature of humanity or what people love and desire. Far from it, he never even considered the simple fact that there were many circumstances different from his own, that such circumstances might give rise to

---

13 On the translation of *daraku*, see Joseph Murphy's comments in Karatani (2001:542n.7), as well my remarks in note 10 of the introduction. The essay "Darakuron" was first published in the journal *Shinchō* in 1946 and was included in the book of the same title published the following year.

a certain thought that was opposed to his own circumstances and to his own thought. (Sakaguchi 1990b:534)

This passage appears almost Marxist in its perspective. However, it was written after most Marxists had undergone ideological conversion. What Ango is trying to say is that Kafū's decadence is nothing more than self-consciousness; he never had any encounter with the other and thus, in other words, he never really "fell." This can apply equally to apostate Marxists. It was not external pressure alone that led to their conversions. Even prior to conversion, though their works may have included the concept of the proletariat, they maintained no conception of the other.

In 1941, shortly before writing "A Personal View of Japanese Culture," Ango wrote an essay called "The Home of Literature" [Bungaku no furusato]. In this essay, Ango cites a number of different narratives, the first of which is Charles Perrault's "Little Red Riding Hood." In contrast to the familiar folktale, this story ends with the young girl, who had gone into the forest to visit her grandmother, being eaten by the wolf disguised as the old woman:

> At that moment, we are suddenly thrust out, feeling confusion as though our preconceived understandings have been betrayed. Yet at the same time, in this sudden shot to the eyes, in the empty, snipped-off margins, do we not see an extremely still, even transparent, heartrending "home"? ...
>
> Just as the fact that there is no moral is itself the moral, the lack of salvation is itself salvation. I myself find here the home of literature, and the home of humanity. This is where literature begins, I feel. I am not saying that only this type of amoral story, one that thrusts us away, qualifies as literature. No, if anything, I don't really value this type of story. For the home of literature may be our cradle, but the work of adults in no way consists of attempting to return home. But I cannot imagine that literature could exist without an awareness and

self-consciousness of this home. Unless the moral of literature, its sociality, is something nurtured from this home, I would have no faith in it. The same is true for literary criticism. (Sakaguchi 1990a:324, 330–31)

Just as he does with the word "fallenness," Ango overturns the accepted meaning of the word "home" [*furusato*]. For Ango, home is not something intimate or familiar but instead signifies a state of being thrust into alterity. We can perhaps demonstrate Ango's topology through comparison with a philosopher who used the same terminology. Heidegger, who saw human existence (*Dasein*) as being-toward-death (*Sein zum Tode*), referred to the flight into everydayness as a fall (*Verfall*). Furthermore, he saw not only modernity but also the entirety of philosophy since Socrates as a loss of the home that is being. In that sense, one can say that to fall signifies the loss of home or of being-with (*Mitsein*). In a political sense, the attempt to return from this fallen state to an original state arrived at Nazism. The Japanese counterpart was "overcoming modernity." For Ango, however, home was something that thrusts people out. He finds it in the exposure of the authenticity of being to the other. If we borrow the words of Levinas, who criticized Heidegger, Ango placed "ethics" at the basis of his thinking. And if Levinas's thought can be said to derive from Judaism, Ango's thought can be said to derive from Buddhism.

In the 1930s, at a time when many intellectuals were attempting to make a return to "Japan" or to a Buddhist "emptiness" from Western knowledge or Marxism, Ango began with the negation of such an attempt. In the first place, he would never have simply become a modernist to begin with. In a certain sense, he never let go of the consciousness of "emptiness." Emptiness signifies that everything exists as relation, without substance. It could thus never be the object of a sentimental return. For emptiness dissolves all things that exist systematically and that are seen as having substance, including beauty, knowledge, and morality. At a time when many understood Buddhism aesthetically, or as a question of internal, individual salvation, for Ango it signified a turn to ethics. Precisely in the fact that he never once spoke positively of Buddhism, he brought his own Buddhist quality to fulfillment.

3. Takeda Taijun

In contrast to Ango, Takeda was one of the many intellectuals who participated in the Marxist movement of the 1930s and underwent ideological conversion. Yet he stands out from the rest on two points. The first is that he was born into the family of a Buddhist monk and for a time became a monk himself. The other is that he was a scholar of Chinese literature. At one time after the war, before deciding to devote himself to writing fiction, he even taught Chinese literature as a professor at Hokkaido University. Nevertheless, these distinctive characteristics frequently lead to one obvious point being overlooked: the fact that Marxism was important to him.

Buddhism and Chinese literature, the two things that make Takeda distinctive, share a similar position in modern Japan. As I mentioned earlier, Buddhism had been one part of a system supporting the Tokugawa order; in the Meiji period, monks were allowed to marry and inherit temple property, becoming a type of landowning class. In particular, Takeda's father was the leader of a religious organization and was both a major landowner and a university professor. While much was made of Buddhism in the intellectual discourse of the 1930s, those who studied Buddhism academically were almost entirely limited to the children of monks. This can be seen in the fact that when Sakaguchi Ango entered Tōyō University in 1926 to study Buddhism, he was the only one among his sixteen classmates who was not the son of a monk. For Takeda, Buddhism was not a matter of concepts but a concrete system and lifestyle—something aspiring intellectuals would not approach. The same can be said for Chinese literature. Chinese learning and literature had been the standard for Japanese intellectuals prior to the Meiji Restoration, but China's position was subsequently superseded by that of the West. After the Sino-Japanese War [1894–

1895] in particular, things Chinese were seen as antiquated objects of disdain and were not deemed worthy of concern for those who considered themselves modern intellectuals. Chinese studies remained within the post-Meiji modern university system, but essentially only as an extension of traditional Chinese learning [*kangaku*].

Takeda nonetheless chose these two domains that had been excluded from the realm of modern knowledge. In one fictional work, he writes as follows: "I became a priest because I am wavering by nature and because at the time there was no sign of anything better to do. I was neither weary of the world nor possessed of an overpowering zeal. I took the easiest road.... Take such a boy, and he will become a fishmonger if his father is a fishmonger, and a landlord if his father is a landlord. And so I became a priest by trade" (Takeda 2007:371–72). He further writes that he chose Chinese literature in college simply because his grades were poor, and he thus did not qualify for any other course of study. Of course, such statements represent Takeda's trademark self-effacement. What this self-effacement conceals, however, is actually something quite different; namely, the importance of the Marxist experience for Takeda. For example, he once wrote as follows about Buddhism:

> Nāgārjuna's concept of emptiness was the most rigorous, advanced system achieved by the natural sciences of the time. It is an incomparably dispassionate natural dialectic, something that tends to keep pious folk at a distance; it is not designed, as it were, to draw people in by generating tears with the signboard of impermanence. There is a habit in Japan of being drawn to such things as an unbroken lineage, hierarchical relationships, and temporal change, but Buddhism originally grasped the universe spatially, confirmed it according to physical chemistry, and emerged as an attempt to eradicate distorted dogma. The kind of lamentation that one finds in the *Tale of the Heike* is no more than the misapprehension of the weak and narrow-minded. (Takeda 1972b:140–41)

Takeda's understanding of Buddhism diverged completely from its commonly known form in Japan. His understanding was not, however, necessarily derived from his academic study of Buddhism. Clearly, Takeda sees the Buddhist consciousness as a kind of dialectical materialism. Takeda had undergone training to be a monk after he had been arrested five times and fallen out of the Marxist movement, but unlike others who moved from Marxism to Buddhism, he can be said to have sought Marxism in Buddhism. The same can be said for his interest in Chinese literature. He turned to Chinese literature because he was a leftist; it cannot be understood apart from this motivation. In fact, it was through the efforts of Takeda and his friend Takeuchi Yoshimi, who wrote on Lu Xun, that Chinese studies in Japan first became something contemporary and actual. Takeda's *Sima Qian: The World of the "Historical Records"* is a product of that effort. Yet this work far exceeds the realm of research on China. It is one of the most essential books of criticism produced in Japan in the twentieth century.

For example, the book begins with Takeda's statement that "Sima Qian was a man who lived on in shame" (1972c:25). The Han-dynasty historian faced a choice between death and castration as his punishment from the emperor, and he chose the latter in order to be able to finish the *Historical Records*. One can say that Takeda projected onto Sima Qian his own experience of having fallen out from the leftist movement and into a dependence on the temple—which is nothing other than a landowner—as well as his experience of being drafted and having to invade his beloved China as a soldier. There was, however, a decisive difference between Takeda and the writer Dazai Osamu, another son of a wealthy landowner, who also committed apostasy from communism and who wrote about his feelings of guilt, anxiety, and irony arising from this experience. For what Takeda writes about is not the psychology of Sima Qian but the structure of the *Historical Records*.

Nonetheless, this sense of shame can be said to exist at the core of Takeda's writing. When he refers to Sima Qian's shame, Takeda does not mean that he suffered a shameful punishment. Rather, he is saying that *to write* is itself something shameful.

No matter why one writes, or what one writes, to write is itself to "live on in shame." In other words, the act of writing can never be legitimized in any sense, and it is precisely this fact that makes writing possible. Takeda's own shame had nothing to do with his becoming a monk. To put it simply, it was a shame that derived from the fact that someone who had fallen out of the Marxist movement would subsequently write anything. Among Japanese intellectuals, Marxism generated a kind of shock that no foreign religion had ever previously produced. Meiji-period Christians committed apostasy without any problem, but in contrast, those who converted away from Marxism were subsequently drawn to religion. It is for this reason that they turned to the Bible or to Shinran.

But why does Takeda insist upon the word "shame" instead of "guilt"? In *The Chrysanthemum and the Sword*, for which anthropologist Ruth Benedict interviewed Japanese Americans interred in wartime camps to help prepare American policy toward Japan, Benedict argues that Japan is a "shame culture," as opposed to the "guilt culture" of the United States (1946:222–27). According to her analysis, guilt is something internal, while shame is external. Generally speaking, this appears valid. One should note, however, that feelings of guilt often erase, by a deep internalization, the sense of shame that is situated in relation to others. In other words, it can erase the very relation to the other. Therefore, although there may be salvation for feelings of guilt, there can be no salvation for shame. The following dialogue appears in one of Takeda's fictional works; it is a dialogue between an elderly intellectual tormented by guilt, who believes that he is going to hell, and the narrator, who has undergone training to be a monk. One can say that both are apostates from left-wing movements:

> "To hell? You are going to hell, sir?"
> "I am. It is a terrible thing, but I am doomed."
> "Really?"
> "Really." He said it with greatest eagerness. "I am filled with sin and guilt. Not that you would understand. It is a terrible thing, but there it is. A fact."

> "Oh, I hardly think so. Imagine it, going to hell."
>
> "I am going to hell." He smiled triumphantly, to brush away my damp sympathy. But in fact I was not sympathizing at all. I had made the remark with what I hoped would suggest the sureness of a prophet and with a spiteful protest against the ease with which he sent himself to hell.
>
> "You are going to heaven."
>
> "Heaven?" His brow clouded.
>
> "Whatever you say, you are going to heaven."
>
> "What makes you so sure?"
>
> "Because we are all going to heaven. It's settled."
>
> He gasped, and looked at me with loathing. (Takeda 2007:371; translation modified)

What "I" expresses here is the "spiteful" critique of the fact that the scholar's guilt is accompanied by self-intoxication. Restated, his "protest against the ease with which he sent himself to hell" signifies a protest against the ease with which he converted *shame* into *guilt*. What Takeda means by shame is something situated in an actual relationship to others—that is, an existence in a state of exposure to others. It is a state that allows for no salvation. This calls to mind Sartre's statement from the same period that "hell is other people." Yet we should also note that this perspective is close to what Ango called *daraku*, a "fallen state." Takeda, while taking on the appearance of Buddhism, was actually criticizing the intellectual bent toward religion. However, just as in the case of Ango, one can say that his type of thinking is in fact Buddhist.

Nonetheless, in Takeda's case, we must consider this consciousness in relation to Marxism. Certainly, Takeda converted away from the Marxist movement. In what sense, however, did he convert? What was Marxism at the time? Marxists of that time had determined that Asia represented a stagnant, undeveloped stage of history. For example, in *The Philosophy of History*, Hegel sees China and India as being at the early stages of the development of spirit: "The English, or rather the East India

Company, are the lords of [India]; for it is the necessary fate of Asiatic Empires to be subjected to Europeans; and China will, some day or other, be obliged to submit to this fate" (1991:142–43). No matter how much one is repulsed by such a statement, this was the reality. Marxism also inherited this type of temporal development and Eurocentrism. The one difference was that Marxists were trying to free Asia from such backwardness and to liberate Asia from the control of the Western powers.

Most likely, Takeda always felt a certain objection to this kind of thinking in a Marxist movement that took its guidance from the Comintern. Apostates from Marxism tended to turn to religion or nihilism, or else followed a trajectory in which they modified the Hegelian-Marxist theory of development in order to posit the liberation of Asia as a "world mission," thereby legitimizing Japanese imperialism. This is a kind of logic that could be produced only by former Marxists. Takeda not only objected to this kind of stance but attempted to critique the Hegelianism that lived on at the foundation of Marxism.

Takeda did not adopt the method of interpreting the *Historical Records* from the perspective of the economic base of the age. If anything, Takeda tried to read in the *Historical Records* a perspective that would oppose and relativize the type of Hegelian / Marxist understanding mentioned above. This was an attempt to grasp history in spatial terms, to evacuate meaning, ideal, telos from "world" history and to see there instead a "system of relationships without a center":

> The emphasis of the *Basic Annals* is not only upon the person of Xiang Yu. Neither is it borne by Gaozu. Rather, the focus is placed on the movement of the opposing elements of Xiang Yu and Gaozu. Without Xiang Yu, there would be no "Basic Annals of Gaozu." The value of the other individual who is placed in opposition would disappear. What is problematized here is not the relationship between king and subject. Rather, it is the relationship between the center of the world and the political figures who surround it. It is the relationship between

two people who are fundamentally opposed. And the investigation of this relationship at some point deepens the content of the *Basic Annals*. (Takeda 1972c:81)

According to Takeda's thinking that was cited earlier, this kind of structuralist reading is Buddhist. For Takeda, Buddhism was not something that perceives "the pathos of things" [*mono no aware*] in the impermanence of all worldly phenomena, or something that transcends historical reality by positing the emptiness of all substance. Rather, it was something that "grasped the universe spatially, confirmed it according to physical chemistry, and emerged as an attempt to eradicate distorted dogma." It involves situating the existing dogma concerning the world, namely the ideas of Hegelianism/Marxism itself, in a historical space that cannot be transcended.

Is that not, however, precisely the standpoint of Marx in *Capital*? Marx writes in the preface as follows:

> To prevent possible misunderstanding, a word. I paint the capitalist and the landlord in no sense *couleur de rose*. But here individuals are dealt with only in so far as they are the personifications of economic categories, embodiments of particular class-relations and class-interests. My standpoint, from which the evolution of the economic formation of society is viewed as a process of natural history, can less than any other make the individual responsible for relations whose creature he socially remains, however much he may subjectively raise himself above them. (1978:297)

For example, Marxists denounce individual capitalists and landowners as bearing responsibility in society. It needs no mention that, like Takeda, virtually all other Marxists of the time came from wealthy families. Their guilt over this fact led them to participate in the movement, but this was nothing more than an attempt to "subjectively raise [themselves] above" social relations. Then, when they defected from the movement, they also subjectively felt this to be a transgression and sought salvation for it. Takeda's point, however, is that the individual bears no "responsibility," yet all individuals exist within "social relations"—this is precisely the meaning of "shame"—and there can be no way to erase this fact. In other words, in the process of falling away from the Marxist political movement, Takeda had grasped, under the label of Buddhism, the perspective by which Marx sees history as a "process of natural history."

In the world of the *Historical Records*, there is no concept or person transcending this world. For example, although Confucianism was the only form of learning and religion officially sanctioned by the state at the time that Sima Qian wrote the *Historical Records*, Confucius is thoroughly relativized in the work as a being in the world, one who is not supported by any separate transcendental meaning. "The world of the *Historical Records*" is something that has no outside; that is, it is a world of interrelationships that cannot be transcended. What Takeda refers to as "the world of the *Historical Records*" is a world without center, or rather a world with multiple centers, a world of chaos that necessarily forces all centers into ruin. Implicitly, this signified the inevitable "ruin" of the Japanese empire.

Takeda's *Sima Qian: The World of the "Historical Records"* was published quietly in 1943, amid the chorus of calls to "overcome modernity" emanating from former leftists, who tried to subjectively raise themselves above the reality of capitalist relations or the relation to Asia. At the time, there was almost no one who could understand his intent. Neither was there anyone to understand it in the postwar period. For eventually, official Marxism as well as the prewar structure that situated an existentialist moment against this Marxism were both resuscitated. No doubt, Takeda's turn toward fiction writing could not have happened without his experience of actually facing "ruin" and "chaos" in Shanghai during the war. Of course, there were many postwar writers who shared such experiences to a greater or lesser extent, but what distinguished Takeda was precisely his consciousness of "the world of the *Historical Records*." Although Takeda's fiction is beyond the scope of this essay, one can say that it was based on an attempt to see in the postwar order the world of the *Historical Records*.

This posed a certain difficulty. For the postwar world was based on a structure of binary opposition between the United States and the Soviet Union; in other words, it was a world that possessed a center. The literature born from the "chaos" of the immediate postwar period was soon absorbed into this stable structure, which was expressed by way of the problematic of "politics and literature." In this context, Takeda's continued fixation on a "world without center" became in a way the subject of awe or reverence, but it also led to his literature being set aside as something inchoate. However, this incompleteness is tied to the fact that he thought about writing in a way that did not fit into the concepts of either Western literature or Japanese literature. This can also be seen in his work on the *Historical Records*.

The writing in the *Historical Records* unquestionably contains a singular richness that is lacking in contemporary historiography and historical fiction. It is a richness that does not emerge from an engagement with "individuals" or with "totality." Rather, the secret resides in the structure of the *Historical Records*, which Takeda discerned:

> What is at issue here is not the fate of individuals but instead the relations between human beings who form the center. Through examination of the "center of the world" from many different points of view as well as of rules of its movement, the historical importance of individual characteristics is clearly demonstrated. It is precisely at this moment that "anger," "laughter," "courage," "impatience," and "wisdom" brilliantly come to the surface of the illustrated tapestry of history. (1972c:82)

The classification of human beings in the *Historical Records* always remains wedded to the concrete, and at the same time, in contrast to modern realism, it is a system of signs densely woven by interrelations, difference, and identity. Most likely, one can say the same thing of Takeda's fiction. Takeda's novels are written like the *Historical Records*. For this reason, however, they necessarily appeared peculiar to those accustomed to modern

Western novels, as well as to those who welcomed efforts in the vein of Sartre after the war.

Today, however, with the postwar world having come to an end, the U.S–Soviet binarism has been replaced by the megacompetition of a single market, while the revival of nationalism and the establishment of the European Union have pushed the formation of economic and political blocs, leading to ideological reconfigurations. In this context, Takeda's work once more takes on fresh meaning. As in the prewar period, postmodernism in Japan emerged on the one hand as a "return to Japan" while giving rise on the other to an "internationalism" on the order of the Greater East Asia Co-Prosperity Sphere, completely erasing the kind of "postwar literature" that Takeda represents. Yet Takeda's *Sima Qian: The World of the "Historical Records"* foresees the eventual dissolution of not only the "postwar world" but also the "world order" that succeeds it.

AGRARIANISM (農本主義 *nōhonshugi*)   Political and philosophical movement that viewed agriculture as the national foundation and the agricultural economy and community as means of overcoming the contradictions of industrial capitalism.

AKUTAGAWA RYŪNOSUKE (芥川龍之介 1892–1927)   Author of numerous masterpieces of short fiction, including "Rashōmon" (1915), "Hell Screen" (Jigokuhen, 1918), "In a Grove" (Yabu no naka, 1922), and "Cogwheels" (Haguruma, 1927). His suicide, marked by a declaration of "vague anxiety about the future," became a defining moment of the age.

ALLIED RED ARMY INCIDENTS (連合赤軍事件 Rengō Sekigun Jiken)   Series of incidents from 1971 to 1972 involving members of the extremist group, including a standoff with police in a villa in the mountain resort town of Karuizawa in February 1972. The ensuing revelation of the group's slaying of its own members is commonly cited as an important inflection point in the demise of the New Left in Japan.

AMPO STRUGGLE (安保闘争)   Mass political uprising of 1959/1960 that unsuccessfully tried to halt the renewal of the U.S.-Japan Security Treaty.

ANGO   *See* Sakaguchi Ango.

BAKIN   *See* Kyokutei Bakin.

BASHŌ   *See* Matsuo Bashō.

BATTLE OF SEKIGAHARA (関ヶ原の戦い)   Decisive military conflict fought in 1600 over control of the realm that led to the establishment of the Tokugawa shogunate.

BUND   A faction of student activists formed in 1956 that led the Zengakuren during the Ampo struggle and that was marked by independence from and disillusionment with the Japanese Communist Party.

BUNKA BUNSEI (文化文政 1804–1830)　Consecutive eras during the Edo period that saw notable achievements in various arts, including fiction, drama, poetry, and painting.

CHEVALIER, MICHEL (1806–1879)　French statesman and economist who advocated free trade.

DAZAI OSAMU (太宰治 1909–1948)　Novelist known for his ironic self-portrayals in his fiction and whose works, including *The Setting Sun* (*Shayō*, 1947), captured the nihilistic sensibility of immediate postwar Japan.

DŌGEN (道元 1200–1253)　Monk of the early Kamakura period known as the founder of the Sōtō school of Zen Buddhism in Japan.

DOPPO　*See* Kunikida Doppo.

EAST ASIAN COOPERATIVE COMMUNITY (東亜協同体 Tōa Kyōdōtai)　Regional economic and political bloc conceptualized in the late 1930s by members of the Shōwa Research Association.

FEBRUARY 26 INCIDENT (二・二六事件 Ni-Ni-Roku Jiken)　Failed 1936 coup d'état led by young army officers of the Imperial Way faction. Although the revolt was put down under orders of the emperor, it marked a key moment in the development of the fascist state.

FREEDOM AND PEOPLE'S RIGHTS MOVEMENT (自由民権運動 Jiyū Minken Undō)　Popular political movement of the early Meiji period that spread throughout the country in the 1870s, advocating the establishment of civil rights and democratic institutions.

FRÓIS, LUÍS (1532–1597)　Portuguese Jesuit missionary who traveled to Japan in 1563 and lived there for the rest of his life.

FUKUMOTO KAZUO (福本和夫 1894–1983)　Leading Marxist theoretician who had a key role in the reconstitution of the Japanese Communist Party in the mid-1920s. He was later criticized by the Comintern and imprisoned from 1928 to 1942.

FUKUZAWA YUKICHI (福沢諭吉 1834–1901)　Influential thinker of the Meiji period and founder of Keiō Gijuku University who propounded ideals of modernization and enlightenment.

FUTABATEI SHIMEI (二葉亭四迷 1864–1909)　Novelist and translator widely credited with writing Japan's first modern novel, *Drifting Clouds* (*Ukigumo*, 1887–1889).

GENROKU (元禄 1688–1704)　Era during the Edo period marked by a flowering of urban culture and remarkable achievements in the arts.

GEN'YŌSHA (玄洋社)　Nationalist association organized in 1881 by disgruntled samurai from the former Fukuoka domain that advocated overseas expansion.

GONDŌ SEIKYŌ (権藤成卿 1868–1937)　Philosopher of agrarianism and critic of the modern state.

GREATER EAST ASIA CO-PROSPERITY SPHERE (大東亜共栄圏 Dai Tōa Kyōeiken)　Wartime concept that cast the Japanese empire as the formation of a regional political and economic bloc to counter Western imperialism in Asia.

HANADA KIYOTERU (花田清輝 1909–1974)　Literary critic active in the postwar intellectual world known especially for his engagement with the avant-garde.

HASHIKAWA BUNZŌ (橋川文三 1922–1983)　Intellectual historian known for his postwar reevaluation of the Japanese Romantic school.

HIDEYOSHI　*See* Toyotomi Hideyoshi.

HIGH TREASON INCIDENT (大逆事件 Taigyaku Jiken)　Incident of 1910 in which twenty-six anarchist and socialist activists were accused of plotting to assassinate the Meiji emperor. After a public trial lasting into the following year, all were found guilty and twelve were executed.

HŌNEN (法然 1133–1212)　Founder of the Pure Land sect (Jōdoshū) of Japanese Buddhism, whose teachings emphasize devotion to the Amida Buddha as opening the path to rebirth in the Pure Land after death.

HONGANJI (本願寺)　Head temple of the main branch of the True Pure Land sect (Jōdo Shinshū) of Japanese Buddhism, which became a powerful institution in the fifteenth and sixteenth centuries. Militarily subdued by Oda Nobunaga in the late sixteenth century, it was subsequently divided into two branches: Nishi (Western) and Higashi (Eastern) Honganji.

IBUSE MASUJI (井伏鱒二 1898–1993)　Novelist best known for his portrayal of the atomic bombing of Hiroshima and its aftermath in *Black Rain* (*Kuroi ame*, 1965).

ICHIKAWA HAKUGEN (市川白弦 1902–1986)　Monk and scholar of Buddhism whose works include *Zen and Contemporary Thought* (*Zen to gendai shisō*, 1967) and *Buddhists' War Responsibility* (*Bukkyōsha no sensō sekinin*, 1970).

IEYASU　*See* Tokugawa Ieyasu.

IKKŌ SECT (一向宗 Ikkōshū)   Meaning "single-minded," a name by which the True Pure Land sect of Japanese Buddhism was called.

IMPERIAL RESCRIPT ON EDUCATION (教育勅語 Kyōiku Chokugo)   Proclamation released in the Meiji emperor's name on October 30, 1890, setting forth moral principles of education centered on the ideal of the national polity.

IMPERIAL WAY FACTION (皇道派 Kōdōha)   Radical faction of primarily young officers in the army formed in the early 1930s and characterized by belief in imperial rule, ardent anticommunism, and agrarianism. Its influence waned after the failed coup d'état of February 26, 1936.

INOMATA TSUNAO (猪俣津南雄 1889–1942)   Marxist economist who helped form the Japanese Communist Party and was a central figure in the Labor-Farmer school.

I-NOVEL (私小説 watakushi shōsetsu)   Form of confessional fiction theorized in the 1920s and considered one of the primary genres of modern Japanese fiction.

INUKAI TSUYOSHI (犬養毅 1855–1932)   Prime minister who was assassinated in the attempted coup d'état of May 15, 1932.

ISE SHRINE (伊勢神宮)   Important site of early *kami* worship and of worship for the ancestral cult of the imperial family that became the center of state Shinto in the Meiji period. It is composed of two complexes of shrine buildings marked by spare wooden architecture, of which the main buildings are rebuilt every twenty years.

ISODA KŌICHI (磯田光一 1931–1987)   Literary critic known for his work on Mishima Yukio and his innovative studies of cultural and intellectual history in works such as *Tokyo as Idea* (*Shisō to shite no Tōkyō*, 1978) and *The Space of Postwar History* (*Sengoshi no kūkan*, 1983).

ITŌ HIROBUMI (伊藤博文 1841–1909)   Powerful statesman of the Meiji period who served as prime minister and later as resident-general of Korea. He was assassinated in Harbin by an activist for Korean independence.

KAFŪ   *See* Nagai Kafū.

KAGA PROVINCE (加賀国)   Province in present-day Ishikawa Prefecture that was under the control of a league of Honganji followers from the late fifteenth to late sixteenth centuries.

KAMAKURA (鎌倉)   City in present-day Kanagawa Prefecture that served as the seat of the military government during the Kamakura period. The term "Kamakura Buddhism" is applied to the developments in Japanese Buddhism during this period.

KATSURA DETACHED PALACE (桂離宮 Katsura Rikyū)   Aristocratic villa (later, an imperial villa) built in the seventeenth century that was lauded by Bruno Taut.

KITA IKKI (北一輝 1883–1937)   Advocate of state socialism and national reform who was executed in the wake of the failed coup d'état of February 26, 1936.

KITAMURA TŌKOKU (北村透谷 1868–1894)   Poet and critic active in the Freedom and People's Rights Movement and a central figure in nineteenth-century Romanticism.

KIYOZAWA MANSHI (清沢満之 1863–1903)   True Pure Land Buddhist priest and philosopher active in the Meiji period.

KOBAYASHI HIDEO (小林秀雄 1902–1983)   Influential literary critic credited with raising criticism to the level of artistic expression and known for his continual rejection of any static ideological position.

KONDRATIEFF, NIKOLAI (1892–1938)   Russian economist who posited the existence of long waves of expansion and depression in capitalist economies.

KONOE FUMIMARO (近衛文麿 1891–1945)   Aristocrat and politician who served as prime minister during the Second Sino-Japanese War and in the lead-up to the Pacific War.

KŌTOKU SHŪSUI (幸徳秋水 1871–1911)   Pioneering socialist and later anarchist thinker who was executed in the High Treason Incident.

KUNIKIDA DOPPO (国木田独歩 1871–1908)   Poet and novelist who had an important role in the establishment of modern Japanese literature, helping to shape the development of a vernacular literary language through his writings and translations.

KYOKUTEI BAKIN (曲亭馬琴 1767–1848)   Fiction writer of the Edo period whose representative works include *Strange Tale of the Crescent Moon* (*Chinsetsu yumiharizuki*, 1807–1811) and *Tale of the Eight Dogs* (*Nansō Satomi hakkenden*, 1814–1842).

KYOTO SCHOOL (京都学派 Kyōto gakuha)   Prominent philosophical school centered on the philosophy department of Kyoto University in the Taishō and Shōwa periods.

LABOR-FARMER SCHOOL (労農派 Rōnōha)   Group of scholars centered on intellectuals affiliated with the journal *Rōnō* (founded 1927) who argued, against the Lectures school, that the Meiji Restoration constituted a bourgeois revolution.

LECTURES SCHOOL (講座派 Kōzaha)   Group of scholars affiliated with the seven-volume *Lectures on the Historical Development of Japanese Capitalism* (*Nihon shihonshugi hattatsushi kōza*), published by Iwanami from 1932 to 1933. The group's main argument, claiming the necessity of a two-stage revolution, was in line with the so-called 1932 Theses issued by the Comintern in May 1932.

MARCO POLO BRIDGE INCIDENT (盧溝橋事件 Rokōkyō Jiken)   Confrontation between Japanese and Chinese forces in July 1937 that led to full-scale war between Japan and China.

MARUYAMA MASAO (丸山眞男 1914–1996)   Widely influential intellectual of the postwar period known for his analyses of Japanese intellectual and political history and whose works include *Studies in the Intellectual History of Tokugawa Japan* (*Nihon seiji shisōshi kenkyū*, 1952; translated 1974) and *Thought and Behaviour in Modern Japanese Politics* (*Gendai seiji no shisō to kōdō*, 1956–1957; translated 1963).

MATSUO BASHŌ (松尾芭蕉 1644–1694)   Revered Edo-period poet and master of the *haikai* genre, a form of linked-verse poetry and the progenitor of what became known as haiku.

MEIJI RESTORATION (明治維新 Meiji Ishin)   Nineteenth-century revolution of Japanese state and society, marked by the dissolution of the Tokugawa shogunate in 1867 and the establishment of a new government in the name of the emperor in 1868.

MINOBE TATSUKICHI (美濃部達吉 1873–1948)   Constitutional scholar and professor at Tokyo Imperial University who developed an interpretation of the constitution positing the emperor as an organ of state. In 1935, his theory was attacked as subverting the national polity, leading to his resignation from the House of Peers and the banning of his publications.

MIKI KIYOSHI (三木清 1897–1945)   Philosopher who studied with Nishida Kitarō and Martin Heidegger and whose work on historical materialism and critique of fascism were influential in the interwar period. He later became a member of the Shōwa Research Association.

MISHIMA YUKIO (三島由紀夫 1925–1970)   Internationally celebrated postwar novelist and playwright whose final series of four novels, known collectively as *The Sea of Fertility* (*Hōjō no umi*, 1965–1971), depicts the course of Japanese history through the device of metempsychosis.

MORI ŌGAI (森鴎外 1862–1922)   Novelist, critic, translator, and army physician who played a defining part in modern literature, introducing various currents of European thought and leaving behind numerous masterpieces of fiction and biography.

MOTOORI NORINAGA (本居宣長 1730–1801)   National Learning scholar of the Edo period known for his studies of the *Kojiki* and *The Tale of Genji* (*Genji monogatari*).

MURAKAMI HARUKI (村上春樹 b. 1949)   One of Japan's most popular contemporary novelists whose early works thematized the dissipation of political struggle and the ascendancy of an increasingly globalized consumer culture in post-1960s Japan.

NAGAI KAFŪ (永井荷風 1879–1959)   Novelist known for his pursuit in his fiction of the vanishing traces of old Edo.

NĀGĀRJUNA (ca. 150–250)   Indian philosopher who founded the Madhyamaka school of Mahāyāna Buddhism

NAKAE CHŌMIN (中江兆民 1847–1901)   Thinker who helped shape the development of democratic ideas and institutions in Japan during the Meiji period.

NAKAGAMI KENJI (中上健次 1946–1992)   Novelist known for his powerful representations of the social and cultural space of the *roji* (alley), Nakagami's imaginative rendering of the outcaste village in Shingū where he was raised.

NAKANO SEIGŌ (中野正剛 1886–1943)   Journalist and right-wing politician.

NATIONAL LEARNING (国学 Kokugaku)   Influential school of thought that rose to prominence in the Tokugawa period, stressing the importance of ancient classics, which were seen as repositories of an originary Yamato spirit prior to the importation of Chinese culture.

NATSUME SŌSEKI (夏目漱石 1867–1916)   Considered one of modern Japan's premier novelists whose works chronicle the inner and intersubjective conflicts involved in the transition to modernity.

NICHIREN (日蓮 1222–1282)   Monk of the Kamakura period and founder of what became known as the Nichiren sect of Japanese Buddhism, also known as the Hokke, or Lotus, sect because of its emphasis on the Lotus Sutra.

NIKKŌ TŌSHŌGŪ (日光東照宮)   Shrine dedicated to Ieyasu, the first Tokugawa shogun.

NISHIDA KITARŌ (西田幾多郎 1870–1945)   One of the most influential philosophers of modern Japan and a main figure in the Kyoto school.

NISHITANI KEIJI (西谷啓治 1900–1990) Prominent Kyoto school philosopher and disciple of Nishida Kitarō.

NOBUNAGA *See* Oda Nobunaga.

NOGI MARESUKE (乃木希典 1849–1912) Army general who served in the Seinan, Sino-Japanese, and Russo-Japanese wars. He committed ritual suicide following the death of the Meiji emperor, an act taken as a form of *junshi*, the suicide of a samurai upon the death of his lord.

ODA NOBUNAGA (織田信長 1534–1582) Daimyo of the Warring States period who achieved military control over much of the realm. Along with Toyotomi Hideyoshi and Tokugawa Ieyasu, he was the first of the three "unifiers" of Japan.

ŌE KENZABURŌ (大江健三郎 b. 1935) One of the most acclaimed novelists of contemporary Japan, awarded the 1994 Nobel Prize in Literature.

ŌGAI *See* Mori Ōgai.

OGURI TADAMASA (小栗忠順 1827–1868) Shogunal retainer of the late Edo period who was executed for his resistance to the new Meiji government.

OKAKURA KAKUZŌ (岡倉覚三, also Okakura Tenshin 岡倉天心 1862–1913) Leading figure in the Meiji-period art world who helped establish the modern study and practice of art in Japan while also introducing the history of Japanese art to the West in works such as *The Ideals of the East* (1903) and *The Book of Tea* (1906).

ŌKUBO TOSHIMICHI (大久保利通 1830–1878) Lower-ranking samurai of the Satsuma domain who had a key role in the Meiji Restoration and the formation of the new government.

OZAKI HOTSUMI (尾崎秀実 1901–1944) Journalist and adviser to Prime Minister Konoe Fumimaro and member of the Shōwa Research Association. He was executed as a spy.

OZAKI KŌYŌ (尾崎紅葉 1867–1903) Prominent novelist of the Meiji period and central figure in the literary group Friends of the Inkstone (Ken'yūsha) whose representative work is *The Golden Demon* (1897–1902).

SAIGŌ TAKAMORI (西郷隆盛 1827–1877) Samurai of the Satsuma domain who had a leading role in the Meiji Restoration and who lost his life after being defeated in the Seinan War.

GLOSSARY 219

SAKAGUCHI ANGO (坂口安吾 1906–1955) Novelist and critic known for his wartime critique of traditional aesthetics and his engagement with the ideological and social collapse of the immediate postwar period.

SAKAI (堺) City in present-day Osaka Prefecture that developed into a largely self-governing trading port in the medieval period.

SAKOKU (鎖国) State policy restricting access to and from the outside world during the Tokugawa period.

SANKIN KŌTAI (参勤交代) Tokugawa policy, aimed at consolidating shogunal power, that required daimyo to maintain residences in Edo, where they were to live for certain periods of time.

SEINAN WAR (西南戦争, also Satsuma Rebellion) Revolt against the new Meiji state led by samurai from the Satsuma domain (present-day Kagoshima), which lasted from February to September 1877.

SHIGA NAOYA (志賀直哉 1883–1971) Critically revered novelist and central figure in the Taishō-period White Birch School (Shirakabaha), known for its cosmopolitan humanism.

SHIKITEI SANBA (式亭三馬 1776–1822) Popular writer of the late Edo period whose representative works include *Bathhouse of the Floating World* (*Ukiyo buro*, 1813–1814).

SHIMAZAKI TŌSON (島崎藤村 1872–1943) Poet and novelist whose *Broken Commandment* (*Hakai*, 1906) is seen as a pinnacle of naturalist fiction in Japan and whose historical epic *Before the Dawn* (*Yoake mae*, 1929–1935) examines the turbulent era surrounding the Meiji Restoration.

SHIMIZU IKUTARŌ (清水幾太郎 1907–1988) Social scientist and critic active in postwar peace and democracy movements who later became a proponent of national rearmament.

SHINRAN (親鸞 1173–1262) Monk of the early Kamakura period and disciple of Hōnen who founded the True Pure Land sect of Japanese Buddhism, whose teachings emphasize the importance of faith and the invocation of the Amida Buddha's name as the basis for salvation.

SHINTO (神道) Array of indigenous practices and beliefs relating to *kami* worship in Japan, established as a state religion in the late nineteenth century.

SHŌWA RESEARCH ASSOCIATION (昭和研究会 Shōwa Kenkyūkai) Served as the brain trust of Prime Minister Konoe Fumimaro and included a wide range of thinkers, including former leftist intellectuals.

SHŌWA RESTORATION (昭和維新 Shōwa Ishin)   Call for a revival of the spirit of the Meiji Restoration and direct imperial rule amid the political and economic uncertainties of the 1920s and 1930s.

SIMA QIAN (司馬遷, J., Shiba Sen; ca. 145–86 B.C.E.)   Historian of the early Han dynasty and author of the *Historical Records* (*Shiji*, 109–91 B.C.E.).

SŌSEKI   *See* Natsume Sōseki.

SUZUKI DAISETSU (鈴木大拙 1870–1966)   Buddhist scholar and thinker known for his explication of Zen Buddhism to Western readers.

TAKEDA TAIJUN (武田泰淳 1912–1976)   Prominent figure in postwar literature whose works were shaped by his experience in and study of China as well as his involvement in Buddhism.

TAKEUCHI YOSHIMI (竹内好 1910–1977)   Influential intellectual and scholar of Chinese literature who wrote on Lu Xun, national literature, and the "overcoming modernity" debate.

TANNISHŌ (歎異抄, *Notes Lamenting Differences*)   Record of Shinran's sayings said to be compiled by his disciples in the late thirteenth century and meant to correct the corruption of his teachings following his death.

TAUT, BRUNO (1880–1938)   German architect who lived in Japan from 1933 to 1936 and wrote a number of books on Japanese architecture and aesthetics.

TEMPLE OF THE GOLDEN PAVILION (金閣寺 Kinkakuji)   Rinzai-sect temple in Kyoto noted for its gold-leaf exterior, it was burned to the ground by a disgruntled acolyte in 1950, an event that served as the background for Mishima Yukio's novel *The Temple of the Golden Pavilion* (*Kinkakuji*, 1956).

THIERS, ADOLPHE (1797–1877)   French historian and politician who took a prominent role in the turbulent politics of nineteenth-century France, including his suppression of the Paris Commune as provisional head of the national government during the Third Republic.

TOKUGAWA IEYASU (徳川家康 1542–1616)   First Tokugawa shogun, who consolidated political control over the realm following the Battle of Sekigahara under an enduring administrative apparatus.

TOSAKA JUN (戸坂潤 1900–1945)   Marxist philosopher who criticized the intellectual movement toward fascism in the prewar and wartime periods.

TOYOTOMI HIDEYOSHI (豊臣秀吉 1537?–1598)   Daimyo of humble origins in the Warring States period who unified the realm under his rule and initiated various reforms, such as the stratification of social classes, that would have a lasting impact on Japanese society.

TSUBOUCHI SHŌYŌ (坪内逍遥 1859–1935)   Novelist, critic, and translator known especially for his theorization of the modern novel in *Essence of the Novel* (*Shōsetsu shinzui*, 1885–1886).

UCHIMURA KANZŌ (内村鑑三 1861–1930)   Prominent Christian thinker who founded the Nonchurch Movement.

UNO KŌZŌ (宇野弘蔵 1897–1977)   Marxist economist who developed original analyses of capitalism in works such as *Principles of Political Economy: Theory of a Purely Capitalist Society* (*Keizai genron*, 1964; translated 1980).

WATANABE KAZUO (渡辺一夫 1901–1975)   Scholar of French literature known for his studies and translations of François Rabelais.

WATSUJI TETSURŌ (和辻哲郎 1889–1960)   Influential philosopher known for writings on ethics, aesthetics, and cultural history.

XAVIER, FRANCIS (1506–1552)   Founder of the Society of Jesus and missionary in Japan from 1549 to 1551.

YAMATO COURT (大和朝廷 Yamato Chōtei)   Central polity, located in the Yamato area of what is present-day Nara Prefecture, that gained authority over a large section of the Japanese archipelago from around the fourth to the middle of the seventh centuries.

YANAGITA KUNIO (柳田国男 1875–1962)   Founder of ethnology (*minzokugaku*) in Japan. His research on folklore, folk customs, and ancient culture influenced a wide range of disciplines.

YASUDA YOJŪRŌ (保田与重郎 1910–1981)   Literary critic and important figure in the Japanese Romantic school whose critique of modernity achieved prominence in the early Shōwa period.

YOSHIMITSU YOSHIHIKO (吉満義彦 1904–1945)   Catholic theologian who wrote on religion, philosophy, and ethics.

ZENGAKUREN (全学連)   Abbreviation of Zen Nihon Gakusei Jichikai Sōrengō (National Federation of Student Self-Governing Associations), a student group that played a key part in the Ampo struggle.

ZENKYŌTŌ (全共闘)   Abbreviation of Zen Gaku Kyōtō Kaigi (All Campus Joint Struggle Committees), student activist groups that came to prominence on university campuses beginning in 1968.

WORKS CITED

Arendt, Hannah. 1973. *The Origins of Totalitarianism*. New York: Harcourt Brace Jovanovich.

Benedict, Ruth. 1946. *The Chrysanthemum and the Sword: Patterns of Japanese Culture*. Boston: Houghton Mifflin.

Benjamin, Walter. 1977. *The Origin of German Tragic Drama*. Translated by John Osborne. London: NLB.

Bourdaghs, Michael K. 2003. *The Dawn That Never Comes: Shimazaki Tōson and Japanese Nationalism*. New York: Columbia University Press.

Bowring, Richard. 1979. *Mori Ōgai and the Modernization of Japanese Culture*. Cambridge: Cambridge University Press.

Burke, Kenneth. 1966. *Language as Symbolic Action: Essays on Life, Literature, and Method*. Berkeley: University of California Press.

Corry, Leo. 1997. "David Hilbert and the Axiomatization of Physics (1894–1905)." *Archive for History of Exact Sciences* 51:83–198.

Defoe, Daniel. 2007. *Robinson Crusoe*. Edited by Thomas Keymer. Oxford: Oxford University Press.

de Man, Paul. 1983. "The Rhetoric of Temporality." In *Blindness and Insight: Essays in the Rhetoric of Contemporary Criticism*. Minneapolis: University of Minnesota Press.

Derrida, Jacques. 1992. "This Strange Institution Called Literature: An Interview with Jacques Derrida." In *Acts of Literature*, edited by Derek Attridge. New York: Routledge.

——. 1994. *Specters of Marx: The State of the Debt, the Work of Mourning, and the New International*. Translated by Peggy Kamuf. New York: Routledge.

Endo, Fuhito. 2002. "Review: Kojin Karatani and the Return of the Thirties: Psychoanalysis in/of Japan." *Semiotic Review of Books* 13, no. 1:2–3.

Freud, Sigmund. 1957. "The Poet and Day-Dreaming." In *Collected Papers*, translated by Joan Riviere. 5 vols. London: Hogarth Press.

———. 1965. *New Introductory Lectures on Psycho-Analysis*. Translated and edited by James Strachey. New York: Norton.

Fróis, Luís. 1991. *Yōroppa bunka to Nihon bunka* (*European Culture and Japanese Culture*). Translated by Okada Akio. Tokyo: Iwanami shoten.

Fujita Shōzō. 1997. *Tenkō no shisōshi-teki kenkyū* (*Research on the Intellectual History of Tenkō*). Vol. 2 of *Fujita Shōzō chosakushū* (*Collected Writings of Fujita Shōzō*). Tokyo: Misuzu shobō.

Fukumoto Kazuo. 1985. *Nihon runessansu shiron* (*On the History of the Japanese Renaissance*). Tokyo: Hōsei Daigaku shuppankyoku.

Fukuyama, Francis. 1998. *The End of History and the Last Man*. New York: Free Press.

Girard, René. 1977. *Violence and the Sacred*. Translated by Patrick Gregory. Baltimore: Johns Hopkins University Press.

Gramsci, Antonio. 1971. *Selections from the Prison Notebooks of Antonio Gramsci*. Edited and translated by Quintin Hoare and Geoffrey Nowell Smith. New York: International Publishers.

Gropius, Walter. 1938. "The Theory and Organization of the Bauhaus." In *Bauhaus: 1919–1928*, edited by Herbert Bayer, Walter Gropius, and Ise Gropius. New York: Museum of Modern Art.

Hanada Kiyoteru. 1946. *Fukkōki no seishin* (*The Spirit of the Renaissance*). Tokyo: Gakansha.

Hardt, Michael, and Antonio Negri. 2000. *Empire*. Cambridge, Mass.: Harvard University Press.

Hartmann, Nicolai. 1960. *Die Philosophie des deutschen Idealismus*. Berlin: de Gruyter.

Hasumi Shigehiko. 1989. *Shōsetsu kara tōku hanarete* (*At a Distance from the Novel*). Tokyo: Nihon bungeisha.

Hegel, Georg Wilhelm Friedrich. 1967. *Hegel's Philosophy of Right*. Translated by T. M. Knox. Oxford: Oxford University Press.

———. 1971. *Hegel's Philosophy of Mind*. Translated by William Wallace. Oxford: Clarendon Press.

———. 1977. *Phenomenology of Spirit*. Translated by A. V. Miller. Oxford: Clarendon Press.

———. 1991. *The Philosophy of History*. Translated by J. Sibree. Buffalo, N.Y.: Prometheus Books.

Heidegger, Martin. 1993. "Declaration of Support for Adolf Hitler and the National Socialist State [November 11, 1933]." In *The Heidegger*

Controversy: A Critical Reader, edited by Richard Wolin. Cambridge, Mass.: MIT Press.
Hirata, Hosea. 2005. *Discourses of Seduction: History, Evil, Desire, and Modern Japanese Literature*. Cambridge, Mass.: Harvard University Asia Center.
Hur, Nam-lin. 2007. *Death and Social Order in Tokugawa Japan: Buddhism, Anti-Christianity, and the Danka System*. Cambridge, Mass.: Harvard University Asia Center.
Ichikawa Hakugen. 1970. *Bukkyōsha no sensō sekinin* (*Buddhists' War Responsibility*). Tokyo: Shunjūsha.
Ikeda Eishun, 1987. "Kindaiteki kaimei shichō to Bukkyō" (Modern Enlightenment Thought and Buddhism). In *Ronshū Nihon Bukkyōshi* (*Collected Essays on the History of Japanese Buddhism*), vol. 8, edited by Ikeda Eishun. Tokyo: Yūzankaku shuppan.
Inamura Ryūichi. 1937. *Shūkyō kaikaku to Nihon nōmin sensō* (*Religious Reformation and Japan's Peasant Wars*). Tokyo: Kaizōsha.
Isoda Kōichi. 1983. *Sengoshi no kūkan* (*The Space of Postwar History*). Tokyo: Shinchōsha.
Jameson, Fredric. 1983. "Postmodernism and Consumer Society." In *The Anti-Aesthetic: Essays on Postmodern Culture*, edited by Hal Foster. Port Townsend, Wash.: Bay Press.
Kamiyama Shigeo. 2003. *Tennōsei ni kansuru rironteki shomondai* (*The Theoretical Problematics of the Emperor System*). Tokyo: Kobushi shobō.
Karatani Kōjin. 1989a. "1970 = Showa 45." Translated by Sandra Buckley. *Polygraph: An International Journal of Culture and Politics* 2–3:74–92.
———. 1989b. *Tankyū II* (*Investigations II*). Tokyo: Kōdansha.
———. 1991. "The Discursive Space of Modern Japan." Translated by Seiji M. Lippit. *boundary 2* 18, no. 3:191–219.
———. 1993a. "Kōtsū kūkan ni tsuite no nōto" (Notes on Communicative Space). In *Yūmoa to shite no yuibutsuron* (*Materialism as Humor*). Tokyo: Chikuma shobō.
———. 1993b. *Origins of Modern Japanese Literature*. Translation edited by Brett de Bary. Durham, N.C.: Duke University Press.
———. 1995. *Architecture as Metaphor: Language, Number, Money*. Translated by Sabu Kohso. Cambridge, Mass.: MIT Press.
———. 2001. "Buddhism, Marxism and Fascism in Japanese Intellectual

Discourse in the 1930's and 1940's: Sakaguchi Ango and Takeda Taijun." Translated by Joseph A. Murphy. In *Approches critiques de la pensée japonaise du XXe siècle*, edited by Livia Monnet. Montreal: Presses de l'Université de Montréal.

———. 2002. *Karatani Kōjin shoki ronbunshū* (*Collected Early Essays by Karatani Kōjin*). Tokyo: Hihyō kūkan.

———. 2004. "Moji no chiseigaku: Nihon seishinbunseki" (The Geopolitics of Letters: The Psychoanalysis of Japan). In *Teihon Karatani Kōjin shū* (*Selected Writings of Karatani Kōjin: Standard Edition*), vol. 4. Tokyo: Iwanami shoten.

———. 2005. "Kindai bungaku no owari" (The End of Modern Literature). In *Kindai bungaku no owari*. Tokyo: Inscript.

———. 2010. "The Irrational Will to Reason: The Praxis of Sakaguchi Ango." In *Literary Mischief: Sakaguchi Ango, Culture, and the War*, edited by James Dorsey and Doug Slaymaker. Lanham, Md.: Lexington Books.

———. n.d. "Representation and Repetition: *The 18th Brumaire of Louis Bonaparte* Revisited." Unpublished translation by Sabu Kohso.

Kawabata, Yasunari. 1981. *Snow Country*. Translated by Edward G. Seidensticker. New York: Perigee Books.

Kelsen, Hans. 2000. "On the Essence and Value of Democracy." Translated by Belinda Cooper. In *Weimar: A Jurisprudence of Crisis*, edited by Arthur J. Jacobson and Bernhard Schlink. Berkeley: University of California Press.

Kita Ikki. 1959a. *Kokka kaizōan genri taikō* (*General Principles of a Plan for National Reform*). In *Kita Ikki chosakushū* (*The Collected Writings of Kita Ikki*), vol. 2. Tokyo: Misuzu shobō.

———. 1959b. *Shina kakumei gaishi* (*The Unofficial History of the Chinese Revolution*). In *Kita Ikki chosakushū* (*The Collected Writings of Kita Ikki*), vol. 2. Tokyo: Misuzu shobō.

———. 2006. "Fundamental Principles for the Reorganization of Japan." Translated by Brij Tankha. In *Kita Ikki and the Making of Modern Japan: A Vision of Empire*, by Brij Tankha. Folkestone, Eng.: Global Oriental.

Kobayashi Hideo. 1995. "Multiple Designs." In *Literature of the Lost Home*, edited by Paul Anderer. Stanford, Calif.: Stanford University Press.

Kohso, Sabu. 1995. "Translator's Remarks: On the English Edition of *Architecture as Metaphor*." In *Architecture as Metaphor: Language,*

Number, Money, by Kojin Karatani. Translated by Sabu Kohso. Cambridge, Mass.: MIT Press.

Kojève, Alexandre. 1980. *Introduction to the Reading of Hegel: Lectures on the "Phenomenology of Spirit."* Translated by James H. Nichols Jr. Ithaca, N.Y.: Cornell University Press.

Kripke, Saul A. 1980. *Naming and Necessity*. Cambridge, Mass.: Harvard University Press.

Kunikida Doppo. 1982. *"River Mist" and Other Stories*. Translated by David G. Chibbett. Tokyo: Kodansha International.

Kushida Tamizō. 1979. "Waga kuni kosakuryō no tokushitsu ni tsuite" (On the Distinguishing Characteristics of Our Nation's Tenancy Fee [1931]). In *Kushida Tamizō zenshū* (*The Complete Works of Kushida Tamizō*), vol. 3, edited by Ōuchi Hyōe. Tokyo: Shakaishugi Kyōkai shuppankyoku.

Laclau, Ernesto. 1979. *Politics and Ideology in Marxist Theory: Capitalism, Fascism, Populism*. New York: Schocken Books.

Lévi-Strauss, Claude. 1966. *The Savage Mind*. Chicago: University of Chicago Press.

Lippit, Seiji Mizuta. 2004. "Kindai gensetsu no chizu ni okeru bungaku to iu toposu" (The Topos of Literature in the Map of Modern Discourse). *Kokubungaku: Kaishaku to kyōzai no kenkyū* 49, no. 1:101–12.

Mandel, Ernest. 1980. *Late Capitalism*. Translated by Joris De Bres. London: Verso.

Maruyama Masao. 1961. *Nihon no shisō* (*Japanese Thought*). Tokyo: Iwanami shoten.

———. 1963. "Thought and Behaviour Patterns of Japan's Wartime Leaders." In *Thought and Behaviour in Modern Japanese Politics*, edited by Ivan Morris. London: Oxford University Press.

Marx, Karl. 1963. *The Eighteenth Brumaire of Louis Bonaparte*. New York: International Publishers.

———. 1978. "Preface to the First German Edition." In *The Marx-Engels Reader*, edited by Robert C. Tucker. 2nd ed. New York: Norton.

———. 2001. *Capital, Volume III*. London: Electric Book Company.

Miki Kiyoshi. 1966. *Pasukaru ni okeru ningen no kenkyū* (*Pascal's Research on Man*). In *Miki Kiyoshi zenshū* (*The Complete Works of Miki Kiyoshi*), vol. 1, edited by Ōuchi Hyōe et al. Tokyo: Iwanami shoten.

———. 1968. *Shinran*. In *Miki Kiyoshi zenshū* (*The Complete Works of Miki Kiyoshi*), vol. 18, edited by Ōuchi Hyōe et al. Tokyo: Iwanami shoten.

Mishima, Yukio. 1974. *The Decay of the Angel*. Translated by Edward G. Seidensticker. New York: Vintage Books.

Mori Ōgai. 1977. *"The Incident at Sakai" and Other Stories*. Vol. 1 of *The Historical Literature of Mori Ōgai*, edited by David Dilworth and J. Thomas Rimer. Honolulu: University of Hawai'i Press.

Murai Osamu. 1995. *Nantō ideorogī no hassei* (*The Birth of the Ideology of the Southern Islands*). Tokyo: Ōta shuppan.

Murakami, Haruki. 1985. *Pinball, 1973*. Translated by Alfred Birnbaum. Tokyo: Kodansha International.

———. 1987. *Hear the Wind Sing*. Translated by Alfred Birnbaum. Tokyo: Kodansha International.

———. 1989. *A Wild Sheep Chase*. Translated by Alfred Birnbaum. Tokyo: Kodansha International.

———. 1991. *Hard-Boiled Wonderland and the End of the World*. Translated by Alfred Birnbaum. New York: Vintage International.

Murakami Yasusuke, Kumon Shumpei, and Satō Seizaburō. 1979. *Bunmei to shite no ie shakai* (*The Family Society as Civilization*). Tokyo: Chūō kōronsha.

Nakagami Kenji. 1996. *Kiseki* (*Miracles*). In *Nakagami Kenji zenshū* (*The Complete Works of Nakagami Kenji*), vol. 10, edited by Karatani Kōjin et al. Tokyo: Shūeisha.

Natsume Kyōko. 1929. *Sōseki no omoide* (*Memories of Sōseki*). Transcribed by Yuzuru Matsuoka. Tokyo: Iwanami shoten.

Natsume Sōseki. 1957. *Kokoro*. Translated by Edwin McClellan. Chicago: Gateway Editions.

———. 2009. *"Theory of Literature" and Other Critical Writings*. Edited by Michael K. Bourdaghs, Atsuko Ueda, and Joseph A. Murphy. New York: Columbia University Press.

Nietzsche, Friedrich. 1969. *Selected Letters of Friedrich Nietzsche*. Edited and translated by Christopher Middleton. Chicago: University of Chicago Press.

Nishida Kitarō. 2004a. "Goshinkō sōan: Rekishi tetsugaku ni tsuite" (Draft of Address to the Emperor: On the Philosophy of History). In *Nishida Kitarō zenshū* (*The Complete Works of Nishida Kitarō*), vol. 10, edited by Takeda Atsushi et al. Tokyo: Iwanami shoten.

———. 2004b. *Nihon bunka no mondai* (*The Question of Japanese Culture*). In *Nishida Kitarō zenshū* (*The Complete Works of Nishida Kitarō*), vol. 9, edited by Takeda Atsushi et al. Tokyo: Iwanami shoten.

Noguchi Yukio. 1995. *1940-nen taisei: Saraba senji keizai* (*The 1940 System: A Farewell to the Wartime Economy*). Tokyo: Tōyō keizai shinpōsha.

Ōe, Kenzaburō. 1974. *The Silent Cry*. Translated by John Bester. Tokyo: Kodansha International.

———. 1996a. *Hiroshima Notes*. Translated by David L. Swain and Toshi Yonezawa. New York: Grove Press.

———. 1996b. "Shisha no ogori" (Lavish Are the Dead). In *Ōe Kenzaburō shōsetsu* (*The Fiction of Ōe Kenzaburō*), vol. 1. Tokyo: Shinchōsha.

———. 1997. *Natsukashii toshi e no tegami* (*Letters to My Sweet Bygone Years*). In *Ōe Kenzaburō shōsetsu* (*The Fiction of Ōe Kenzaburō*), vol. 9. Tokyo: Shinchōsha.

Okakura, Kakuzō. 1964. *The Book of Tea*. New York: Dover.

———. 1970. *The Ideals of the East: With Special Reference to the Art of Japan*. Rutland, Vt.: Tuttle.

———. 1980. "Taitō kōgeishi" (History of Far Eastern Art). In *Okakura Tenshin zenshū* (*The Complete Works of Okakura Kakuzō*), vol. 4, edited by Kumamoto Kenjirō et al. Tokyo: Heibonsha.

Ooms, Herman. 1985. *Tokugawa Ideology: Early Constructs, 1570–1680*. Princeton, N.J.: Princeton University Press.

Rousseau, Jean-Jacques. 2002. *The Social Contract*. In *"The Social Contract" and "The First and Second Discourses,"* edited by Susan Dunn. New Haven, Conn.: Yale University Press.

Ruiz de Medina, Juan Garcia. 1988. *Harukanaru Kaori: Jūrokuseiki Kankoku kaikyō to Nihon Iesusukai* (*Distant Koryo: The Opening of the Sixteenth-Century Mission in Korea and the Society of Jesus in Japan*). Tokyo: Kondō shuppansha. [Japanese translation of *Orígenes de la iglesia Católica Coreana*]

Russell, Bertrand. 1905. "On Denoting." *Mind* 14, no. 56:479–93.

Sakagami Takashi. 1977. "Daini teisei to kokumin keizaikan no niruikei" (The Second Empire and Two Perspectives on the National Economy). In *Furansu burujoa shakai no seiritsu: Daini teiseiki no kenkyū* (*The Birth of French Bourgeois Society: Research on the Second Empire*), edited by Kawano Kenji. Tokyo: Iwanami shoten.

Sakaguchi Ango. 1986. "Discourse on Decadence." Translated by Seiji M. Lippit. *Review of Japanese Culture and Society* 1:1–5.

——. 1990a. "Bungaku no furusato" (The Home of Literature [1941]). In *Sakaguchi Ango zenshū* (*The Complete Works of Sakaguchi Ango*), vol. 14, edited by Karatani Kōjin and Sekii Mitsuo. Tokyo: Chikuma shobō.

——. 1990b. "Tsūzoku sakka Kafū" (Kafū, the Popular Writer). In *Sakaguchi Ango zenshū* (*The Complete Works of Sakaguchi Ango*), vol. 14, edited by Karatani Kōjin and Sekii Mitsuo. Tokyo: Chikuma shobō.

——. 1991. "Yōroppateki seikaku, Nipponteki seikaku" (European Character, Japanese Character). In *Sakaguchi Ango zenshū* (*The Complete Works of Sakaguchi Ango*), vol. 15, edited by Karatani Kōjin and Sekii Mitsuo. Tokyo: Chikuma shobō

——. 1999. "Kongo no jiin seikatsu ni taisuru shikō" (My Thoughts on the Future of Temple Life [1927]). In *Sakaguchi Ango zenshū* (*The Complete Works of Sakaguchi Ango*), vol. 1, edited by Karatani Kōjin and Sekii Mitsuo. Tokyo: Chikuma shobō.

——. 2005. "A Personal View of Japanese Culture." Translated by James Dorsey. In *The Columbia Anthology of Modern Japanese Literature*, edited by J. Thomas Rimer and Van C. Gessel. Vol. 1, *From Restoration to Occupation, 1868–1945*. New York: Columbia University Press.

——. 2010. "Discourse on Decadence." Translated by James Dorsey. In *Literary Mischief: Sakaguchi Ango, Culture, and the War*, edited by James Dorsey and Doug Slaymaker. Lanham, Md.: Lexington Books.

Sartre, Jean-Paul. 1988. "What Is Literature?" In *"What Is Literature" and Other Essays*. Cambridge, Mass.: Harvard University Press.

Schmitt, Carl. 1985. *Political Theology: Four Chapters on the Concept of Sovereignty*. Translated by George Schwab. Cambridge, Mass.: MIT Press.

——. 1988. *The Crisis of Parliamentary Democracy*. Translated by Ellen Kennedy. Cambridge, Mass.: MIT Press.

Sōda Kiichirō. 1930. "Nishida tetsugaku no hōhō ni tsuite" (On the Method of Nishida Philosophy). In *Sōda Kiichirō zenshū* (*The Complete Works of Sōda Kiichirō*), vol. 4, edited by the Sōda Hakase Kinenkai. Tokyo: Iwanami shoten.

Sorel, Georges. 1999. *Reflections on Violence*. Edited by Jeremy Jennings. Cambridge: Cambridge University Press.

Suzuki Daisetsu. 1968. *Nihonteki reisei* (*The Japanese Spirit*). In *Suzuki Daisetsu zenshū* (*The Complete Works of Suzuki Daisetsu*), vol. 8. Tokyo: Iwanami shoten.

Takeda Taijun. 1972a. "Metsubō ni tsuite" (On Ruin). In *Takeda Taijun zenshū* (*The Complete Works of Takeda Taijun*), vol. 12. Tokyo: Chikuma shobō.

——. 1972b. "Okamoto Kanoko *Seisei ryūten*" (Afterword to Okamoto Kanoko's *Samsara* [1949]). In *Takeda Taijun zenshū* (*The Complete Works of Takeda Taijun*), vol. 12. Tokyo: Chikuma shobō.

——. 1972c. *Shiba Sen: Shiki no sekai* (*Sima Qian: The World of the "Historical Records"*). Tokyo: Kōdansha.

——. 2007. "The Misshapen Ones." Translated by Edward G. Seidensticker. In *The Columbia Anthology of Modern Japanese Literature*, edited by J. Thomas Rimer and Van C. Gessel. Vol. 2, *From 1945 to the Present*. New York: Columbia University Press.

Takeuchi Yoshimi. 1980a. "Nihon no Ajiashugi" (Japan's Asianism). In *Takeuchi Yoshimi zenshū* (*The Complete Works of Takeuchi Yoshimi*), vol. 8, edited by Iikura Shōhei, Hashikawa Bunzō, and Matsumoto Ken'ichi. Tokyo: Chikuma shobō.

——. 1980b. "Okakura Tenshin." In *Takeuchi Yoshimi zenshū* (*The Complete Works of Takeuchi Yoshimi*), vol. 8, edited by Iikura Shōhei, Hashikawa Bunzō, and Matsumoto Ken'ichi. Tokyo: Chikuma shobō.

——. 1981a. "Nashonarizumu to shakai kakumei" (Nationalism and Social Revolution). In *Takeuchi Yoshimi zenshū* (*The Complete Works of Takeuchi Yoshimi*), vol. 7, edited by Iikura Shōhei, Hashikawa Bunzō, and Matsumoto Ken'ichi. Tokyo: Chikuma shobō.

——. 1981b. "Nihonjin no Ajia-kan" (Japanese Views of Asia). In *Takeuchi Yoshimi zenshū* (*The Complete Works of Takeuchi Yoshimi*), vol. 5, edited by Iikura Shōhei, Hashikawa Bunzō, and Matsumoto Ken'ichi. Tokyo: Chikuma shobō.

——. 2004. "Overcoming Modernity." In *What Is Modernity? Writings of Takeuchi Yoshimi*, edited and translated by Richard F. Calichman. New York: Columbia University Press.

Tansman, Alan. 2008. "Japanese Bridges: A Translation of Yasuda

Yojūrō's 'Nihon no Hashi.'" *Journal of Japanese Studies* 34, no. 2:257–61.

Taut, Bruno. 1962. *Nihonbi no saihakken* (*The Rediscovery of Japanese Beauty*). Translated by Shinoda Hideo. Tokyo: Iwanami shoten.

Tosaka Jun. 1935. *Nihon ideorogī* (*The Japanese Ideology*). Tokyo: Hakuyōsha.

Treat, John Whittier. 1995. *Writing Ground Zero: Japanese Literature and the Atomic Bomb*. Chicago: University of Chicago Press.

Wallerstein, Immanuel. 1980. *The Modern World-System II: Mercantilism and the Consolidation of the European World-Economy, 1600–1750*. New York: Academic Press.

Watanabe Kazuo. 1943. *Raburē oboegaki: Sono ta* (*"Notes on Rabelais" and Other Writings*). Tokyo: Hakusuisha.

Watsuji Tetsurō. 1962. "Nihon ni okeru Bukkyō shisō no ishoku" (The Transplantation of Buddhist Thought in Japan). In *Watsuji Tetsurō zenshū* (*The Complete Works of Watsuji Tetsurō*), vol. 4, edited by Abe Yoshishige et al. Tokyo: Iwanami shoten.

Watt, Ian. 1957. *The Rise of the Novel: Studies in Defoe, Richardson, and Fielding*. Berkeley: University of California Press.

Wilson, Edmund. 2003. *To the Finland Station*. New York: New York Review of Books.

Wittgenstein, Ludwig. 1958. *Philosophical Investigations*. Translated by G. E. M. Anscombe. Oxford: Blackwell.

Yabe Teiji. 1958. *Konoe Fumimaro*. Tokyo: Jiji tsūshinsha.

Yamaguchi Masao. 2003. *Afurika* (*Africa*). Vol. 4 of *Yamaguchi Masao chosakushū* (*Collected Writings of Yamaguchi Masao*), edited by Imafuku Ryūta. Tokyo: Chikuma shobō.

Yasuda Yojūrō. 1988. *Nihon Rōmanha no jidai* (*The Age of the Japanese Romantic School*). In *Yasuda Yojūrō zenshū* (*The Complete Works of Yasuda Yojūrō*), vol. 36. Tokyo: Kōdansha.

Yoshimitsu Yoshihiko. 2008. "The Theological Grounds of Overcoming Modernity." In *Overcoming Modernity: Cultural Identity in Wartime Japan*, edited and translated by Richard F. Calichman. New York: Columbia University Press.

Yoshimoto Takaaki. 2008. "On *Tenkō*, or Ideological Conversion." Translated by Hisaaki Wake. *Review of Japanese Culture and Society* 20:99–119.

Yusa, Michiko. 2002. *Zen and Philosophy: An Intellectual Biography of Nishida Kitarō*. Honolulu: University of Hawai'i Press.

Žižek, Slavoj. 2004. "The Parallax View." *New Left Review* 25:121–34.

——. 2006. *The Parallax View*. Cambridge, Mass.: MIT Press.

agrarianism, 36, 39n.6, 61
Akutagawa Ryūnosuke, 73
allegory, xxii, xxiin.7, xxiv, 91–96, 98–100, 103, 114, 120, 129
Allied Red Army, 82
Althusser, Louis, 13, 184
"Ampo struggle of 1960," xxii, 52, 53, 96n.3, 97–100, 111, 113
Ango. *See* Sakaguchi Ango
Annales school, 50
Arendt, Hannah, xii, 21
Asianism, 57–59, 59nn.2,3, 60–62, 72, 106–7, 110–11, 168

Bakhtin, Mikhail, 191
Balzac, Honoré de, 123
Barthes, Roland, 188
Bashō. *See* Matsuo Bashō
Bateson, Gregory, 133
Baudelaire, Charles, 18
Benedict, Ruth, 203
Benjamin, Walter, xxiin.7, 18, 91–92
Bergson, Henri, 104
Bolshevism, 13
Bonaparte, Louis Napoléon, xx–xxi, 3–5, 6n.2, 9–11, 13, 15–19, 22–23, 29, 35, 37n.4, 40–41
Bonapartism, 4, 6, 6n.2, 7, 18–19, 23, 34, 41
Bourdaghs, Michael K., xxiiin.9
Buddhism, xxvi, 66–68, 76, 173–86, 186n.9, 194–97, 199–204, 206–7
Bund faction, 112
Bunka Bunsei eras, 48

Burke, Kenneth, 8
Byōdōin (Buddhist temple), 189

Caesar, Julius, 6n.2, 20, 170
capitalism, xx, 1, 19, 24, 32, 42, 59n.3, 167, 185; global, x–xiii, xvii–xviii, 2, 23–25, 31n.1, 43–45, 53, 175; industrial, ix, 33, 38, 61, 179; in Japan, ix, xvi, 29–30, 30n.1, 33n.2, 38, 43n.9, 56, 61, 64n.5; late, xi, 2, 42–43, 45; mercantile, 32
Chevalier, Michel, 22
Chikazumi Jōkan, 179n.4
Chōmin. *See* Nakae Chōmin
Christianity, 49, 66–67, 76, 174n.1, 175–77, 179, 182, 191–92, 195, 203
Cold War, xii, xvi, 25, 45, 50, 82–83
Coleridge, Samuel Taylor, 157
Communist Party, 12, 29
Confucius, 207
Control faction, 40
Corry, Leo, 141n.4
Cromwell, Oliver, 37
Cultural Revolution, 72, 79

Dante Alighieri, 153, 158
Dazai Osamu, 202
de-Asianization, xxiii, 59, 61, 64, 65n.5
Defoe, Daniel, 94
de Man, Paul, xxiin.7
Derrida, Jacques, xviin.1, xxxn.12
Descartes, René, x
Dōgen, 173–74, 174n.1
Don Quixote (Cervantes), 136

Doppo. *See* Kunikida Doppo
Dostoyevsky, Fyodor, 124
Durrell, Lawrence, 151n.1, 151–54

East Asia Cooperative Community, 41, 61n.4
emperor: figure of, 3–4, 12, 15–16, 20, 30; of Japan, xxi, 31–33, 36–41, 39n.6, 48, 51, 54, 56, 62–63, 68–72, 82, 99, 109, 139, 167, 168, 176, 182, 184, 187; Louis Bonaparte as, 3, 10–11, 15–17, 22, 35; Meiji, 38, 74, 78; Shōwa, vii, xvi, 47, 78n.9, 82–84; Taishō, 38
Endo, Fuhito, xxin.6
Engels, Friedrich, 6, 6n.2, 7, 8n.3, 177

fascism, xx, 5–7, 10–11, 13, 23, 31, 34–36, 42n.8, 104; in Japan, xx, xxvi, 5, 11–12, 23, 31, 33–34, 36, 39, 41, 61, 71, 183–87, 193
Faulkner, William, 165
February 26 Incident, 39, 53, 68, 72, 139, 164
Fichte, Johann Gottlieb, 143, 183
Fordism, 25, 44
Foucault, Michel, 50, 136
Franco-Prussian War, 37n.4
Frankfurt school, 12, 34
Freedom and People's Rights Movement, 37, 37n.4, 56–57, 58, 60, 64n.5, 73, 76–77
French Revolution (1789), 19, 21, 35, 37, 37n.4, 57, 59, 64n.5, 79
French Revolution (1848), 7–10, 15–17, 35
Freud, Sigmund, 2, 12, 29, 164
Fróis, Luís, 192–93
Fujita Shōzō, xxiiin.9
Fukumoto Kazuo, 191, 191n.11
Fukuyama, Francis, 1
Fukuzawa, Yukichi, xxiii, 64, 64n.5
Futabatei Shimei, 90, 120

Gen'yōsha (ultranationalist society), 61

Girard, René, 103
globalization, xii–xiii, xviii, 1, 24–26
Gödel, Kurt, 141n.4, 142
Goethe, Johann Wolfgang von, 91
Gondō Seikyō, 39n.6
Gramsci, Antonio, 6n.2, 191
Great Depression, 5, 44
Greater East Asia Co-Prosperity Sphere, viii, 45, 53n.1, 61n.4, 83, 167, 184, 209
Gropius, Walter, 190

Hanada Kiyoteru, 191
Hardt, Michael, xiii
Hashikawa Bunzō, 52, 79
Hasumi Shigehiko, 124
Hegel, Georg Wilhelm Friedrich, 14, 19–21, 68–69, 93, 143–44, 152–60, 162–65, 170, 204–6
Heidegger, Martin, 3, 14, 14n.4, 15, 180, 183–85, 199
High Treason Incident, 53, 197
Hilbert, David, 141, 141n.4
Hirata, Hosea, xix, xixn.4
Hiromatsu Wataru, 8n.3
Hiroshima, atomic bombing of, 93–94, 94n.2
history, repetition of, vii–viii, ix, xiii, xvi–xviii, xx–xxi, xxix, 1–3, 5, 6n.2, 16, 19–22, 26, 29, 34–36, 43–44, 51, 53–54, 61, 63, 68, 79, 81, 83, 94, 98, 103, 114, 129, 132, 153, 156, 159, 163, 167–68, 171
Hitler, Adolf, 11–15, 35, 53n.1, 105, 128
Hobson, John A., 25
Hōnen, 173
Hōryūji (Buddhist temple), xxvii, 189
Hugo, Victor, 10
Hur, Nam-lin, 177n.3
Husserl, Edmund, 79, 195

Ibuse Masuji, 94
Ichikawa Hakugen, 186n.9

ideological conversion, xxiii, xxiiin.9, xxvi–xxvii, 61–62, 102, 110–12, 179–80, 198, 200, 203–4
Ikeda Eishun, 179n.4
imperialism, ix–xiii, 2, 5, 21–22, 25, 33n.2, 42n.8, 44–45, 59n.3; of Japan, 38, 43, 45, 58, 60–61, 64–66, 80, 106–7, 110, 184, 187, 205
Imperial Rescript on Education, 38
Imperial Way faction, 39, 41
Inomata Tsunao, 33n.2
I-novel, 64, 87, 91, 120, 153, 153n.3, 154
intercourse (*kōtsū*), xix, 65, 80, 131, 193
interiority, xxiv–xxvi, xxviii, 74, 76–77, 82, 122, 129
Inukai Tsuyoshi, 40n.7
Iraq War, xiii
irony, xxiv–xxv, 79–81, 122, 126, 128, 135–37, 139–40, 143, 148–49, 164, 202
Ise Shrine, 187, 190
Isoda Kōichi, 111
Itō Hirobumi, 57, 58

Jameson, Fredric, 136
Japanese Romantic school, 52, 55, 78, 80–81, 164, 181
Jünger, Ernst, 42

Kafka, Franz, 93
Kafū. *See* Nagai Kafū
Kamiyama Shigeo, 33n.2
Kant, Immanuel, xvii, 119–20, 140, 143, 154, 183
Katsura Detached Palace, xxvii, 187, 190
Kawabata Yasunari, 81, 81n.11
Kelsen, Hans, 8, 8n.3
Kierkegaard, Søren, 66, 159
Kishi Nobusuke, 111
Kita Ikki, 36, 37n.4, 39, 39n.6, 40, 42, 68–70, 80
Kitamura Tōkoku, 76, 113
Kiyozawa Manshi, 179, 179n.4
Kobayashi Hideo, 146–47, 181
Kohso, Sabu, xviiin.3, xixn.4

Kojève, Alexandre, 159, 177
Kondratieff, Nikolai, 2, 2n.1, 23
Konoe Fumimaro, xxi, 36, 40, 40n.7, 41–43, 43n.9, 61n.4, 148, 185
Kōtoku Shūsui, 66
Kripke, Saul, 146
Kristeva, Julia, xxix
Kuhn, Thomas, 50
Kunikida Doppo, xxiv–xxvi, 121–24, 128–29, 137
Kushida Tamizō, 30n.1
Kyokutei Bakin, 77, 168
Kyoto school, 42, 54–55, 180–82, 184–85

Labor-Farmer school, 29–30, 30n.1, 31, 33n.2
Lacan, Jacques, xxin.6, 13
Laclau, Ernesto, 30n.1
landscape, xxv, 95, 121–24, 127, 129, 137, 149
Lectures school, 29–30, 30n.1, 31–32, 33n.2, 43n.9
Lelouche, Claude, 123
Lenin, Vladimir, xi, 25
Levinas, Emmanuel, 199
Lévi-Strauss, Claude, xxv, 51, 130–31
liberalism, x–xiii, 2, 5, 13, 42, 45, 183
Luther, Martin, 174n.1, 177
Lu Xun, 202

Machiavelli, Niccolò, 17–18
Madame Bovary (Flaubert), 136
Manchukuo, 80
Mandel, Ernest, 2n.1
Marco Polo Bridge Incident, 42
Maruyama Masao, 34, 36
Marx, Karl, viii, xvii, 8n.3, 12, 25, 33, 59n.2, 72, 79, 81, 159, 184, 207; *Capital*, viii, xx, 1–4, 10, 23–26, 31–32, 34, 206; *The Communist Manifesto*, 77; *The Eighteenth Brumaire of Louis Bonaparte*, viii, xx, 1–7, 8n.3, 12–13, 15–16, 18–19, 22–23, 26, 29, 31–35, 37, 40

Marxism, xxiiin.9, xxvi–xxvii, 6, 6n.2, 8n.3, 11–12, 29, 32–34, 41, 61, 63–64, 94, 152, 180, 197–99, 200–207
Matsuo Bashō, 95
Meiji Restoration, xvii, xxi, 29–30, 36, 36n.3, 37, 37n.4, 45, 53–58, 64, 67–69, 71, 76, 78–80, 110, 200
Miki Kiyoshi, 41–42, 180, 185
Minobe Tatsukichi, 38
Mishima Yukio, xvii, xxi, xxiv, xxix, 52–53, 72, 75, 78–79, 81, 81n.12, 82–83, 109, 114, 139–40, 154, 157–58, 162–65, 171
Mito school, 70
Mori Ōgai, 73, 73n.7, 77n.8, 78
Motoori Norinaga, 57, 59n.3, 187
Murai Osamu, 70
Murakami Haruki, xxi, xxiv–xxvi, xxix, 117–49, 165, 168
Murakami Yasusuke, 43n.9
Murphy, Joseph, xxviiin.10, 197n.13
Mussolini, Benito, 35, 103

Nagai Kafū, 197–98
Nakae Chōmin, 57, 60
Nakagami Kenji, xxi, xxix, 152n.2, 165–71
Nakano Seigō, 41
National Learning, 36, 36n.3, 57, 59n.3, 69, 187, 193
Natsume Kyōko, 78n.10
Natsume Sōseki, xviii, xxvi, xxix, 47, 63, 74–78, 78n.10, 113–14, 122, 161
Negri, Antonio, xiii
neoliberalism, ix, xi–xii, 43, 45
New Left, 52, 72, 82, 99
Nichiren, 173–74, 174n.1
Nietzsche, Friedrich, 66, 104, 159, 170, 170n.5, 171
Nikkō Tōshōgū Shrine, 187
Nishida Kitarō, 54, 62, 68, 76, 113, 182–86, 186n.9
Nishitani Keiji, 181, 185
Nogi Maresuke, xvii, 53, 72–75
Noguchi Yukio, 42n.8

Oda Nobunaga, 176
Ōe Kenzaburō, xxi, xxii–xxv, xxix, 87–114, 118–20, 126, 129, 131, 139, 147–48, 151, 151n.1, 153–58, 161–62, 164–65, 168
Ōgai. *See* Mori Ōgai
Oguri Tadamasa, 37n.4
Okakura Kakuzō, xxiii, 57, 64–66, 68, 80, 180, 185, 185n.8
Ōkubo Toshimichi, 58, 110
Ooms, Herman, 177n.2
Orikuchi Shinobu, 96n.4
overcoming modernity: discourse of, xxiii, xxv–xxvi, xxviii, xxix, 42–43, 148, 178, 181, 185–86, 188–89, 191, 193–94, 199, 207; symposium on, xxvi–xxvii, 54–55, 72, 99, 181
overdetermination, 13
Ozaki Hotsumi, 41, 61n.4
Ozaki Kōyō, 90

parallax, xvi–xviii, xxii–xxiii, 48, 51, 113
Paris Commune, 37n.4
Perrault, Charles, 198
Persian Gulf War, xiii
proper names, xix, xxi–xxii, xxiv, 87–90, 92–95, 98–100, 102, 117–18, 121–22, 127, 143–47, 159–60, 162, 171
Proust, Marcel, 153
psychoanalysis, xxin.6, 12, 34. *See also* Freud, Sigmund

Rabelais, François, 18, 191
regionalism, xi, 45, 59n.3
Romanticism, xxii, 120, 122, 147–48, 157–58, 164, 180–83. *See also* Japanese Romantic school
Roosevelt, Franklin Delano, 5, 23
Rousseau, Jean-Jacques, 13–14
Russell, Bertrand, 145–46
Russian Revolution, 5, 34, 39, 48
Russo-Japanese War, 53, 63–67, 69, 71–72, 80
Ryōanji (Buddhist temple), rock garden at, 190

Saigō Takamori, 53, 57–59, 59n.2, 61, 78, 110
Sakagami Takashi, 23n.5
Sakaguchi Ango, xxvi–xxviii, xxix, 186, 188–200, 204
Sartre, Jean-Paul, xxix, 88, 204, 209
Saussure, Ferdinand de, 118–19, 134, 143, 145–46
Schlegel, Friedrich, 128, 140, 164–65, 170
Schmitt, Carl, 13, 15
Schopenhauer, Arthur, 178
Seinan War, 37, 53, 58, 59n.2, 73–74, 110
Shiga Naoya, 73
Shikitei Sanba, 77
Shimazaki Tōson, 36n.3
Shimizu Ikutarō, 112
Shinran, 173–74, 174n.1, 179, 179n.4, 180, 203
Shinto, 68, 178, 182, 186n.9
Shōwa Research Association, 36, 41
Shōwa Restoration, xvii, xxi, 36, 38, 41–42, 45, 53, 68, 70, 78, 80–81, 110
Shūgakuin Detached Palace, 190
Sima Qian, xxvi, 186, 202, 205–9
singularity, xix, xixn.4, xxii, xxviii, 92–94, 98, 101, 125, 160, 169, 171
Sino-Japanese War, ix, 38, 53, 58, 60, 65n.5, 66, 200; Second, 42
Socrates, 80
Sōda Kiichirō, 182, 182n.6
Sorel, Georges, 102, 106
Sōseki. *See* Natsume Sōseki
Spinoza, Baruch (Benedict) de, x
Sterne, Laurence, 77
Suzuki Daisetsu, 173, 186n.9
Swift, Jonathan, 18, 77

Taishō democracy, xx, 33, 38, 71
Takeda Taijun, xxvi–xxviii, xxix, 186, 200–209
Takeuchi Yoshimi, xxii, xxvi, 52, 54–55, 58, 59n.2, 62, 66, 99, 106, 148, 202
Taut, Bruno, xxvii, 186–88, 190
Temple of the Golden Pavilion, 82
Thiers, Adolphe, 23
Tokugawa Ieyasu, 176, 187
Tokugawa shogunate, 36, 37n.4, 41, 55, 176–78
Tokyo Olympics, 53, 53n.1, 63, 72
Tosaka Jun, 182
Toyotomi Hideyoshi, 176
Tsubouchi Shōyō, 77, 77n.8

Uchimura Kanzō, 66
Ueno Chizuko, 70
Uno Kōzō, 33n.2

Wallerstein, Immanuel, x, 31n.1, 193
Wang Yangming school, 57
Watanabe Kazuo, 191
Watsuji Tetsurō, 66–67, 173, 180–81
Watt, Ian, 89
Weimar Republic, 15, 35
Wilson, Edmund, 18,
Wittgenstein, Ludwig, 51
Wordsworth, William, 157–58

Xavier, Saint Francis, 175, 194–95

Yamaguchi Masao, 70
Yanagita Kunio, 69–70, 90, 96n.4, 180
Yasuda Yojūrō, 55, 72, 78–81, 122
Yoshimitsu Yoshihiko, 181
Yoshimoto Takaaki, xxiiin.9

Žižek, Slavoj, xvii, xviin.2

WEATHERHEAD BOOKS ON ASIA

Weatherhead East Asian Institute, Columbia University

LITERATURE   David Der-wei Wang, Editor

Ye Zhaoyan, *Nanjing 1937: A Love Story*, translated by Michael Berry (2003)
Oda Makato, *The Breaking Jewel*, translated by Donald Keene (2003)
Han Shaogong, *A Dictionary of Maqiao*, translated by Julia Lovell (2003)
Takahashi Takako, *Lonely Woman*, translated by Maryellen Toman Mori (2004)
Chen Ran, *A Private Life*, translated by John Howard-Gibbon (2004)
Eileen Chang, *Written on Water*, translated by Andrew F. Jones (2004)
Writing Women in Modern China: The Revolutionary Years, 1936-1976, edited by Amy D. Dooling (2005)
Han Bangqing, *The Sing-song Girls of Shanghai*, first translated by Eileen Chang, revised and edited by Eva Hung (2005)
Loud Sparrows: Contemporary Chinese Short-Shorts, translated and edited by Aili Mu, Julie Chiu, and Howard Goldblatt (2006)
Hiratsuka Raichō, *In the Beginning, Woman Was the Sun*, translated by Teruko Craig (2006)
Zhu Wen, *I Love Dollars and Other Stories of China*, translated by Julia Lovell (2007)
Kim Sowŏl, *Azaleas: A Book of Poems*, translated by David McCann (2007)
Wang Anyi, *The Song of Everlasting Sorrow: A Novel of Shanghai*, translated by Michael Berry with Susan Chan Egan (2008)
Ch'oe Yun, *There a Petal Silently Falls: Three Stories by Ch'oe Yun*, translated by Bruce and Ju-Chan Fulton (2008)
Inoue Yasushi, *The Blue Wolf: A Novel of the Life of Chinggis Khan*, translated by Joshua A. Fogel (2009)
Anonymous, *Courtesans and Opium: Romantic Illusions of the Fool of Yangzhou*, translated by Patrick Hanan (2009)
Cao Naiqian, *There's Nothing I Can Do When I Think of You Late at Night*, translated by John Balcom (2009)
Park Wan-suh, *Who Ate Up All the Shinga? An Autobiographical Novel*, translated by Yu Young-nan and Stephen J. Epstein (2009)
Yi T'aejun, *Eastern Sentiments*, translated by Janet Poole (2009)
Hwang Sunwŏn, *Lost Souls: Stories*, translated by Bruce and Ju-Chan Fulton (2009)
Kim Sŏk-pŏm, *The Curious Tale of Mandogi's Ghost*, translated by Cindy Textor (2010)
Xiaomei Chen, editor, *The Columbia Anthology of Modern Chinese Drama* (2011)
Qian Zhongshu, *Humans, Beasts, and Ghosts: Stories and Essays*, edited by Christopher G. Rea, translated by Dennis T. Hu, Nathan K. Mao, Yiran Mao, Christopher G. Rea, and Philip F. Williams (2011)

HISTORY, SOCIETY, AND CULTURE   Carol Gluck, Editor

Takeuchi Yoshimi, *What Is Modernity? Writings of Takeuchi Yoshimi*, edited and translated, with an introduction, by Richard F. Calichman (2005)
Contemporary Japanese Thought, edited and translated by Richard F. Calichman (2005)
Overcoming Modernity, edited and translated by Richard F. Calichman (2008)
Natsume Sōseki, *Theory of Literature and Other Critical Writings*, edited and translated by Michael Bourdaghs, Atsuko Ueda, and Joseph A. Murphy (2009)

GPSR Authorized Representative: Easy Access System Europe, Mustamäe tee 50, 10621 Tallinn, Estonia, gpsr.requests@easproject.com

www.ingramcontent.com/pod-product-compliance
Lightning Source LLC
Chambersburg PA
CBHW050901300426
44111CB00010B/1324